GREAT DISASTERS IN HISTORY

GREAT DISASTERS IN HISTORY

Herbert Genzmer

Sybille Kershner

Christian Schütz

Bath · ew York · Singapore · Hong Kong · Cologne · Delhi · Melbourne

Contents

FAMINE AND DROUGHT 96

PLAGUES AND EPIDEMICS 118

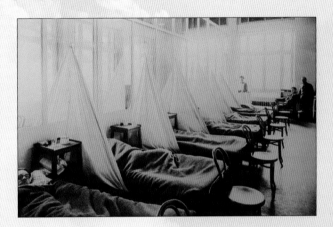

WAR AND TERROR 160

DISASTERS IN THE AIR 204

DISASTERS AT SEA 238

THE CURSE OF TECHNOLOGY 270

PREFACE

Literally translated, the Greek word *katastraphei*, from which "catastrophe" is derived, means a sudden turn of events bringing calamity, collapse, and doom. That is how the word catastrophe is understood today: as a disaster, an often unanticipated event that results in great misfortune. Our definition of the word presupposes that we live a life of peace and security that is suddenly, unhappily disrupted precisely when it is least expected. Of course, this is not entirely true. In this age so rich in disasters, we are constantly reminded that calamity is always close by, even if we have been fortunate enough not to have experienced it or suffered its effects directly.

A book about disasters could be much thicker and heavier than this volume. Even if the selection of events was limited to those that have occurred since the beginning of the last century, they would fill every chapter in this book. The volcanoes and earthquakes that have long plagued humankind continue to do so today. Storms and floods still inundate large parts of the planet, claiming as many victims as ever. Along with disease and epidemics, hunger and draught have been our constant companions since time began. Diseases thought to have been eradicated have made threatening comebacks. War and terror can strike anywhere, and are being waged in many places even as we write these lines. Horrors in the air and at sea and travel-related disasters of all kinds are nearly everyday occurences. Last but not least, there is the curse of technology. Almost any innovation that provides us with the level of comfort we have come to take for granted, including many of our most praiseworthy technological advances, can turn against us with fateful consequences. The production of nuclear energy can lead to a meltdown; chemicals that kill weeds or keep our homes free from pests can poison and kill thousands.

Of course, this book also includes accidents and disasters that took place a long time ago. Our earth is a fragile planet, and its history is full of dramatic and momentous events that shaped its structure long before humans arrived on the scene. Since our appearance, however, we have increasingly contributed to these events; indeed, most are now a direct consequence of our existence. In these days of live media reports from around the globe and immediate discussion and analysis of every event, these questions have come to the fore: How do people deal with catastrophe? How would I react to a disaster? How can anyone process the flood of catastrophic news that engulfs us daily? Other questions are more practical. How can the scale of a disaster be measured? By counting the number of people it leaves dead, or the tears of the mourning relatives and devastated survivors? Should we calculate the years that humanity, or a group of people, have fallen behind in their development because of the catastrophe? Damage can always be measured in monetary terms, with insurance companies on hand to provide the necessary data. None of these, however, are the true benchmark. It is the element of surprise, the unimaginable horror of the unexpected disaster that sets the standard.

The selection of disasters presented in this volume are largely chosen with this benchmark in mind. What is the worst catastrophe of all? A tsunami? A broken dam? The collision of two jumbo jets? A nuclear meltdown? All these horrific scenarios have already happened to some degree, and have been presented to us in real time, but we have to assume that nothing so iniquitous could happen to us personally. This is the only way people can continue living their lives. Such events will always catch us unawares, no matter how well we try to prepare ourselves to face the worst; we never can, not really. There is always something just around the corner that will take our breath away.

VOLCANOES, FIRE, AND EARTHQUAKES

For many people, the planet earth is a safe, secure place to settle down, raise families and live one's life in peace. In some parts of the globe, however, earthquakes, fire, and volcanic eruptions pose a constant threat to this sense of security. Volcanic eruptions have extinguished whole cultures, while earthquakes have demolished entire great cities, and continue to do so. Fire not only consumes land and property, it can exact a horrifying death toll if not quickly brought under control.

A Civilization Disappears

VOLCANIC ACTIVITY ON SANTORINI

Santorini is a barren island of volcanic origin in the eastern Mediterranean, where the Eurasian and African continental plates meet. Like the much larger island of Crete to the south, Santorini was home to the legendary Minoan civilization that flourished 3,600 years ago, a uniquely sophisticated culture. With wealth earned by trading throughout the Mediterranean, the Minoans built multistory buildings and palaces decorated with colorful murals. No one knows just what caused the end of the Minoan civilization. One theory proposes that it was snuffed out by one of the greatest volcanic disasters in history.

An island of many names

Santorini has had many names, including Thera ("The Wild One"), a reference to constant volcanic activity in the vicinity.

There are more than 2,000 islands scattered throughout the eastern Mediterranean. Two hundred of these make up the Aegean Sea's famous Cycladic Islands. The Greeks gave them this name, which is derived from *kyklos*, ("circle") because the islands were arranged in a ring around the sacred island of Delos. The Cycladic Islands are small, barren, rocky, and mostly uninhabited. Only eight of the group's islands have an area larger than 40 square miles. The southernmost of the Cycladic Islands has borne many names during its long history. In antiquity it was called Kallisti ("the Beautiful One"), then Strongyle ("the Round One") and, once its violent geological nature had been revealed, Thera ("the Wild One"). Since the thirteenth century its name has been Santorini after its patron saint Santa Irini.

Santorini today is a crescent shaped island, its unusual shape the result of millennia of eruptions and earthquakes, large and small. The violent activity of the earth's crust in this region is due to the shifting of the Eurasian and African continental plates that meet almost exactly underneath the island. Underwater, the cooled magma seeping from far beneath the earth's surface continually forms new volcanic cones. The ancient Greek geographer and historian Strabo (63/64 BCE–24 CE) once described

"When I look up from the glowing hearth below, my eyes take in the fairy-tale beautiful landscape. The black wall of the crater, rising high above the white houses of the island looking like a necklace of white coral set against black velvet and rugged cliffs ... that soar against the background of the deep blue sky ..."

Franz Spunda (1889–1963), Austrian author

(secondhand) the birth of a new islet formed by a cone growing large enough to project above the surface of the sea.

The rugged coast of Santorini is one of the most beautiful in the world.

Santorini's volcanic history

Nine major eruptions have taken place since the 197 BCE event referred to by Strabo. Historical sources document volcanic activity in 46 BCE, 726, 1570, 1707, 1866, 1925, 1939, 1950, and 1956. Some periods of activity lasted for several years, involving many small eruptions and earthquakes. The island has been at rest since the last eruption, but hissing steam vents, hot springs, sulfurous vapors, and other escaping gases are evidence of its underlying potential for violent activity. In 1956 two major earthquakes, with epicenters near the islands of Amorgos and Ios, shook Santorini. One of them had a magnitude of 7.7 on the Richter scale. Several villages near the towns of Oia and Fira were almost completely destroyed. The island's distinctive crescent shape came into being 3,600 years ago during the greatest eruption of them all. The so-called Theran eruption was the largest and most violent the world had ever seen.

The Theran eruption

Recent work by a group of scientists from Copenhagen supported by radiocarbon dates from Aarhus University date the Theran eruption to the year 1645 BCE. At that time, the island was probably the one called Strongyle ("Round One") in Bronze Age texts. Prior to the disaster, it was perfectly round in plan with a centrally situated volcano. The quantity of magma thrown up by the Theran eruption has been measured at 1,050 billion cubic feet, which is comparable to 7 cubic miles of lava. The escaping magma was so rich in gases that it foamed, giving it a volume three times its actual mass. Pumice and ash

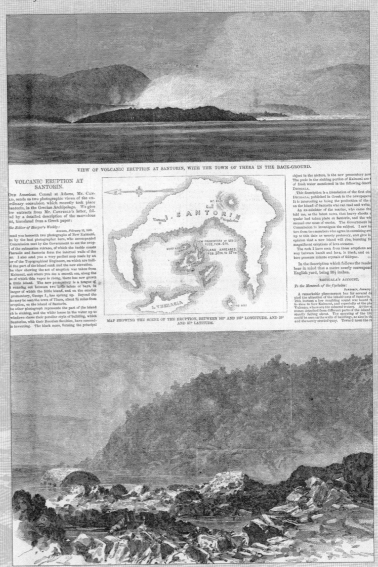

This illustration from the American magazine Harper's Weekly *depicts the most recent eruption on Santorini in 1956.*

The Minoan culture

The Minoan or Cretan-Mycenaean civilization had expanded to the Santorini in the Bronze Age, arriving from Crete via the Cycladic Islands. Minoan culture consisted of a network of trade relationships connecting ethnically diverse geographical regions over long distances. Flourishing trade in grain, pottery, marble, copper and tin, the latter an important raw material for the production of bronze, formed the basis of the wealth of the Minoans. Its fast sailing ships could navigate the open seas in an era when most vessels could only operate in coastal waters. The Minoans may have traveled as far as Sicily or even Spain in search of trade opportunities.

were ejected as well, with fine particles of ash catapulted into the stratosphere to a height of 22 miles above the earth's surface.

The density of the particles and dust in the stratosphere caused far-reaching climatic changes, and the eruption may also be responsible in part for the barrenness of the islands in this region to this day. Ash and pumice from the Theran eruption can still be found in quantity throughout the eastern Mediterranean, and particles of it have been found in ice cores from central Greenland and Alaska. Santorini itself is still covered with a layer of pumice as much as 160 feet thick.

The expulsion of such an enormous amount of lava emptied the magma chamber inside the

Traces of contacts with Minoan civilization can be found everywhere on Santorini. Here, a Minoan-style fresco from the city of Akrotiri depicts two young men boxing.

This fresco found in Akrotiri shows a harbor scene with a Minoan fleet. The wealth of this civilization is clearly depicted in this and other monumental works of art from the island.

volcanic cone so completely that it collapsed in on itself. In its place, a so-called caldera formed. The island became crescent shaped when seawater flooded the caldera.

A monstrous tidal wave

The eruption of the volcano at the center of the "Round One" extinguished all life on the island. When the empty magma chamber of the volcanic cone collapsed, only the edges of the island were left above water. What remained were the large, crescent-shaped island of Santorini and the small islets of Therissia and Aspronisi in a bay formed by the waters of the flooded caldera. Over time, seeping magma has rebuilt the volcanic cone, contributing to the formation of the additional islets of Palea Kameni and Nea Kameni, both of which currently barely project above the bay's surface.

The collapse of the volcano's magma chamber triggered a tidal wave that is estimated to have traveled at a speed of around 220 miles per hour. Simulation studies suggest that it reached a height of over 820 feet. It would have reached Crete in about half an hour, destroying all the coastal settlements. On Santorini itself, the eruption buried what may have been the first European city under a thick layer of lava,

pumice, and ash. The well-preserved remains of this city were found in 1967 near the village of Akrotiri. Some people believe the Theran eruption may have formed the basis for the Greek myth of Atlantis.

The effect of the disaster on the region as a whole is far from certain. No contemporary documentary evidence has survived; our main sources are Greek mythology and the Hebrew Bible, both of which mention widespread, terrible destruction by tidal waves. The myth of Deucalion and Pyrrha recounts a flood sent by Zeus to punish humankind. Another myth tells of Poseidon's fury, abandoning Attica to be consumed by floods after he failed to win control over the city in his contest with Athena. Scholar Anthony Kontaratos has interpreted references in the Old Testament to the destructive flooding of Egypt and the sulfuric fumes poisoning the atmosphere of Sodom as possible references to the Theran eruption. We do know that Kallisti, "the Beautiful One," as the island was next called, was not resettled until the thirteenth century BCE.

Buried beneath 160 ft of pumice and ash, the city of Akrotiri was destroyed by the Theran eruption more than 3,500 years ago.

The Roman emperor, with lyre in hand, surveys "his handiwork." Nero's role in the Great Fire of Rome can probably be traced back to Early Christian propaganda.

ROME BURNS

HISTORY'S FIRST AND MOST DEVASTATING CITY FIRE

On the night of July 18th in the year 64 CE, the eternal city was transformed into a sea of flames. As much as one half of Rome was badly damaged or destroyed. Whenever the question of the arsonist comes up, it is always Emperor Nero who is named, although he was not in Rome when the fire broke out. Many historians now believe that a small and utterly run-of-the-mill fire broke out near the Circus Maximus. It was able to devour half of Rome because the predominantly wooden buildings and crowded conditions inside the city walls made it particularly vulnerable. Nero may have used the disaster as an excuse for persecuting the Christians, whom he blamed for the fire. Afterward, the city was completely rebuilt according to Nero's plans.

The largest city of the known world

In 64 CE, around 1 million people lived in Rome, often packed together in multistoried buildings. Historians of the day report almost daily fires of various degrees of severity. The majority of the buildings were built of wood, and the alleys between them were narrow. Romans cooked over open fires and there were few mechanisms in the poorer areas of the city for fire prevention or control. The most disastrous fire in the city's history was probably caused like so many others before it: someone was cooking and failed to watch the fire, possibly in one of the street kitchens in the commercial area surrounding the Circus Maximus.

Most of the businesses were constructed of wood, and in no time at all they were ablaze.

Not only historians busy themselves with the Great Fire of Rome. It has also been a popular subject for artists like Raphael (1483–1520), whose interpretation is shown here.

The Great Fire of London in 1666

Another devastating city fire took place in England over four days in 1666. The Great Fire of London broke out on September 2, consuming almost a third of the city. When it was over, 85 churches and 13,000 houses had been reduced to ashes, with more than 100,000 people made homeless. The official number of deaths—just nine—was remarkably low. The fire began in a bakery near the Thames after a baker forgot to extinguish the embers in his oven. It quickly spread, fanned by a strong southwest wind. Soon it could no longer be brought under control. London at the time was one great firetrap that fire brigades could only access with difficulty. The streets of London were so narrow, especially in the poorer quarters, that fire brigades could hardly gain access to the fires. Houses were daubed with flammable tar for weatherproofing, and their bay windows jutted out so far over the streets that the buildings opposite one another almost touched. Another factor was the means citizens had at hand for lighting their household fires, which was no easy task in the seventeenth century, before the invention of matches. Tinder and embers were used instead, kept as charcoal embers in a bucket and carried from house to house. For all these reasons, outbreaks of fire were a daily occurrence in London. It was only a matter of time before a conflagration such as that of 1666 befell the city.

Strong winds helped the fire spread, jumping quickly from shop to shop, engulfing entire streets in minutes. During the six days it raged, three of Rome's fourteen districts were completely destroyed, with another seven seriously damaged. Two-thirds of the city was no longer inhabitable. The death toll is unknown.

Eyewitness report by the historian Tacitus

Inconceivable chaos reigned in the streets of burning Rome. The historian Tacitus vividly described the disaster: "Terrified, shrieking women, helpless old and young, people intent on their own safety, people unselfishly supporting invalids or waiting for them, fugitives and lingerers alike—all heightened the confusion. When people looked back, menacing flames sprang up before them or outflanked them.

When they escaped to a neighboring quarter, the fire followed—even districts believed remote proved to be involved. Finally, with no idea where or what to flee, they crowded on to the country roads, or lay in the fields. Some who had lost everything—even their food for the day—could have escaped, but preferred to die."

The people needed someone to blame

Throughout the history of humankind, people have always needed someone to blame for disasters. Those in power have often satisfied this need by providing a scapegoat. Many rulers have been happy to turn disaster into an instrument of politics, fabricating guilt as a means of achieving their larger goals. In this case, Emperor Nero (ruled 54–68) was under increasing pressure from his advisors to assign responsibility for the fire. Finally, the unpopular Christians were announced as the arsonists, setting off a long period of persecution—which, however, was nowhere near as violent as some later Christian historians would have us believe.

Was Nero responsible for setting the fire?

Today historians know that the legends about Christians martyred by Nero first emerged more than 300 years later, during the fourth century. These legends required that Nero not only blame Christians for setting the fire, but that he himself must also be the arsonist. Historians now say that the cruelty that later generations attributed to Nero is subject to doubt. His treatment of the Christians, together with the story that he burned down the city so that he could build "his Rome" more magnificently splendid than before, are all probably more legend than reality.

He did, of course, build a magnificent new palace after the fire, and he was indeed subject to violent fits of temper and madness, all of which served to support the later propaganda. Two days before the devastating fire, he is supposed to have said, while arguing about a translation of a Greek play with one of his advisors, that the work should not begin with "When I am dead, may fire devour the world," but rather "As long as I live, fire must devour the world." Like many other emperors, Nero is reported to have constantly complained that his imperial eyes were insulted by the ugliness of

The legend that Nero played music while Rome burned has endured over many centuries.

Claudius Caesar Augustus Germanicus, called Nero

Nero was born Lucius Domitius Ahenobarbus in the year 37, in Antium. When his mother, Agrippina the Younger, married the later Caesar Claudius (41–54) his name was changed to Claudius Caesar Augustus Germanicus. It was his mother's ambition to see her son on the imperial throne. Nero realized this at the age of 17, in the year 54, when his stepfather Claudius died. At the age of 16, he married his stepsister Octavia. In 62 he married Poppaea Sabina, who bore him a daughter, Claudia. Four years later he married Statilia Messalina. During the last years of his life he had his rivals murdered, including his stepbrother, his wife Octavia, and even his own mother. Tainted by these murders and his increasing paranoia, he was declared an enemy of the state by the Senate. Shortly thereafter, he committed suicide. The Senate condemned him posthumously to damnatio memoriae (deletion from memory). This meant that all his statues and inscriptions would be destroyed. Only a few portraits have survived.

Rome's buildings. Nevertheless, this hardly proves that he burned down the city so that he could rebuild it. We know for certain that Nero had traveled to his birthplace, Antium, on the Latium coast south of Rome two days before the fire broke out. When he returned four days later and found Rome in flames, he is said to have surveyed the 800-year-old city from a tower of his palace and spoken of the beauty of the flames and the intoxicating spectacle of destruction. Here the legend of Nero the monster takes over, claiming that he reached immediately for his lyre and began singing verses about the fall of Troy.

The Christian Church promotes the image of Nero as a monster

In comparison to some of the Julio Claudian Roman emperors who preceded him, such as Augustus (27 BCE–14 CE), Tiberius (14–37), or Caligula (37–41), Nero was relatively harmless. He lost quite a bit of his own wealth during the Great Fire, including his palace and its extensive collection of art. Since the emperor was responsible for housing and feeding all of the citizens who had lost their homes, he also had to pay out a great deal of money to support the fire's victims. The arson theory publicized by Suetonius (70–140), an author who specialized in unsubstantiated rumors and anecdotes, seems unlikely given the circumstances. As for Nero's direct involvement in martyring Christians, it is know for certain that Nero was in Greece at the time when the Christians were put on trial. It is entirely possible that he did not know they were being persecuted at all. Although a violent man himself, Nero was no fan of organized terror and had even tried to abolish the gladiatorial games. It was largely the emboldened Christian Church that, from the fourth century onward, must be held responsible for propagating stories about his cruelty and involvement in the Great Fire of Rome.

St. Peter's Square from the top of St. Peter's Cathedral, seat of the Roman Catholic Church. The Catholic Church probably presented persecution of Early Christians with more drama than historical accuracy.

The worst eruption of Vesuvius in 72 years took place in 1944, when an enormous shroud of smoke darkened the entire region.

BURIED UNDER A CLOUD OF HOT ASH

THE ERUPTION OF VESUVIUS

The volcano of Vesuvius is on the Gulf of Naples. The bustling towns of Pompeii, Herculaneum, and Stabiae were settled on its slopes. In 79 CE, Vesuvius proved false the assumption that it was extinct with an eruption that buried the cities under a rain of ash, costing an estimated 17,000 people their lives. Archaeologists rediscovered the ruins of Pompeii in 1709; excavations that followed revealed the victims' suffering to the world.

The eruption of a volcano thought to be extinct

Mount Vesuvius on the Gulf of Naples in the Campania region of Italy is the only volcano on the European mainland that is still intermittently active. Its height is constantly changing due to minor eruptions that alter its basic topography. In 1998 it measured 4,196 feet, but today it is only 3,878 feet high. The mountain is categorized as what is known as a double volcano. The peak of Monte Vesuvio, a volcanic cone, is encircled by the caldera of Monte Somma. Its magma chamber is located 3 miles beneath the surface. The Monte Vesuvio cone visible today sits within the curve of the bowl-like depression of the Monte Somma caldera, 2 miles in diameter. Amazingly, there is good evidence that, in antiquity Vesuvius was widely considered to be extinct. The presumption was disproved, however, when it destroyed the Roman towns of Pompeii, Herculaneum, and Stabiae in a massive eruption in the year 79. Further serious eruptions occurred in 1631, 1872, 1906, and 1944.

Pliny the Younger

Gaius Plinius Caecilius Secundus (61–113) was born in Como and died as consul of Bithynia, a region located in what is now Turkey. He was a Roman senator and author. His uncle, Pliny the Elder (23–79) was a civil servant responsible for the Roman fleet in the Gulf of Naples. The correspondence of Pliny the Younger, including his letters to the emperor Trajan, was rediscovered in the sixteenth century. His letters provide today's readers with detailed insight into many aspects of life in ancient Rome.

An eruption as early as 1740 BCE?

Recent excavations have shown that several enormous, devastating eruptions predated the year 79 event, with the earliest dating to 1740 BCE. This so-called Avellino Eruption buried ancient settlements near the present-day villages of Avellino, Nola, and San Paolo Bel Sito under several feet of ash. Construction of a freeway in 1972 and of a supermarket in Nola in 2001 uncovered household articles, dead pets and livestock, as well as houses that showed evidence of the hurried departure of the region's population. In contrast to the later eruption in 79, the Bronze Age inhabitants clearly had a chance to flee to more distant settlements, which were located about 20 miles from the volcano. Things were different 1,800 years later. Pompeii alone had a population of around 20,000, and many of them probably lost their lives in the sudden eruption.

This painting of the harbor of Naples with Vesuvius erupting in the background dates from 1777.

This guard dog fell victim to the volcanic eruption. His owner did not unchain him so that he could escape.

The wrath of the gods

Early in the afternoon of August 24th in the year 79, the inhabitants of the towns on the slopes of Vesuvius suddenly noticed that an enormous cloud was forming in an otherwise cloudless, bright blue sky. The cloud varied in color from dirty grey to pure white and had the shape of a slowly opening umbrella. An eruption that had gone unnoticed was spewing thousands of tons of dust and ash into the sky. As the cloud of volcanic debris sank slowly back down to earth, it continued to expand until it blotted out the sun. The people finally noticed that Vesuvius was the source of this sinister cloud when, a short time later, a thick, hot rain of ashes began to fall. Large, heavy,

volcanic projectile rocks fell first, followed by fine, glowing-hot ash. Ships approaching the coast near Rectina ran aground as they tried to rescue the desperate people running down the slopes to the bay. The seabed has already risen due to the quantity of falling boulders, rocks, and ash. This is why, today, it is no longer possible to approach the coast by ship. Sailing out of the ancient harbor bay is no longer possible because the water is too shallow.

The rain of ashes

As night fell, Vesuvius' eruption could be seen and heard for miles. Bright flames blazed in the darkness, turning night into day. The streets and squares of the towns of Pompeii, Herculaneum, and Stabiae were clogged with ash and pumice. Earthquakes shook the buildings, many of which swayed on their foundations and collapsed. The people who had not been able to escape fled indoors

The hollow spaces left in the ash by the decayed corpses were filled with plaster to produce startlingly detailed casts of the victims at the moment of death.

A letter from Pliny the Younger describing what happened to him and his mother on the second day of the eruption

"The ash was not yet falling very densely. I looked around: a thick black cloud threatened us from behind, pouring over the land like a flood wave. "Let us leave the road while we can still see," I said, "or we will be trampled underfoot by the mass of people in the darkness." We had just sat down to rest as the darkness closed over us. It was not like the darkness of a moonless or cloudy night, it was as if the light were to be extinguished in a closed, windowless room.

One could hear women's screams, the crying of children, and men calling ... many begged for help from the gods, but the large majority thought that there were no gods anymore and that the universe was lost in eternal darkness ... A faint light returned, but we considered it a warning of approaching flames rather than daylight. But the flames stayed some distance from us. Then the darkness engulfed us again, and ash began to rain down anew, this time in large dense amounts. We rose to free ourselves from time to time, otherwise we would have been buried beneath it."

to avoid the rain of burning ash. They may have felt safe there, ready to wait out the end of what did not appear to be such a great disaster after all. Apart from the earthquakes and the rain of hot ash, there was no visible flow of lava running down the mountainside. At the time of the eruption, Pliny the Younger (61–113) was just 18 years old and staying at the house of his uncle, Pliny the Elder (23–79) in the small town of Misenum some 25 miles from Vesuvius. On the evening of the first day, he wrote a letter to Cornelius Tacitus, reassuring him that the ash rain was no great threat.

Smoke and ash darken the skies

People who persisted in running through the streets trying to get away tied cushions to their heads and shoulders to protect themselves from the rocks hailing down on them. Although pumice is porous and not very heavy, it does have sharp edges. Larger chunks can cause serious injury. On the second day, long past the time when the sun should have been high in the sky, the darkness of the night continued. The dense rain of ash and hot embers completely blocked out the sun's rays. That ash rain, underestimated by the people who chose to remain in the cities on Vesuvius' slopes, was proving itself to be lethal by the early hours of the morning. The ash and smoke made it difficult to breathe. People began to suffocate, falling dead in their homes or out in the street, looking as if they had fallen asleep. The negative impressions of many bodies, human and animal alike, were preserved in their death throes under a layer of ash several feet thick.

The uncovered ruins of Pompeii are a magnificent museum of Roman art, architecture, and lifestyles.

Inhabitants look on helplessly as lava flows along the main street of San Sebastiano during Vesuvius' eruption in 1944.

UNTAMABLE FORCES OF NATURE

FACTS ABOUT VOLCANOES

Varieties of volcanoes

The form and structure of volcanoes vary widely. Some are immense mountains with perfect cinder cones built up over the course of many centuries. Others are little more than fissures in the earth or crevices in the seabed. The earth's crust is not a rigid shell, but is made up of shifting tectonic plates. Most volcanoes are found where tectonic plates meet or collide. These plate seams are places where the earth not only moves, but where the earth's crust is notably thin and friable. About half of the world's 550 active volcanoes can be found in the Pacific Ocean, where they form what is called the "Ring of Fire." There are also volcanoes in the Mediterranean basin, in Africa, and on the seafloor of the Atlantic.

Types of volcano

There are two basic types of volcano:

(a) Composite or stratovolcanoes are usually tall and conical in form. Their structure consists of alternate layers of lava, volcanic ash, and cinders. They can also be called subduction volcanoes because they are always found in subduction zones, where two or more tectonic plates meet. Examples of composite volcanoes are Mount Fuji (Japan), Mount St. Helens (USA), and Vesuvius (Italy).

(b) Shield or lava volcanoes are flatter and often cover a broad area. They are formed from extremely fluid lava that flows faster and further than the rocky mix of ash and cinders characteristic of lava from the composite type. Shield volcanoes can be found both within tectonic plates, where they are called hot-spot volcanoes, and at plate seams where the plates in question are moving away from each other. The volcanoes of the Hawaiian Islands and Iceland belong to this group.

Types of eruption

Volcanoes differ not only in their shape, but also in the way they erupt. The lava of composite volcanoes usually contains a high proportion of steam (water vapor) and silica. The thick consistency of composite volcano lava keeps these gases from escaping, increasing the pressure within the volcanic cone. Eventually, the pressure is relieved by an eruption of incredible force, such as that of the Bronze Age Theran eruption that blew apart the island of Santorini. The crust over a suddenly emptied magna chamber can collapse like the roof of a house. The crater created when the magma chamber collapses is called a caldera, which is Spanish for "cauldron."

Geologists categorize certain composite volcanoes as super volcanoes. When a super volcano erupts, it releases destructive power comparable to the impact of a small asteroid. Such eruptions are counted among the worst natural catastrophes the world has ever seen. During a prehistoric eruption in what is now Yellowstone National Park in the USA, a super volcano explosion sent a steaming mixture of

gas, lava, and ash up to 30 miles into the stratosphere at supersonic speed. The material fell back to earth as thick clouds of burning ash. When the volcanic material hit the ground, particles of ash and lava raced over the surface at speeds of up to 250 miles per hour. No land vehicle and few aircraft could move fast enough to escape anything moving at such a speed. Temperatures within the ash cloud soared to 1,100–1,300 °F. Everything in its path was incinerated before being buried under the lava. The eruption of Vesuvius in the year 79 is an example of this kind of explosion, though on a lesser scale. Composite volcanoes are found all over the world. When they erupt, twilight can last for weeks as the clouds of ash darken the skies. Ash catapulted into the atmosphere by composite volcanoes can actually cool the earth's atmosphere, leading to crop failure over large areas.

The lava from shield volcanoes, in contrast, has a much lower level of water vapor and silica. Gases are able to escape more easily, which means that the volcanoes seldom erupt explosively. Instead, they emit a steady stream of thin, fast flowing lava. Hotspot shield volcanoes can, however, occasionally erupt with explosive force. When the volcano is over a hotspot, the magma burns its way through the earth's crust like a blowtorch. An eruption occurs when the heat has melted so much rock that the earth's crust can no longer remain intact under the pressure.

The procedures for investigating and monitoring volcanoes are becoming more accurate as technology continues to develop. In the end, however, no one will ever be able to prevent a volcanic eruption or any of the related disasters that result from them.

EARTHQUAKES, TSUNAMIS, AND FIRE

THE LISBON EARTHQUAKE AND FIRE

At 9:30 in the morning of November 1, 1755, a powerful earthquake rocked the Portuguese capital of Lisbon. Two additional quakes followed a short time later. The Lisbon earthquake was one of the worst natural disasters of the modern age. The port city of Lisbon was completely destroyed: its churches, palaces, bridges, and towers collapsed into piles of rubble. As if the earthquake were not bad enough, it was followed by a series of tsunami waves up to 50 feet high that completely flooded the center of the city. Finally, a gigantic dust cloud darkened the sky and a fire broke out, one that would devour what little remained standing of the great city of Lisbon.

Rubble and ashes on All Saints' Day

On the morning of All Saints' Day 1755, the earth under Lisbon shook three times, leaving one of the most powerful and wealthiest cities in Europe a wasteland of rubble and ashes. More than 60,000 of the city's 275,000 inhabitants lost their lives. The quake was felt all over the European continent. The magnitude of the earthquake has been calculated at approximately 9 on the Richter scale.

Half an hour after the three quakes, a 50-foot tall tsunami made its way up the Tagus River from the Atlantic. The low-lying heart of

This engraving shows the tsunami waves rolling up the Tagus, flooding the city and killing thousands.

Lisbon was completely flooded. The tsunami swept away people on the shore and sank overloaded boats trying to escape to safety on the opposite side of the river. The rescue boats sank, and their passengers drowned.

The all-consuming fire that followed left the city in ashes. Narrow streets were blocked by debris from the earthquake, and fire brigades could not reach the source. The inferno soon grew to catastrophic proportions. After five days, Lisbon had been burnt to the ground.

Lisbon was not the only city destroyed. The tsunami devastated the entire Atlantic coastline of Portugal, Spain, and Morocco, reaching up the Guadalquivir, one of the longest rivers in Spain, as far as Seville. Thousands fell victim to the earthquake in the Moroccan cities of Fez and Marrakech. The water levels of lakes in Scotland and Switzerland rose and ships were torn from their anchor as far away as Sweden. In Lisbon itself, the flood and the blaze that followed were by far more destructive than the earthquake that had triggered them.

Where did the earthquake originate?

The cause of the earthquake is still uncertain. Some 250 years after the calamity, geologists are still groping in the dark for its geological origins, unsure as to the exact location of its epicenter. It is theorized to have been near the Azores, a group of Portuguese islands in the Atlantic between Europe and North America,

several hundred miles from the mainland coast. This is the only theory that explains the devastating tsunami that hit the Atlantic coast after the earthquake.

An earthquake of magnitude 7.9 occurred off the coast of Portugal in 1969. At the time, experts thought the epicenter could have been the same as in 1755. However, the 1969 earthquake produced a tidal wave of less than 2 feet. Due to the great difference in the size of the waves, most scientists have concluded that the epicenters were not identical, leaving the cause and location of the 1755 quake unexplained.

Crisis management under the Marquês de Pombal

For the first time in history, a kind of crisis management followed on the heels of the 1755 disaster in Lisbon. King José I assigned his secretary of state, Sebastián José Carvalho e Melo (1699–1782), the task of dealing with the devastation. His answer to the king's question of what should be done was "bury the dead, take care of the living." Thanks to this pragmatic approach, the city was reported free of debris only one year later. In addition, the enlightened Carvalho e Melo laid the foundations of modern seismology by recording the observations of survivors as to the extent and strength of the quake and its aftershocks.

Earthquake researchers today still refer to the important data he gathered. In a society

Sebastian José de Carvalho e Melo, later Marquês de Pombal, was the crisis manager who took over the reconstruction in 1755.

shaken to its core, he turned the discussion away from questions of sin or guilt. In focusing on the disaster itself he set the stage for the study of risks and precautionary measures that

In the view of many scientists, the Lisbon earthquake was the first disaster to be followed by a modern recovery and reconstruction plan.

The most powerful earthquakes since the start of the 20th century

Date	Location	Magnitude	Victims
4/04/1905	Himalaya (India)	8.6	19,000
1/31/1906	Columbia/Ecuador	8.9	1,000
8/17/1906	Central China	8.6	20,000
8/18/1906	US West Coast	8.3	>3,000
12/17/1920	Central China	8.6	200,000
5/22/1922	Russia/Kamchatka	8.3	unknown
2/3/1923	Central Japan	8.5	142,000
9/1/1923	Russia/Kamchatka	8.3	3,000
3/2/1933	India/Nepal	8.9	>10,000
1/15/1934	Indonesia	8.4	unknown
2/1/1938	Central Chile	8.5	28,000
1/25/1939	Southern Japan	8.3	>1,000
12/7/1944	Southern Japan	8.3	>1,000
12/20/1946	Himalaya (India and Tibet)	8.4	>1,000
8/15/1950	Russia/Kamchatka	8.7	0
11/4/1952	Southern Chile	8.9	>2,000
5/22/1960	Russia/Kuril Islands	9.5	unknown
10/13/1963	Alaska	8.5	125
3/28/1964	Alaska	9.2	0
2/4/1965	Indonesia/Sri Lanka	8.7	280,000
12/26/2004	India/Thailand	9.0	>1,000
3/28/2005	Sumatra	8.7	unknown

could be taken to avoid future catastrophes. In 1769, the king expressed his gratitude by granting him the title of Marquês de Pombal. The marquês was innovative in other fields, including law and human rights. Making the most of his high-profile position, he abolished slavery, expelled the Jesuits, and granted Brazilian native peoples legal parity with the Portuguese.

The Enlightenment and the Lisbon disaster

The eighteenth century, the Age of Enlightenment, was characterized by the belief in the rational structure of the world, science and the steady progress of human knowledge. The death of so many people in Lisbon and the sight of one of Europe's most important trade centers in ruins wreaked havoc with earlier religion-focused ideas about the world and humanity's role within it. Loss of faith in the certainty of God's will made way for the rationalism of the Enlightenment to flourish. The earthquake was not simply a natural disaster, but a watershed in people's relationship to natural disasters. For the first time in history, terms such as catastrophe and risk were discussed where formerly the wages of sin and the biblical flood would have served as reference points. This earthquake was not a judgment by God, for how could a benevolent God have allowed his own houses of worship to be destroyed? The power of the Church as an institution was shaken to its foundations by this new way of thinking. The French philosopher Voltaire (1694–1778) published his *Poem on the Lisbon Disaster* in 1756, strengthening secularism throughout Europe and accelerating the onset of the modern age.

The religious interpretation of disasters had reached its limits. Science, particularly geology and the methodical observation of nature, could now replace the religious logic of the biblical

Justice and rationality

"The Lisbon earthquake triggered a fierce discussion in 18th-century intellectual Europe about the justness of God and the rationality of the world. The Indian Ocean tsunami disaster of December 2004 makes the subject current once again."

Dr. Volker Sellin,
Professor of Modern History,
University of Catania, Italy

flood, which held all disasters as varieties of God's punishment for human sinfulness. From now on, earthquakes and floods were understood as natural calamities. This is why the repercussions of the 1755 Lisbon earthquake were so far-reaching, and why the disaster still resonates today. Generations of theologians, philosophers, and authors were shaped by this event. The greatest thinkers of the age tried to analyze the meaning of what happened on that All Saint's Day in 1755.

Nothing in this view of the present-day harbor district of Lisbon reminds anyone of the disaster of 1755.

The ruins of the Convento de Carmo in Lisbon were left standing as a memorial to the destruction.

Ash Rain,
Tidal Waves,
and Balls of fire

THE KRAKATOA ERUPTION OF 1883

Krakatoa, one of Indonesia's more than 1,700 islands, is located in the Sunda Strait between the islands of Sumatra and Java. It is the site of a volcano, rather inconspicuous to look at, but which is nevertheless one the most devastating in the world. In August 1883, Krakatoa erupted with a force that was felt as far away as Australia. The roar of the blast was heard on the island of Rodriguez near Mauritius some 2,900 miles away. A tidal wave followed close on its heels. The 130-foot tsunami waves swept more than 36,000 people to their deaths.

Eyewitness report

"The eye-stinging rain of sand and stones, the pitch blackness all around us, only punctuated by the continual bursts of flashes of lightening both great and small, and the constant thunderous roar of Krakatoa, made our situation truly terrifying ... and in the flood waves raged hundreds of billions of tons of whipped-up, roaring, foaming water."

W. J. Watson, captain of the freighter *Charles Bal*, which was on its way from Belfast to Hong Kong.

An eruption that eclipsed the sun

In May 1883, a series of volcanic eruptions began on a small island east of Java. Their early shock waves were felt 90 miles away in the Indonesian capital city of Jakarta. Clouds of steam and ash rose high into the sky, and a pumice and ash rain fell upon the land. Smaller eruptions and minor earthquakes continued throughout the entire summer, reaching their

Indonesia is regularly subject to volcanic eruptions, including that of Galunggung on Java in the 1980s.

crescendo on August 22nd, 26th, and 27th. Over the course of those three days, more than 4 cubic miles of ash and rock exploded from the earth, reaching an altitude of 50 miles. The devastating eruption released energy equivalent to between 10,000 and 100,000 atomic bombs the size of the one dropped on Hiroshima. Survivors told tales of the terrifying, near total darkness that engulfed them shortly after the eruption began: they would not see the sun again for nearly a week. Glowing hot streams of rock, gas, and ash, a so-called pyroclastic flow, erupted into the black skies at speeds of up to 500 miles per hour, providing the only illumination in the eerie darkness. Towns and villages on neighboring islands were destroyed, with many people killed. Lava bombs the size of pumpkins were reported raining down on the

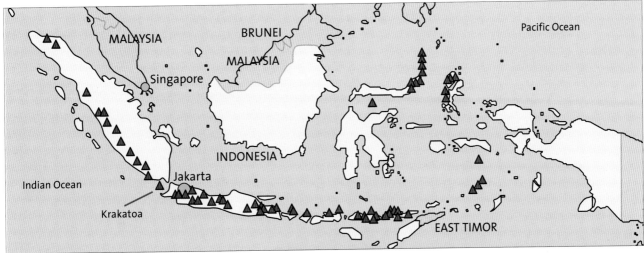

Many of the world's most active volcanoes can be found on the islands of Indonesia.

town of Telukbetung on Sumatra's southern coast. For more than 200 years, a lava plug, a stopper of hardened magma and rubble, had acted as a stopper, keeping the Krakatoa volcano from erupting. Meanwhile, the pressure inside had steadily increased until its top was finally blown away. The ash released by the eruption traveled as far as the Coconut Islands, approximately 1,200 miles away. The sea surrounding the volcano was so thickly covered in pumice that it looked like solid ground. Over the next few months, these floating fields of pumice were washed around the globe as far away as Africa.

Fiery-red sunsets around the world

No other volcanic eruption over the last 2,000 years has had the global repercussions of the terrible explosion of Krakatoa in1883. It had immediate consequences for the world climate. Temperatures in the northern hemisphere sank by an average of 2 °F. As a result, summers were unusually cool and rainy, leading to catastrophic crop failures. The shock wave of the explosion ran around the globe several times. It could be felt from London to San Francisco for more than two weeks. Wind carried dust particles from the eruption around the world, producing spectacularly colored sunsets from

The front page of the Illustrated London News *of September 8, 1883 shows pictures of the 1883 eruption of Krakatoa.*

The Krakatoa
eruption of 1883
was powerful
enough to split
the island in two.

New Zealand to Iceland, as the fine silicates in the air altered the angle of light refraction. Artists all over the world captured these glowing red sunsets in their work. The sky in the famous painting *The Scream* by Edvard Munch (1863–1944) is based on colors the painter observed in Copenhagen years after the eruption. The particles remained in the atmosphere for as much as three years.

The flood after the final eruption

All the earthquakes and eruptions, however, were only a prelude to events yet to come. During the final eruption on August 27th, the cauldron of the volcano collapsed in on itself, and 11 square miles of Krakatoa Island sank into the now empty magma chamber beneath the sea. The shock wave thus generated knocked down walls in Batavia, 90 miles away. The collapsing chamber triggered a total of ten gigantic tidal waves. These flooded the island, submerging two-thirds of its remaining landmass beneath the waves.

In total darkness, tsunamis raced toward the coasts of the neighboring islands at speeds of more than 60 miles per hour. When shallower coastal areas slowed the waves' forward motion, they grew to monstrous heights, up to 130 feet. Within two hours of the final eruption, the coastal regions of Sumatra and Java were completely inundated. In the harbor of Telukbetung, the Dutch gunboat *Berouw* was seized by a

wave and tossed several miles inland, where it remains to this day, a memorial in the jungle. Within a 5-mile radius of the volcano, 36,418 people lost their lives in the floodwaters, and 295 towns and villages were completely lost.

Plate tectonics

It was the German polar researcher and geophysicist Alfred Wegener (1880–1930) who, in 1915, first proposed the theory that the continents had somehow drifted apart. Unable to explain the mechanism for such movement, he was ridiculed by his contemporaries. Today, continental drift is part of the larger study of plate tectonics. According to the theory of plate tectonics, the earth's crust can be likened to a jigsaw puzzle of plates, 150 miles thick, that are either moving toward one another, away from one another or grinding up and down alongside each other.

Today we know that a chain of volcanoes, like pearls on a necklace, marks the points where various plates converge. Where these subduction zones, the term for places where the plates slide underneath one another, occur, the pressure that builds up within a magma chamber can be extreme, leading to explosive volcanic eruptions, including the one on Krakatoa. The worst volcanic disaster in recorded history took place immediately above the continental seam where the Indo-Australian and Eurasian plates meet.

The "son of Krakatoa"

The Krakatoa volcano remains very active to this day. Only forty years after the last catastrophic explosion, a new volcano began to grow where the original cauldera sank into the sea. The volcanic cone broke through the surface of the water in 1930, and has reached a height of 1,500 feet. The locals call it Anak Krakatoa, "son of Krakatoa." In recent years it has repeatedly drawn attention with new, relatively minor eruptions that nevertheless incite fear and terror among the people of the region.

A quote attributed to the philosopher Will Durant may best describe the level of insecurity felt by those who live in the vicinity of volcanoes like Krakatoa, where it can certainly be said that "civilization exists by geological consent — subject to change without notice."

Fields of volcanic ash can still be found all over the island.

Anak Krakatoa, the "son of Krakatoa," rumbles ominously. Rising from the sunken caldera of the old volcano, the youngster erupts almost continuously, as here in 1969.

The Day the Sky Caught Fire

THE SAN FRANCISCO EARTHQUAKE OF 1906

At 5:13 a.m. on April 18, 1906, San Francisco was hit by an earthquake of force 8.25 on the Richter scale and then ravaged by an unquenchable four-day-long fire that followed. Although the quake itself lasted hardly more than a minute, 490 city blocks including 25,000 buildings were destroyed. Of the roughly 400,000 inhabitants at the time, 250,000 were made homeless, and more than 3,000 people were either killed by the quake or died in the flames.

The biggest earthquake of all time

The San Francisco earthquake was one of the worst earthquakes of all time, and it put an abrupt end to the *belle époque* of the golden city on the Pacific. A foreshock occured along the San Andreas fault and throughout the Bay Area (the region around San Francisco Bay) at 5:12 a.m. on April 18, 1906. The city center was shaken within moments, as the epicenter lay just a short distance from the city limits. Shockwaves were felt from Oregon in the north to Nevada and Los Angeles to the south. The city's various geological ground formations reacted to the earthquake in different ways: the greatest damage was suffered by the areas of the city wrung from the bay through the process of land reclamation. In contrast to rocky areas, the devastation here was total.

As powerful and damaging as it was, however, the earthquake itself was not responsible for the great devastation the city suffered: it was the terrible fire triggered by it that ravaged the city. The primary causes of the conflagration were short-circuits on damaged power lines and escaping gas, but overturned heating stoves (mostly coal- or wood-fired) also started fires that could not be brought under control, especially since water mains had been broken by the quake. After the catastrophe, the number of fatalities officially reported was less than 700, but that figure has been corrected to something over 3,000, owing in part to the report's exclusion of the city's many inhabitants of Chinese descent.

Flames lit up the sky

Unimaginable panic erupted among the survivors of the quake as the fire took hold all around them with frightening speed, for it was not only gas pipelines that had been damaged: the city's water supply had also been interrupted. The gas fed the flames and there was no water to put them out. On all sides, helpers tried to bring in water to extinguish the burning houses, most of which were built of wood. Flames lit up the early morning sky, and by dawn an enormous pall of smoke, visible from afar, lay over the city.

Thick clouds of smoke darken the sky above San Francisco.

Terrible tragedies took place in the devastated metropolis. Eyewitnesses reported three men on the roof of the burning Windsor Hotel on Market Street, for example, who could not possibly be rescued. To save them from being burnt alive or leaping in desperation to certain death, the police officer responsible gave the order to shoot them. At another location, a man lay trapped under rubble as the fire approached. Helpers were unable to free him. As his feet began to burn, he begged to be put out of his misery. A police officer approached him, wrote down his personal details, and killed him with a shot to the head. Other tragedies occured at the ferries, where tens of thousands of people attempted to escape the flames as many more panic-stricken people fought their way onto ships than the ferries could possibly hold. On the same day, the mayor of the city at the time, E. E. Schmitz, gave the order that anyone caught looting or engaged in other criminal activity should be shot.

The earthquake and fire left behind destruction on an unbelievable scale: San Francisco lay in ruins.

Predicting the unpredictable

An earthquake is a convulsion on the earth's surface triggered by sudden activity in the earth's crust or upper mantle, primarily at geological faults. A total of more than one million earthquakes occur each year, of which only very few, a handful at most, take on catastrophic dimensions. The Pacific Rim is an especially active center of earthquakes. At the San Andreas fault, which was responsible for the earthquake of 1906, the Pacific and North American continental plates come up against each other. The fault stretches for 738 miles through California. One of the world's foremost seismological institutes is located at the University of California at Berkeley, where scientists investigate earthquakes and endeavor to make exact predictions. A further great quake, "the Big One," is constantly being predicted for San Francisco or Los Angeles, or at least preys on people's minds. Toward the end of 1980, a man entered a betting office in Las Vegas and wagered $5,000 that Los Angeles would be destroyed on New Year's Eve. He lost his bet. Nevertheless, the quakes happen, weekly—indeed, daily—and they are felt all over the state. On October 18, 1989, a quake with a magnitude of 7.1 shook San Francisco, leading to 272 deaths and billions of dollars in damage. Three years

Market Street, one of the city's most important arteries, was almost entirely destroyed.

In 1906, the city's wooden Victorian houses were almost all burnt down or so badly damaged that they had to be demolished.

later, on June 28, 1992, a quake of 7.4 that lasted 30 seconds occurred near Los Angeles. Almost a thousand aftershocks of up to 7.0 on the Richter scale followed; damage "only" ran into the millions because the epicenter lay in the sparsely inhabited Mojave Desert.

Although it is still not possible for experts to foretell when an earthquake will take place, they can now predict with some degree of accuracy what will happen if one occurs at any given time. For example, it has been calculated that a quake in

Los Angeles at 2:30 a.m. would result in around 3,000 fatalities and 12,000 injuries; however, an earthquake during the evening rush hour after 4:30 p.m. would claim 23,000 lives and casualties of almost 100,000. Los Angeles is spread over a much wider area with lower-built housing than San Francisco, where, by contrast, the main causes of death and injury would be masonry falling from facades, collapsing buildings, and glass splinters raining down as windows burst.

Psychological effects

A doctor once wrote that people never get used to earthquakes. On the contrary, a kind of hypersensitivity is noticeable in most cases. Those who have been affected experience fear at the slightest vibration, even when it is only caused by a truck driving past. After a quake many people refuse to sleep in their houses, preferring to camp out in tents due to their fear of being buried under the rubble of a subsequent aftershock. Many people leave regions that have been hit by earthquakes and move to safer locations.

At the same time, however, earthquakes can also exercise a positive effect on the array of feelings people experience, namely when a kind of indifference or even arrogance sets in after surviving the catastrophe. The doctor mentioned above wrote that some individuals lose their inhibitions, while others free themselves from unpleasant circumstances, gaining advantages for themselves and the conditions of their lives from the worldly damage around them. Most survivors really do feel they have been given the gift of a new life. Others, wrote the Russian author Maxim Gorki in 1909, draw the conclusion that daily life and the so-called existential order is no more than a gigantic, slowly unfolding catastrophe, venting itself in occasional eruptions.

Bridges also collapsed in 1989 as if they were merely children's toys.

Stock market hit

The San Francisco earthquake was a serious blow not only for the city and its inhabitants, but also had devastating effects on American financial markets—at least temporarily—when a wave of panic hit the stock exchange at the end of April, 1906. Especially badly hit were the shares of the insurance companies, whose values slid precipitously. The USA's leading fire insurance company of the time, the Aetna Fire Insurance Company, declared that the fire damage in San Francisco following the earthquake had used up all the reserves they had amassed over the previous forty years.

CAN DISASTER BE PREDICTED?

ALL ABOUT EARTHQUAKES

Pressure builds in Southern California

An earthquake is preceded by a number of indicators, including fluctuations in groundwater levels, changes in the electrical resistance of soil, visible bulging of the ground, and unusual animal behavior. Scientifically speaking, most of these have proven to be inconsistent.

An earthquake is only certifiably imminent when geologists register movement along the edges of tectonic plates. Tremendous tension and pressure build up when the continental plates grind against one another. Even with these indications, however, precise prediction is still extremely difficult. Movement detection equipment like a seismograph can tell scientists that an earthquake will occur, but not when.

In southern California, the North American and Pacific tectonic plates regularly slide along each other, locking up from time to time along the San Andreas fault. The locking up can cause the ground to buckle, creating the small quakes that are a part of life in California. Training for earthquakes has become an integral part of everyday life. Schools, offices, and hospitals are posted with signs making people aware of what they should do in case of an earthquake: if you feel the earth move, stand in a doorframe or crouch under a table.

Although the northern and central sections of the San Andreas fault have both been subject to massive, pressure-reducing earthquakes within the last 150 years (in San Francisco in 1906 and the Napa Valley in 1857), there has been no major earthquake in Southern California for nearly 300 years. This means that "the Big One" is imminent. Lasers are being used to monitor "hot" spots on the San Andreas fault. Every seismic disturbance, however slight, is recorded immediately.

Earthquake prediction in China

In 1975, something happened in China that had never before succeeded with such precision. For the first time ever, scientists predicted an earthquake. On February 4th, at 7:36 p.m. a quake with a magnitude of 7.3 struck the northern Chinese city of Haicheng. Had authorities not recommended evacuation prior to its occurrence, it would have threatened the lives of millions. Instead, "only" 2,041 people lost their lives instead of the hundreds of thousands expected from a densely populated area hit by an earthquake of that magnitude. A year later, over 200,000 people were killed in a comparable major earthquake in Tangshan.

The Chinese government provided little information as to how the impossible had been achieved at Haicheng. Propaganda disseminated at the time patriotically claimed that the alarm had been raised based on measurements taken by heroic private individuals. In fact, only scientists were involved in the data collection and prediction.

Despite the success at Haicheng, experts still consider precise prediction of earthquakes to be virtually impossible. Scientists all over the world continue to work on systems that will make accurate earthquake prediction a reality.

Animals and fireballs

In many cultures around the world, animals and their behavior are thought to be sure indicators for an earthquake. Unusual animal behavior was reported from Tangshan and its surroundings shortly before the 1976 quake. Fish sprang from their aquariums, chickens ran around chaotically in the middle of the night, and rats fled houses to roam the streets. Other phenomena were observed as well. The water level of a well sank several yards three times on the day before the earthquake, noxious gases escaped from the ground, well rims developed cracks and fissures, and fireballs were seen in the sky. Flickering lights were noted, as were deep rumbling noises, like thunder, emanating from the earth.

The San Andreas fault is one of the earth's most tectonically active zones.

Most scientific authorities reject reliance on animal behavior alone to predict earthquakes. However, combining animal observation with advanced technological resources may help "round off" a prediction, provided, of course, that each kind of data supports the other.

The Richter scale

The American seismologist Charles F. Richter (1900–1985) developed the first objective means of measuring the destructive power of earthquakes. There are other ways, including the Shindo scale used in Japan and the Mercalli intensity scale, named after Italian volcanologist Giuseppe Mercalli (1850–1914). The Shindo and Mercalli methods, however, are subjective, based on visible and tangible effects of an earthquake. In contrast, orders of magnitude on the Richter scale are objective and open-ended. The magnitude is based on scientific measurement of amplitude, indicated by the degree of horizontal displacement—how far the earth is moving in either direction while shaking—recorded on an instrument called a seismometer.

The Richter scale is named after its inventor, Charles F. Richter (1900–1985).

The seismometer has a long history. The Chinese scholar Zhang Heng (78–139) is credited with inventing the first version in 132, a bronze cauldron with eight bronze dragons descending from its rim, each with a ball in its mouth. The dragon's jaws were wired to a pendulum swinging inside the pot. In the event of a seismic disturbance, the pendulum would swing, making the dragons' jaws open. The balls fell from the dragon's jaws and struck a gong, warning everyone within hearing distance that an earthquake was imminent. Zhang Heng designed his cauldron not just to study earthquakes, but to also predict them. Modern seismologists continue along his path.

Razed to the Ground

THE TANGSHAN EARTHQUAKE

In the pre-dawn hours of July 28, 1976, at 3:42 a.m., an unexpected earthquake of magnitude 8.2 on the Richter scale devastated the city of Tangshan in the northeastern province of Hebei, China. At least 250,000 people were killed out of a population of around one million, and some set the death toll as much as three times higher; a further 200,000 were badly injured. The Tangshan earthquake claimed more lives than any other earthquake disaster of the twentieth century. If the higher figures for the death toll are accurate, it may have been the deadliest earthquake of all time.

In 1976, an earthquake of magnitude 8.2 rocked Tangshan in China. Nearly every building was destroyed, and 800,000 people were trapped in the rubble.

800,000 people buried under the rubble

The inhabitants of Tangshan, an important industrial and mining city, were asleep in their beds when the earthquake hit in the early morning hours of July 28, 1976. Eyewitness reports describe the city shaking "like a sieve." The first and most devastating series of tremors lasted no more then 15 seconds. The epicenter lay some 6.8 miles under the surface of the earth, but directly below the city. Including the initial aftershocks, the quake was over within two minutes, which was, however, more than enough time to raze the city to the ground. Nearly every building in the city collapsed, burying almost 800,000 people under the rubble. Tangshan was not even thought to lie in a zone prone to earthquakes, and as a result, its building codes did not require any of the special safety measures that are common in place in threatened areas. Walls tumbled down like dominoes, roofs collapsed, and floors

telescoped, crushing the sleeping population of Tangshan in their beds.

Buried alive inside a coal mine

Not everyone in Tangshan was asleep, of course. Miners on the night shift were buried alive as they worked deep beneath the earth. With so many coal mines winding their way beneath the city streets, whole blocks of houses, with their inhabitants still inside, just vanished into the earth when the mine shafts collapsed during the quake. In the hours after the disaster, the city was cloaked in a gigantic cloud of dust. Miraculously, many people were able to free themselves from the fallen buildings and began searching for relatives and neighbors trapped in the rubble. The survivors found themselves in a totally devastated city, without water, without food, and without electricity. An incredible 90 percent of homes and about 80 percent of industrial buildings simply no longer existed. Nearly all the water-pumping stations and the city's entire water supply network were completely destroyed, and 20 percent of the waste treatment plants were unusable. Through it all, buildings continued to collapse and the bridges spanning the river began to sway on their damaged foundations.

Aftershocks

Fifteen hours after the quake hit, a major aftershock measuring 7.2 on the Richter scale hit the city in the afternoon, killing many of the people still pinned in the rubble awaiting rescue. Many more aftershocks would follow, each one raising the death toll further. The aftershocks were strong enough to cause structural damage as far away as Beijing, some 85 miles away. In the end, the disaster rendered more than 5 million homes in China completely uninhabitable.

Medical assistance

More than 700,000 people were in desperate need of medical care, but the hospitals had been destroyed, and many of the medical staff buried under the rubble. The doctors who arrived from other cities to help had to operate in the midst of an entirely chaotic situation. Medical instruments were in short supply. Doctors and nurses, working non-stop to help the injured, sterilized all their equipment in saline solution and operated with the help of acupuncture when anesthesia ran out. Soldiers arrived to pump drinking water from the wells and parachute food packages into the devastated city. Although the railroad tracks were badly twisted and tangled, more than 40,000 workers were brought in to repair them right away. Amazingly, they finished the job within just six days, permitting steady resupply and the evacuation of the injured. The opening of

Worst earthquakes in northern Asia

1293: Kamakura, Japan: 300,000 dead	1850: Sichuan, China: 300,000 dead
1556: Shaanxi, China: 800,000 dead	1857: Tokyo, Japan: 107,000 dead
1596: Isumi, Japan: 2,000 dead	1920: Gansu, China: 200,000 dead
1705: Edo (today Tokyo), Japan: 20,000 dead	1923: Tokyo, Japan: 143,000 dead
1730: Kamikawa (Hokkaido), Japan: 137,000 dead	1976: Tangshan, China: 250,000 dead (official death toll)
	1996: Kobe, Japan: 6,000 dead

Distraught people wander through their destroyed city. More than 7,200 multigenerational families were completely extinguished, with all their members killed in the quake.

Although the rail tracks were badly mangled by the earthquake, the main route was repaired in six days.

The Chairman of the Communist Party of China, Hua Guofeng, applauds the workers rebuilding Tangshan.

the railroad was crucial. All roads leading to Tangshan were either blocked with debris or so fractured by fissures and crevasses that they were completely impassable.

The vast numbers of corpses resulting from the disaster were quickly buried, most near the site of their former homes. Within a few days, this led to a public heath crisis when heavy rainfall caused flooding that floated many of the dead out of their shallow graves to the surface. Every one of the tens of thousands of corpses had to be exhumed and reburied more carefully outside the city.

Ideology over humanity

The extreme variation in the information released concerning the death toll of the Tangshan earthquake was due to the chaotic political situation in the People's Republic of China at the time. That year, 1976, was the last of the Cultural Revolution, during which there was a tendency to play down the consequences of disasters of all kinds. China thus reported an earthquake with a magnitude of 7.8, despite the fact that international sources measured it at 8.2. The reported death toll fluctuated between the extremes of 250,000 and 750,000, as different sources released widely varying figures. Just one week after the disaster, an article appeared in the Beijing *People's Daily* newspaper that reflected the spirit of Chinese politics at the time. The article told the story of Che Cheng-min, a member of the communist party, a politburo representative and citizen of Tangshan. The article tells how Cheng-min heard the cries of his 13-year-old and 16-year-old children after he had managed to free himself from the rubble. He was about to begin digging them out as well when he heard the voice of the chairman of the Tangshan politburo, who was trapped in a collapsed building nearby. Without hesitation, he went first to free the chairman, for the chairman must live to organize the rescue efforts for the people. The chairman was rescued and survived. Cheng-min's children, however, died before they could be rescued. The article emphasized that our hero showed no sign of regret or grief. Ideology had won out over humanity. He had sacrificed his children for the good of his fellow citizens.

Reconstruction

Three years after the earthquake, after the regional infrastructure had been restored and the dead properly buried, all of China, according to the propaganda, joined in the task of rebuilding the destroyed city. The fear of another quake was so great that discussions

about whether or not to rebuild the city at the same location lasted three years. It was a further ten years before the city, razed to the ground, rose from the ruins. Today, Tangshan is a city of millions once again. The fear remains, but the people have learned to live with the ever-present possibility of disaster. Tanghan has been officially declared "China's Bravest City." A memorial in city center commemorates the disaster, and China's only earthquake museum is located nearby.

This memorial bearing the names of the victims was erected on the 30th anniversary of the Tangshan earthquake.

Ash was catapulted some 11 miles into the stratosphere. The columns of smoke could be seen from a great distance.

A MOUNTAIN EXPLODES

THE ERUPTION OF MOUNT ST. HELENS

Because of its symmetrical beauty, Mount St. Helens in the state of Washington is also known as the Mount Fuji of America. Eternal ice and snow shimmer idyllically on its peak— or did so until the catastrophe of May 18, 1980, when the volcano erupted—completely unpredicted—after an earthquake triggered a landslide of the entire northern flank. The release of pent-up pressure caused the numerous explosions that followed, and an avalanche of rocks, boulders, ash, and ice destroyed everything in its path for hundreds of miles. More than sixty people lost their lives in this natural catastrophe.

Naming the mountain

Between 1792 and 1794, Commander George Vancouver and his crew aboard the expedition ship HMS *Discovery* explored the Pacific coast of North America. Early on in this journey, in October of 1792, they gave the towering volcano on the west coast of America the name Mount St. Helens—after the British diplomat Alleyne Fitzherbert (1753–1839), who bore the title of Baron St. Helens.

Mount St. Helens is surrounded by several "brother" peaks. Mount Adams lies at a distance of about 30 miles; roughly 48 miles away is the gigantic cascade volcano Mount Rainer; and Mount Hood soars into the sky above the neighboring state of Oregon.

History of eruption

Despite this density of great volcanoes in northwestern North America, there are only a few reports of eruptions. Until 1980, the volcanoes of the region were considered to be "alive" but not active. Today Mount St. Helens is classified as a dangerous volcano, yet until that day in May of 1980, reports of volcanic activity had been sparse. Evidence could be found for four major eruptions that have taken place over the last 520 years, each of which had ejected as much as 1,308,000 cubic yards of ash and stone into the atmosphere, in addition to dozens of smaller eruptions. An eruption occured in 1480 that, according to contemporary estimates, was four times more forceful than that of 1980. Impressive as that is, there is geological proof of even more violent activity during the 50,000 years this powerful volcano has been in existence.

Lava bulge

A lava bulge is the result of many smaller eruptions. Its creation is comparable to an upright tube of toothpaste, which squeezes out lava that is so rich in silicon and so viscous when cool that it can scarcely flow, if at all. At the upper, outer edge, the lava cools and a skin forms that tears from time to time when additional lava forces its way up from below. Occasionally small eruptions may occur, during which parts of the upper skin are catapulted into the air due to greatly increased pressure inside the volcano. If the lava bulge inside the crater of Mount St. Helens were to continue to grow at its current rate of around 3.6 cubic miles a year, it would take almost a hundred years for the crater to refill itself to its level prior to the 1980 eruption.

In more recent times, there must have been an eruption in the year 1800. Missionaries, fur trappers, and traders heard reports of clouds of ash and ash rain from Native Americans of the Sanspoil and Spokane tribes. In November 1842, the clergyman Josiah Parrish in Oregon, about 80 miles southwest of Mount St. Helens, witnessed an eruption. According to his report, the earth shook and ash rained down from a darkened sky. On the following day, Mount St. Helens had spread its ash over the Columbia River like a snow shower.

Mount St. Helens rising majestically above picturesque Spirit Lake.

A river meanders its way through a field of pumice stone, the surface of which is permeated by salts, in Mount St. Helens National Park in Washington.

Vast areas of woodland caught on fire following the eruption.

opened up to settlers at a very late point in US history. It was not until the second half of the nineteenth century that Oregon and Washington were first settled by Europeans; Oregon became a state in 1859 and Washington only attained this status in 1889. Settlement was extremely sparse until the early years of the twentieth century. Thus it is not surprising that no exact details of volcanic activity prior to that time exist.

An earthquake triggers the catastrophe

Like most volcanoes of the Cascade Range, Mount St. Helens is a great cone filled with basalt, lava, and other types of rock. Several lava bulges had formed on its slopes prior to 1980. The region around the volcano was a nature reserve, a paradise for hunters, anglers, and hikers. Its thick woods, rich in fauna, as well as the trout and salmon that were plentiful in its clear streams and rivers, were an invitation to visitors.

During the two months in 1980 prior to the catastrophic eruption, more than 10,000 earth-

It is thought that there had been more or less continual volcanic activity at Mount St. Helens up until 1857. Thereafter, there were reports of smaller eruptions in 1898, 1903, and 1921, although there are no supporting records of these events. In light of what has become known since 1980, these must have been smaller eruptions or steam explosions with little ejection of rock. It is interesting to bear in mind that this region of the USA was only

quakes were registered in Washington state, including several steam explosions. At the same time, the swelling of the lava bulge on the north flank, known as Goat Rocks, increased by more than 262 feet.

At 8:32 a.m. on May 18, 1980, an earthquake of magnitude 5.1 occured directly underneath the volcano. This was the trigger for the enormous eruption that quickly followed in its wake. Within a few seconds, the entire north flank of the moutain exploded, creating one of the most gargantuan rock and debris avalanches of all time, advancing at a speed of 60 miles per hour. Within seconds, the temperature in the danger zone had soared to over 570°F. Snow and ice on the peak of Mount St. Helens melted, creating raging torrents that poured down the slopes into the valleys, destroying all life in their path. Within minutes, a cloud of ash formed over the volcano that rose more than 11 miles upward. The wind blew nearly 600 million tons of ash over almost 23,000 square miles of the northwestern USA. By lunchtime the ash cloud in the stratosphere had reached the state of Idaho, and by 3:00 p.m. it reached Montana, from where it started to move south owing to the prevailing winds. At the end of the day, it had arrived in Colorado to the southeast. On this day, the volcano lost significant height: within a few hours the peak of the mountain, now absent, was transformed into ash and dust and rained down over the northwestern USA to form a blanket of debris.

Witnesses in various states described the explosion as deafening, and the ash rain as a fine gray sand smelling of sulfur.

Since the 1980 eruption, a new lava bulge measuring 3,600 feet in diameter and 820 feet high has formed on Mount St. Helens. It is estimated to contain around 3,200,000,000 cubic feet of lava.

Fifty-seven people lost their lives as a direct result of the catastrophe. The eruption was also indirectly responsible for seven further victims who died in a plane crash and a severe road accident, thus establishing the total number of fatalities as sixty-four.

Smoke and ash were catapulted out of Mount St. Helens in Washington state by the massive volcanic eruption of May 18, 1980.

DESTRUCTION AT DAWN

THE KOBE EARTHQUAKE

The people of Kobe, Japan, had reason to feel secure despite the fact that they lived in a region prone to earthquakes. There had been no major earthquake in Japan for forty-seven years. The science of earthquake detection was well developed and the people of Japan well trained in how to behave should disaster strike. Surely, were an earthquake to threaten, it would not be a big one. This security was shattered as a massive earthquake hit Kobe as dawn broke on January 17, 1995. Houses collapsed, roads were torn apart like paper, and rail ties were twisted off the tracks. Over 6,000 people lost their lives, and more than 300,000 were rendered homeless.

The wooden houses of Kobe could not withstand the earthquake.

Destroyed within 20 seconds

People in western Japan have always felt relatively safe from major earthquakes, despite the fact that Japan, like the entire region surrounding the Pacific Ocean, is a particularly earthquake-prone region of the world. This is because it lies at the conjunction point of three tectonic plates. Earthquakes can and do occur when these continental plates shift and thus grind against each other.

At 5:46 a.m. local time on January 17, 1995, what is now known as the Kobe earthquake took place along the Nojima fault, located some 10 miles underground. Although it only lasted a mere 20 seconds, it would prove to be the most costly earthquake of all time. Its magnitude reached 7 on the Shindo scale, which is the system most commonly used in Japan (see box on p. 50). A 7 on the Shindo scale is approximately equal to an earthquake with a magnitude of 7.2 on the Richter scale. The earthquake was so strong that its rumblings caused fear and terror among the inhabitants of Osaka, another city about 20 miles away. The primeval fear of earthquakes and other natural disasters, so long dormant in Japan, had been awakened once again.

Many structures designed to be earthquake safe were damaged or destroyed. The quake claimed over 6,300 lives.

Deceptive safety

Japan has always led the world in the design and engineering of earthquake-proof buildings. Some of the world's first earthquake-safe houses and skyscrapers were built in Japan. Despite the extensive research that had gone into their construction, nearly all the buildings in Kobe collapsed or suffered severe damage during the 1995 earthquake. Theoretically, Japan should also have been exceptionally well prepared to react to a disaster of this kind. The Japanese knew from lengthy experience how to behave during an earthquake. Every school and workplace conducts regular earthquake drills. Never-

An eyewitness pays tribute to Kobe's *yakuza* (gangsters), the Yamaguchi-Gumi
"I shudder to think what would have happened if there had been no help from the Yamaguchi-Gumi.

I will never forget what they did for us. As long as I live I will tell my grandchildren and great-grandchildren about it, for one who forgets gratitude is no longer human."
Tetsu Tanimura, journalist

theless, no one had reckoned with a quake as strong as this one taking place within such a short span of time. The earth shook for less than 20 seconds. Everything was over well be-

Deep fissures were torn in the ground after the Kobe earthquake.

Offerings of flowers and food were set out all over Kobe in remembrance of lost relatives and friends.

fore Kobe's citizens could gather their wits and react. At the time of day when the earthquake hit, most people were still at home in bed or eating breakfast. This was a bit of good luck. Had offices, businesses, shops, and streets not been relatively empty, the number of people killed and injured would have been much higher. Commuters jamming the trains and buses on their way to work just two hours later would have paid the greatest price.

The cost of the destruction

The disaster of 1995 was the worst earthquake in western Japan since 1923. In addition to the houses that collapsed and buried their inhabitants, a 3-mile stretch of the four-lane Hanshin freeway, built high on pilings and considered earthquake-safe, gave way. Steel and concrete debris crashed down onto the road below; the lights of crushed cars were visible inside the mountains of rubble. The quake destroyed more than 150,000 buildings; then fire broke out. Hundreds of fires burnt to the ground an area greater than 250 acres. Over 300,000 of the city's 1.4 million inhabitants found themselves homeless, and six months after the disaster, 17,000 people were still living on the streets. The harbor, once the heart of an international shipping port with the greatest volume of non-oil shipments in the world, was heavily damaged. As a port city, Kobe has yet to recover. The financial cost of the damage was estimated at around $100 billion, more than half of which was spent rebuilding Kobe's transportation network and other infrastructure.

Criticism of disaster management

It was a long time before all those who had lost their homes finally had a roof over their heads again. Gas, water, and electrical systems had been completely destroyed. It was deemed too expensive to repair them, meaning that Kobe's citizens had to wait until completely new utility systems could be built. Rainfall levels had been so low the previous summer of 1994 that the city's resevoirs were almost empty at the time of the earthquake. When the post-earthquake fires broke out, often quite a distance away from each other, the fire department was unable to keep them from spreading. Critics of the disaster management and recovery efforts suggested that too much time and money had been

Measuring an earthquake

The strength of an earthquake can be quantified in a number of ways. The Richter scale, the most commonly used system, is based on measurement of the seismic intensity of tremors over time and the amount of energy released by a quake. In contrast to the open-ended Richter scale, the Japanese-derived Shindo scale is a closed system based on subjective criteria including visual assessment of the damage and subjective experience of the quake. Developed by Japanese scientists in 1949, it scores each earthquake from zero to seven:
ZERO: a tremor can be registered, but is not generally noticed
ONE: a weak tremor, noticed by a few sensitive people.
TWO: a tremor felt by most of the people in an affected area.
THREE: a moderate earthquake that everyone notices. Buildings sway and windows break.
FOUR: a medium earthquake with strongly swaying buildings. People walking on the street or driving a car will feel it.
FIVE: a strong earthquake, collapsing walls and streetlights.
SIX: a destructive earthquake. Up to 30% of buildings collapse.
SEVEN: the strongest quake. Fissures open in the ground and more buildings collapse. Transportation and other infrastructure is destroyed.

Wrapped in a blanket, 12-year-old Emi Shimazu sits in front of the ruins of her home following the 1995 earthquake.

devoted to quantifying data about earthquakes, time and money that might have been better spent formulating concrete plans about what to do in the aftermath of a major event.

In the days and weeks that followed, drinking water, food, blankets, warm clothing (Kobe is cold in January), and many daily necessities were in short supply. The government provided almost no emergency accommodation for the homeless, leaving the population to make do on their own. The few passable roads, such as the highway to Osaka, were choked with traffic as Kobe's survivors made the journey to buy essential supplies. Contributions from abroad and some government aid helped a little. The *yakuza*, members of a criminal organization normally the subject of fear and loathing, helped greatly. Using dubiously won "connections," the gangsters of the *yakuza* stepped forward and distributed generous aid to those in need.

The yakuza and the earthquake

The Japanese Prime Minister, Tomiichi Murayama (born 1924), visited the disaster area and promised immediate help. He did not, however, keep his promise. Desperately needed water, wool blankets, tents, and toilets failed to arrive. People waited in mile-long lines for water and food. Help came in the form of the *yakuza*, a mafia-like criminal organization. Its members used speedboats and helicopters to bring aid into the destroyed city. The motto of the *yakuza*

is *jingi*, which means, broadly, "justice." The *yakuza* code of honor demands that mercy be shown when somebody is in difficulty. This is why, they said, they intervened in the face of much resistance from the police and other authorities. It is estimated that the *yakuza* provided some $10 million in aid in the aftermath of the Kobe earthquake.

Critical voices claimed that what looked like charity was in fact done to further the gangsters' own best interests. The *yakuza* needed to reestablish the status quo so that they could resume their criminal activities as fast as possible.

A still-intact school provided shelter from the cold for the victims of the earthquake of January 1995.

WALLS OF FLAME REACHING TO THE SKY

THE GALICIAN FOREST FIRES IN SPAIN, 2006

Forest fires in southern Europe are an annual event. Still, the summer of 2006 was exceptional. During the first two weeks of August alone, more than 2,055 fires were reported in Galicia, a province of Spain. Four people lost their lives in the flames. Thousands of firefighters, soldiers, and volunteers fought wildfires that devoured more than 195,000 acres of forest. Investigations showed that most of the blazes were started deliberately, and arson was blamed for as many as 80 percent of the fires.

fires. Between the years 2000 and 2004, around 22,000 fires were registered annually; in 2005 the number climbed to almost 26,000. In 2006, prior to the devastating fires that took place in August, over 270,000 acres of land had already been torched, and some three-quarters of that land was in the province of Galicia. The World Wildlife Fund (WWF) estimated the cost of the environmental, economic, and social damage at more than $7,000 per acre, even without taking into account the long-term effects of erosion and the subsequent loss of soil fertility. Some of these wildfires were natural, set off by lightening strikes, but most were not. A considerable body of evidence shows that the great majority were the result of arson.

Fire is a terrifying natural force. Observers compare fighting a fire in a forest to holding off sheets of flames falling from the sky.

Spain's rapidly expanding steppe

The weather in Spain is characterized by aridity. The country is home to Europe's most rapidly expanding steppe, which in the summer becomes a tinderbox-dry mixture of grass- and scrubland. Every summer brings drought and wild-

Organized gangs of arsonists?

With arson blamed for most of the 2006 fire season in Galicia, the Spanish police arrested more than sixty suspects, fourteen of whom were charged and imprisoned. Seven were admitted to psychiatric institutions. Twenty-eight

were released on probation, and the remainder were freed for lack of evidence. One of those taken into custody was a member of the local voluntary fire department! In Spain, these part-time firefighters are paid according to the number of incidents they respond to.

There was also evidence that pointed to organized bands of arsonists. A major part of the Spanish drug trade operates out of Galicia. Perhaps the arsonists sought to divert author-ities' attention by creating a fiery chaos in the hills. In most cases, the main motive was economic. Many experts have since concluded that the fires were an attempt to raise the price

The biggest fire ever
The biggest wildfire ever occurred in October 1871 near the city of Peshtigo, Wisconsin. More than 385 square miles of forest were destroyed after strong winds fanned the flames over several days. A total of 1,500 people died, and nine towns were burnt to the ground.

of timber, which at the time was at a historic low. Local foresters may also have wanted to cash in on European Union subsidies available to those willing to plant quick-growing euca-lyptus trees to supply the paper industry. Most of the blame was laid at the door of land speculators seeking to clear land for grazing or building. There were also a few pyromaniacs involved, driven by a pathological desire to see things burn. The Spanish minister of agricul-ture, Alfredo Suárez Canal, concluded that this "new type" of arsonist had clearly intended to cause the greatest possible damage, proven by the number of fires deliberately set near towns and villages. Though the government called on the country to fight this "terrorism by fire," it would soon be revealed that the Spanish gov-ernment itself was not without blame.

Arsonists continued to set new fires while others were fighting to save their lives and property.

Villagers look on helplessly as the fire approaches.

Galicians spent the summer of 2006 fighting virtually non-stop against the devastating forest fires. Four people lost their lives and hundreds were injured.

Criticism of the government

The WWF's forestry experts estimate that almost $2 billion went up in flames in 2006, in part because government authorities did not take adequate precautions against forest fires. Noting that the number of forest fires in Spain had increased ten-fold since the 1960s, urgent action was recommended.

Fires in other countries

Every summer, fires devastate enormous areas of forest and scrubland in Greece, Italy, and southern France. Portugal was badly hit in 2005, with an area of approximately 615,000 acres devoured by flames. The EU commission is promoting the European Forest Fire Information Service (EFFIS), a commission designed to serve as a platform for the exchange of information between the nineteen partici-

pating countries with a goal of improving risk assessment and prevention.

Forest fires also hit the USA every year, concentrated in the western part of the country. Every year, the citizens of Los Angeles County wonder whether the advancing fires will be stopped before they reach their homes, and every year thousands of people are forced to flee from the flames.

Considering that forest fires are "regular" disasters in both Spain and Portugal, the laws in place to protect the forests from fire were remarkably lax. There were few rangers roaming the hills to enforce the controls that did exist. Next to no one in Spain was employed clearing undergrowth, a common procedure that helps keep fire from spreading out of control. The increasing number of forest fires is also related to how a forest is used. Rural depopulation had led to an exponential increase in unmanaged forests. This failure of forestry policy, along with the summer heat wave, drought, and human perfidy, all contributed to the disaster.

Conspiracy theories

One reason proposed for the high number of fires throughout Spain in 2005, the year before the Galician fires, was the passing of the "mountain law" by the Spain's socialist government. The law banned the use of land for building or agricultural purposes for up to thirty years after a fire. The law was scheduled to take effect after the summer of 2005. It is therefore prob-

ably correct to surmise that a high proportion of that year's fires were the result of people trying to gain land for speculation and development before the mountain law made forest clearance difficult, if not impossible. In the summer of 2006, the number of fires declined throughout Spain, with the exception of the province of Galicia, where they increased sharply. What could explain the discrepancy?

The government saw itself confronted by what it referred to as a "campaign by fire." Spanish Interior Minister Alfredo Pérez Rubalcaba believed that the Galician fires were less a natural phenomenon than a series of strategically planned political attacks. He blamed the conservative People's Party (PP) that had been a power in Galicia for decades and accused them of trying to draw attention to the political incompetence of the socialists, who had replaced them in office, by sending the government scrambling to fight thousands of fires. What is now clear is that every one of the many potential causes of the Galician fires played a role in the disaster. There were so many fires that every variety of arsonist was likely involved, for a wide variety of reasons. In the end, it was heavy rainfall that finally snuffed out the fires of 2006. What might the next summers bring?

The flames continued to spread despite firefighters working around the clock.

Inhabitants of the affected areas desperately tried to stop the flames.

STORMS
AND FLOODS

Wind and water are essential for life on earth, yet they can also be deadly. It is not uncommon for storms and floods to obliterate human works like mere playthings. Scientists interpret the recent increase in extreme weather conditions as the consequence of damaging ecological imbalance: there have never been more victims to mourn or greater material damage than today. The living organism we call the world is unwell.

THE STORM SURGE THAT CHANGED COASTLINES

Dredger barges raise temporary dikes.

THE GREAT NORTH SEA FLOOD OF 1953

In medieval times, the European North Sea coast was regularly devastated by storm tides and flood surges. The worst of these events would be given the name of the saint on whose feast day the disaster occurred. The destructive force of these surging floodwaters was such that, over the centuries, they have repeatedly altered the line of the coast itself. The most devastating of these pre-modern floods occurred in 1362 on the name day of St. Marcellus. In a single night, the St. Marcellus storm, driven by hurricane-force winds, created the Dollart, a bay near the Dutch-German border with an area of 40 square miles. In 1953, the most powerful North Sea storm surge of the modern era brought catastrophic floods to the low-lying coastlands of the Netherlands, Belgium, and Great Britain. The Delta Works project, a comprehensive realign-ment and rebuilding of the Dutch lowlands, as well as the construction of the Thames Barrier downriver from London, were both direct results of this disaster.

Historical North Sea storm floods

Since very early times, people living in low-lying North Sea coastal areas have tried to protect themselves and their property from floodwaters. An extensive system of dikes was constructed through well-organized communal efforts, the European equivalent of the levees found in the United States. People in coastal areas built their houses perched on artificial mounds called *warften*, which elevated them above land that was technically below sea level. Nevertheless, nature, ever unpredictable, has always managed to regain the upper hand in the end. Every few generations, storm surges occur of such ferocity that dikes and dams thought to be secure cannot hold back the floodwaters. The first great flood documented by historical sources hit the North Sea coast on February 17, 1164, the Juliana Flood, named for the feast day celebrated the day before the disaster struck. The storm surge created an enormous new bay on the coast of the Netherlands, the Jadebusen, which is still there today.

The Grote Mandrenke

The most famous pre-modern North Sea coastal disaster is probably the Marcellus Flood of 1362. The German North Sea coastline was left utterly changed by the strength and volume of its immense storm surge. The sea devoured enormous areas of what had been fertile marshlands, destroying a great many flourishing villages and small towns as the flood tide moved inland. The Marcellus Flood topped even the tallest dikes of the time by more than 6 feet. Popularly known as the *Grote Mandrenke* ("great drowning of men"), some sources mention more than 100,000 victims.

Naturally, efforts were made to counter the ever-present threat of inundation with ever higher and broader dikes. Most medieval dikes were relatively short, approximately 13 feet tall, whereas modern versions can be twice that high atop a base that is more than 300 feet wide. Nevertheless, nature continues to fight back, eager to challenge the sense of security these bulwarks against disaster are meant to provide.

Debris and household possessions float in the water-filled streets of the flooded town of Stellendam, Holland one night after the flooding.

The Thames Barrier

The Thames Barrier in the London suburb of Woolwich is the world's largest mobile flood control structure. Planning for this gigantic bulwark began following the storm surge and floods of 1953. Construction took place from 1974 to 1984. The ten rotating floodgates rest on the bed of the Thames so as not to hinder the flow of shipping traffic on the river. They can be closed within 15 minutes in the event of a storm surge, protecting London and the low-lying Thames Valley from flooding.

Hurricane over the North Sea

During the last days of January 1953, a low pressure weather system formed to the south of Iceland and began to move in the direction of Scotland. A storm developed on its heels, pushing the low further southeast. By midday on January 31, 1953, the storm, which had developed hurricane-force winds, held the entire North Sea in its grip. The surging storm increased the height of the already seasonally high, record-breaking tides along the Dutch coast. In many places, seawater was already beginning to crash up and over the dikes. The pressure produced by the storm prevented the tidal waters from draining back away from the coast: there would be no ebb tide that evening. In the early morning hours of February 1, the storm still raged unabated, and sea level rose to 16 feet above normal. The dikes could not hold back water that high. The first of them was breached around 3 a.m. Unimpeded, the worst storm surge of the last 500 years rushed in and struck the Netherlands full force.

The consequences

Meteorologists had long underestimated the extent of the floods that could result when—as in 1953—a high spring tide is chased by a cyclonic storm. The lack of warning was also an issue. Disaster struck in the middle of the night, too late to warn people living in the low-lying areas, let alone evacuate them. In 1953, a last minute warning via radio or television was impossible. There were no regularly scheduled broadcasts at night, making it unlikely that anyone would be listening. When the dikes began to break, eventually breaching in more than 100 locations, everyone was completely unpre-

The Delta Works

The Delta Works are a gigantic protective system of dams and surge barriers. An integral part of the reconstruction of the Dutch coastline following the 1953 disaster, the Delta Works completely altered the coastal lowlands to ensure that such a catastrophe could never happen again. The great North Sea flood of 1953 devastated the deltas of the Maas and Waal Rivers, where the dikes had failed. The solution was to block the estuaries with storm surge barriers, shortening the length of exposed Dutch coastline by more than 370 miles. The most technically complex section is the Oosterscheldekering, a storm surge barrier with 62 gigantic sluice gates that can be closed within an hour should danger threaten.

pared. More than 1,800 people drowned in the Netherlands alone, as well as with 200,000 farm animals, and 500,000 acres of agricultural land, inundated by saltwater, were rendered unusable. The neighboring country of Belgium was also gravely affected. The death toll in England was over 300, with 100,000 acres of arable land ruined. The people who lived along the North Sea coast were badly shaken. With the dikes now exposed as insufficient, planning for the installation of giant, artificial, protective barriers began immediately after the disaster. The Dutch "Delta Works" and British "Thames Barrier" were the result.

The local population returned to their destroyed villages after the dikes were repaired. Months later, their fields, streets, and homes were still a sea of mud and debris.

Cadets Caught in a Hurricane

THE SINKING OF THE TRAINING SHIP PAMIR

The sailing ship *Pamir* was a training and transport vessel that ran into a hurricane in the Atlantic Ocean. In service primarily to train the German merchant marine's next generation of officers, the *Pamir* was also loaded with a cargo of barley from Argentina. Fifty-two of the ship's crew of eighty-six were trainees, among them cadets, an apprentice ship's carpenter, and other young men. The *Pamir* sank in the storm, killing eighty sailors. Subsequent investigation blamed the ship's owners and the onboard command for the catastrophe.

The four-masted bark Pamir *was a training ship as well as a freighter.*

The eight sisters

The long-established Hamburg shipping company, F. Laeisz, was famous for constructing fast sailing ships that have always borne names beginning with the letter "P." These ships, employed primarily in the saltpeter trade with Chile, were known among seamen as the "Flying-P liners." The last of their kind ever built were a series of eight, four-masted barks that began sailing between 1903 and 1926. Similar to each other in size and construction, they were referred to as the eight sisters. Their names were *Pangani*, *Petschili*, *Pamir*, *Peking*, *Passat*, *Pola*, *Priwall*, and *Padua*. Three of these sisters still survive today: the *Passat* and *Peking* as museum ships in Lübeck and New York respectively, and the *Padua* as a Russian training ship now sailing under the name *Kruzenshtern*.

The history of the Pamir

The *Pamir* left Hamburg harbor on its maiden voyage to Chile in October 1905. Built as a freighter, the ship worked the saltpeter route between Germany and Chile for the next nine years until the outbreak of World War I. The *Pamir* was at sea in the Atlantic at the time war was declared. Unable to penetrate the British blockade of the English Channel to reach its home port, the *Pamir* spent the next six years anchored in a quiet bay on the Island of Parma, waiting for the war to end.

In 1920, the Pamir returned to Hamburg and resumed her Chilean trade route from 1924 to 1931. Over the next two decades, the ship sailed under several flags, first out of Finland and then New Zealand, before finally being sold to a Belgian scrap yard. A year later, the *Pamir* and her sister ship, the *Passat*, were purchased by a German syndicate. Following a general refitting in Kiel, both ships were returned to service. In 1954 they were part of a foreclosure sale, and a consortium of forty German shipping companies acquired both ships at auction for use as training vessels.

The Pamir capsizes

On September 21, 1957, the *Pamir* was returning to Germany from Argentina with more than 4,000 tons of barley in her hold. Most of the barley was not in sacks, but stored in bulk, and therefore not secured against slippage or shifting. At 8:00 hours ship's time, the radio operator received a warning about Hurricane Carrie, which was forecast to cross the shipping route. The outer edges of the storm reached the ship just one hour later. Hurricane force winds battered the sailing ship. By the time the *Pamir*'s final SOS was sent, its sails had been shredded and it was listing more than 45 degrees. The ship could not be righted because the cargo had shifted, throwing off its center of gravity. A

The New York freighter rescued the five occupants of lifeboat no. 5 after they had spent two days on the open sea.

final, unintelligible radio message was sent around 16:00 hours. Shortly thereafter, the ship capsized. It drifted with its keel upturned in the raging Atlantic Ocean for a further 20 minutes. Many crewmen were hopelessly trapped inside the ship's hull with no chance of escape. The lifeboats could not be let down due to the extreme list of the ship. Those who survived the sinking of the *Pamir* were left with three damaged lifeboats found floating in the debris-filled ocean. Thirty seamen were able to climb into the lifeboats, where there was no food or drinking water.

Only six survivors

After the *Pamir*'s SOS raised the alarm, no fewer than seventy-eight different ships sailed to the area to begin an immediate search for survivors. They were joined the next day, after the storm has abated, by eleven airplanes. At the time, this was the largest search and rescue mission every undertaken for a disaster at sea. Two days later, the steamer *Saxon* came upon the *Pamir*'s no. 5 lifeboat. It was no more than a wreck, with neither bow nor stern, but did carry five of the last remaining survivors. Only two hours earlier, a sixth sailor had swum away, never to be seen again. Only one other crewman survived. He was found a day later, the sole survivor of the second lifeboat. Eighty seamen had been killed in the disaster, including all the ship's officers.

The investigation by the Lübeck Maritime Board of Inquiry

The sinking of the *Pamir* caused great consternation in Germany. Not a single member of the ship's command had survived, making it difficult to come to any definitive conclusions as to what decision or circumstances or why might have been responsible for the disaster.

The sinking of the *Pamir* was thoroughly investigated nonetheless, bringing to light a wide range of evidence, all of which pointed to negligence both on the part of the ship's owners and of those in command onboard. The sails had obviously been struck much too late, perhaps because the captain thought it was still

The Pamir's masts and its rigging were impressive.

The emotions of the survivors of the Pamir swung between relief at being rescued and grief for their lost comrades.

possible to sail away from the hurricane. The cargo of barley was transported unsecured, leaving it to shift around the hold in the high waves and wind. Many of the ship's hatches had been left open, bringing in water that further increased the list of the ship. The ballast tanks had been filled with bulk barley. Had the tanks been empty, it would have been possible to flood them with water in an emergency. This would have improved the ship's stability to the point that it might have survived the storm. The captain had not dared to flood the tanks because of the risk of the barley swelling to the point of bursting the hull. Overall, the ship's command lacked the experience necessary to safely transport such a cargo, for which they and their crew paid the ultimate price.

One captain's experiment

The captain of one of the Pamir's sister ships, the Passat, doubted that swelling barley could really have burst the Pamir's steel-plated hull. He decided to conduct a small experiment to see if this was ever a genuine possibility. He filled a glass with barley, added water, and observed the reaction. The captain noted that the actual increase in the volume of the barley was minimal, even after it had soaked in water for four days. Two months later, the captain's simple experiment saved the crew of the Passat

from meeting the same tragic fate as the Pamir. The Passat, also laden with barley, sailed into heavy seas and, like the Pamir, began to list badly. The captain immediately ordered the lower tanks to be flooded, and the Passat was able to right itself at once. Nevertheless, the time of the Flying-P Liners as training and transport ships was coming to an end. The Passat was taken out of service and anchored in the harbor of Lübeck, Germany, where it remains as a museum ship today.

The sailing ship Kruzensthern, formerly the Padua, sits at anchor in New York harbor. A sister ship of the Pamir, she is today a Russian training vessel.

STORM SURGE IN HAMBURG

THE 1962 FLOOD OF A HANSEATIC CITY

In 1962, the Federal Republic of Germany was shaken when disaster hit the former Hanseatic city of Hamburg. A storm surge flooded the completely unprepared city. Some 75,000 of the city's inhabitants lost their homes, and 315 people were killed.

The hurricane approaches

On the evening of February 15, 1962, there were storm warnings for the North Sea. The low pressure system "Vincinette" was heading from the Arctic Sea toward the northern German coast. By the next day the storm had developed into a hurricane with winds of up to 125 miles per hour, and a storm tide was forecast. Hamburg, however, lies 60 miles inland. It was considered well protected from coastal flooding, which, in the past, had dissipated on the lower reaches of the Elbe River before coming anywhere near the city. That this storm might be different was never considered. Hamburg, it was assumed, would not be in danger, and so its citizens received no warning of what was to come.

The dikes are breached

But the events of the night of February 16 to 17 did not play out as expected. The cyclonic storm pushed surging seawater further up the Elbe than anyone had thought possible. More than sixty sections of the Elbe dikes were breached that night; 20 percent of Hamburg was soon underwater. The disaster struck a completely unprepared populace with no emergency disaster plan, alternative power source, or experienced personnel on hand. There was no means to react quickly and it was much too late for evacuation. The low-lying district of Hamburg-Wilhelmsburg suffered the most: of the flood's 315 victims, 222 died there.

The "flying angels"

A crisis task force was rapidly assembled under the leadership of Helmut Schmidt, the city's representative in the German senate. Immediate assistance was requested from military aircraft because the flooded areas could not be reached by land. Seventy-one helicopters from the German armed forces and twenty-five US Army aircraft were deployed. They worked nonstop bringing aid to trapped survivors, rescuing them from roofs. Hundreds of military boats were also brought in, making it possible to evacuate 20,000 people from the disaster area.

The homes and streets behind the breached dikes were completely flooded.

HG 98-HAMBURG 17/2/62 DEICHBRUCH UND ÜBERFLUTETE STRASSENZÜGE IN DEM HAMBURGER ELBVORORT FINKENWERDER.   UPI-TELE

Helmut Schmidt

Chancellor of the Federal Republic of Germany from 1974 to 1982, Helmut Schmidt (born 1918), was Hamburg's Senator for Internal Affairs at the time of the storm surge. Formerly a member of the armed forces committee of the German parliament, he had strong contacts to the military. He was thus able to bypass the usual bureaucracy and call in soldiers who could be deployed quickly. This was the first civilian disaster response in the history of the Federal Armed Forces. Although this deployment was not legally covered by the German constitution, the political courage and resolution Schmidt showed during the crisis greatly increased his stature within the country. The newly formed, post-World War II German Armed Forces were widely praised for their role in combating the disaster.

Rescuers moved slowly through the flooded districts of the city.

Aftermath

For 315 people in Hamburg, rescue came too late. The regional death toll of 340 included five members of the rescue forces, all victims of the floodwaters. The dikes were raised and strengthened in the aftermath of the catastrophe and emergency disaster plans were drawn up. Happily, in 1976 the dikes held against a storm surge that was 3 feet higher than the one that struck Hamburg on that terrible February night in 1962.

The desperate residents of the flooded districts were evacuated by boat.

A church spire towers over the Italian village of Longarone. On October 9, 1963, a wave of water washing over the Vajont Reservoir Dam completely destroyed the village.

FLOOD WAVE IN A RESERVOIR

A FLOOD WAVE SURMOUNTS THE VAJONT DAM

Today, Italy's Monte di Toc and the Vajont reservoir stand as symbols of a disaster that claimed more than 2,000 lives on October 9, 1963. More than forty years after this fateful night, the national power company, ENEL, still maintains a catwalk over the dam so that visitors can view the scene of the disaster. On that fateful day, a monstrous wave, triggered by a landslide, surmounted the crest of the Vajont Dam and roared its way down through the narrow valley. Within minutes, the village of Longarone at the other end of the valley had been obliterated.

Ambition and greed

The Vajont valley is located in the foothills of the Alps north of Venice. The valley is narrow, steep, and rich in water, all qualities that made it an ideal location for a hydroelectric dam. The people in charge of the power company SADE (Società Adriatica di Elettricità) invested in the construction of what they hoped would be a lucrative enterprise. The rapidly expanding cities of Milan and Turin in the Po valley would make ideal potential customers for the electricity produced.

In 1940, SADE petitioned the government for the right to build an enormous dam in the Vajont valley. Experts on the SADE payroll were happy to provide an overwhelmingly positive geological appraisal of the valley's topography and sedimentation. Resistance from local inhabitants was ignored. The project's organizers were not adverse to fomenting disputes between the valley's villages, which could not agree on who owned the rights to various tracts of communal land. One village was able to sell land to SADE without proving their legal ownership of the property.

Construction began in 1957 with many of the land ownership issues still unresolved. All of the necessary authorizations had not been granted when the engineers decided to raise the height of the dam from 650 feet to 855 feet in order to increase the volume of the reservoir to 5,300 million cubic feet. The intent was to make the Vajont project the largest concave dam in the world, a status accordingly celebrated in the SADE- controlled press.

The Vajont Dam disaster in literature and film

The Vajont reservoir disaster has been the subject of several books as well as the film Vajont by Italian director Renzo Martinelli, which debuted in European movie theaters in 2001. The film was based on a book written by Italian journalist Tina Merlin. For many years, Merlin extensively researched and wrote about the causes of the catastrophic incident, in particular giving voice to the perspective of the peasants who lived below the dam. She was indicted for her allegedly exaggerated accounts of the disaster, but a court in Milan later found her innocent of all charges. For the film, the giant tsunami wave pouring over the crest of the dam was reconstructed using computer animation.

Filling the reservoir

The dam was finally completed in September 1959. The first attempt at filling the reservoir followed. Within a year, there were indications that disaster lay ahead when a powerful mud-

The survivors still suffered from shock long after the disaster.

slide crashed down into the reservoir from the towering Monte di Toc to the south. The mountain's slope was now split by a crevasse more than a mile wide that even the most biased geologist could not ignore. There was fear that a further mudslide would cut the reservoir in two. The only precaution taken was to build a canal that would connect both halves should this occur; it was not anticipated that a flood wave of significant size could also result. In 1962, SADE was incorporated into the newly founded state power company ENEL (Ente Nazionale per l'Energia Elettricà), but at the Vajont dam and reservoir, it was business as usual. The third and final test filling began in April 1963 as the cracks in the mountainside became ever larger. A few weeks before the disaster, geologists conducted an intense survey in the surrounding area of the now 4-mile-long, 985-foot-wide reservoir. The results were so worrying that the mayor of one of the nearby villages advised people to leave the area. Only a few people followed his advice, and the state made no preparations for evacuation.

The mountainside tumbles down

The more water filled the reservoir, the more alarming the portents of coming disaster became. Villagers heard underground rumblings and ancient mountain paths became suddenly impassable due to landslides. ENEL still grimly clung to its project. The reservoir could not be allowed to drain because the dam was intended to generate power using that water. The disaster struck at midday on October 9. The employees of ENEL looked on as the mountainside very slowly began to slide. Finally, at 10:39 p.m., the situation raged completely out of control. From one moment to the next, the speed of the slide increased to 60 miles per hour. Mud and rock raced down the slopes of the Monte di Toc, crashing into the reservoir.

People in the Piave valley clean up after the 650-foot flood wave.

The displaced water formed two gigantic flood waves that swept up the opposite slopes of Monte di Toc, washing away the villages of Erto and Casso. One of the two waves continued on, arching over the crest of the dam. The dam itself held, but 1,700 million cubic feet of water from the 600-foot-high wave poured down into the Piave valley below it. The village of Longarone, just 2 miles away, was totally destroyed within a few minutes; two thousand people perished. The immense mass of swiftly flowing water left standing nothing but a tree and the church bell tower, the latter pointing skyward like the finger of fate. Nothing else remained of the once flourishing village. The dam itself was virtually undamaged, but the reservoir had completely vanished. The basin behind the dam was now filled with mud, rock and debris.

A natural disaster?

The Vajont dam still stands today, its reservoir emptied. The dam, once the highest in Europe, was left in place as a memorial, serving as a warning of the responsibility humankind bears when it tries to hold back the forces of nature. Investigations into the disaster, drawn out over many years, resulted in just one conviction and a ten-year prison term, of which only one year was actually served. The responsibility of the authorities and the project manager remains a matter of some controversy. Far too many warning signals were underestimated or ignored. Experts concluded that filling the reservoir, due to the so-called capillary effect, had altered the moisture levels of the soils and sediments of Monte di Loc to the extent that rainwater could no longer run off efficiently. Instead, the different layers of sediment remained wet and slippery until they finally culminated in a mudslide. Rapid draining of the reservoir's water, officials argued, would not have been able to prevent the landslide that caused the disaster. That the misbegotten dam, and the filling of its reservoir, had been responsible for the catastrophic flood wave that obliterated Longerone, remains officially unacknowledged.

A priest blesses the coffins of the victims of the Vajont disaster, which claimed around 2,000 lives.

SWATHES OF DESTRUCTION

THE SUPER OUTBREAK: 148 TORNADOES RAMPAGE THROUGH AMERICA

In April 1974, 148 tornados raged across the United States within eighteen hours. This disaster, known as the Super Outbreak, left more than 300 people dead and caused some $3,500,000,000 in damage. Thirteen states were afflicted by this—the biggest series of tornadoes there has ever been—and suffered serious damage. According to recent research, such an intense series of tornadoes can be expected to occur only once every 500 years.

It began in Illinois

The weather forecast for North America on Wednesday April 3, 1974 anticipated some rain showers on the East Coast and thunderstorms in the Midwest. Children went to school, adults went to work, people carried on as usual. Then, around lunchtime, the first tornado developed over Morris, a small town in Illinois—a relatively harmless whirlwind that was more of a local land spout than a genuine tornado. Further eastward, it had been sunny all day, but then a storm front moved in an easterly direction and the accompanying tornadoes grew in intensity. By the time the tornadoes reached the eastern border of the state of Illinois, they had already accounted for the first two deaths, and individual twisters were attaining category F3, which means they were strong enough to overturn trucks.

A threatening tornado approaches. An apparently peaceful country idyll can be totally devastated in mere minutes.

Rotating storms

Many different terms are used to describe rotating storms: cyclones, typhoons, tornadoes, hurricanes. What all these storms have in common is that they consist of fiercely rotating winds that spin around a vertical axis, clockwise in the southern hemisphere and counterclockwise in the northern hemisphere. Cyclone, typhoon, and hurricane are various regional terms for tropical rotating storms that develop over the oceans, drawing their strength from moisture rising from the warm water. They are given different names depending on the region in which they develop. In the Caribbean and southeastern USA they are called hurricanes, in the Indian Ocean (especially in the Bay of Bengal) they are known as typhoons, and elsewhere the term cyclone is used. Tornadoes, in contrast, are rotating storms that develop over land when strong differences in temperature and pressure exist vertically in the air mass. Nature's attempt to equalize such differences in pressure gives rise to powerfully rotating winds that can be observed especially well over the North American mainland. There they achieve rotational speeds of up to 290 mph.

The tornadoes reach Indiana

Monticello, Indiana experienced the first F4 tornado, which rampaged over almost 120 miles before it dispersed. In the process, it created the longest swathe of destruction caused by any tornado during the Super Out- break. This tornado alone left nineteen dead and more than 300 seriously injured. Within

An F4 tornado is already capable of shifting wooden houses with weak foundations or even overturning them, as shown in this photo from Texas.

A tornado of category F5 on the Fujita scale is capable of literally sucking away large chunks of paved road.

minutes, the small town of Monticello was transformed into a scene of unimagineable destruction. Even massive official buildings such as the courthouse, the local high school, and a Presbyterian church suffered serious damage. The headquarters of the local TV channel was simply blown away, almost without a trace.

The ordeal of the small town of Xenia

The storm front, in which new tornadoes were continually forming, moved eastward and reached the bordering state of Ohio just before 5 p.m. The thirty-seventh tornado of the day developed into a tornado of category F5, the highest category of tornado that has ever been measured on earth to date. With wind speeds of more than 290 miles per hour, such a tornado rips apart anything that lies in its path—even road surfaces are literally sucked from the ground. It struck the small town of Xenia, Ohio, which lies in an area that was already known to the Native Americans as the "place of deadly winds." Indeed, local records report more than twenty tornadoes since 1884 alone. The 1974 tornado left thirty-four dead, 1,150 people injured, and an additional 10,000 homeless. Nine schools, nine churches, and approximately 180 businesses were destroyed, and half of the town lay in ruins.

One Super Outbreak tornado hit the town of Xenia, Ohio. One wall of this house was blown away, yet the furniture remained almost undamaged inside it; even the pictures are still hanging on the walls.

13 states declared disaster areas

For eighteen hours, the storm front continued its progress, continually forming local tornadoes as it moved along. Later, 148 tornadoes were registered in total, six of them reaching the feared level of category F5. In the end, the entire American Midwest was hit by this series, as well as New York state in the east and Alabama and Georgia to the south. To the north, the effects were felt as far away as the Canadian province of Ontario. The terror finally ended at 7 a.m. the following morning. The Super Outbreak had claimed between 315 and 330 lives, left behind inconceivable damage, and entered the record books as the biggest tornado series in American history.

The Fujita scale

The storm researcher Tetsuya Fujita (1920–1998) developed a scale for categorizing tornadoes according to their wind speeds and destructive potential. The scale comprises 13 categories, from F0 to F12, of which only the first five levels have been observed to date. From F6 upward, the categories are thus theoretical.

Categ.	Maximum wind speed	Damage
F0	< 73 mph (116 km/h)	Shallow-rooted trees and billboards overturned
F1	112 mph (180 km/h)	Tiles peeled off roofs, moving vehicles blown off roads
F2	157 mph (250 km/h)	Roofs torn off, large trees uprooted, light objects become dangerous missiles
F3	206 mph (330 km/h)	Trains derailed, cars overturned, forests uprooted
F4	260 mph (415 km/h)	Wooden houses with weak foundations blown some distance, trucks overturned
F5	318 mph (510 km/h)	Wooden houses destroyed, paved roads partially sucked from the ground

HURRICANE WINDS AT FASTNET ROCK

The disaster at the 1979 Admiral's Cup

In the night of August 13, 1979, an armada of sailing yachts in the Atlantic off the coast of Ireland was struck by hurricane force winds. The 303 sailboats were taking part in the final leg of the Admiral's Cup, a venerable race from southern England to Fastnet Rock, the southernmost point of Ireland. A low pressure weather system unexpectedly changed direction, striking the unprepared racing yachts with winds up to gale force 11. Seventy-five boats capsized and fifteen competitors were killed. Nearly all the yachts were severely damaged, including some of the largest, most technologically advanced sailboats ever built.

Ireland

Fastnet

United Kingdom

Atlantic Ocean

Plymouth

Scilly Islands

Cowes

The classic Fastnet Race starts in Cowes, England. The turning point is Fastnet Rock off the southern coast of Ireland, from where the course leads back to Plymouth.

Fastnet Rock

In the folksong "The Boatman of Kinsale," Irish balladeer Thomas Osborne Davis sang of "the wind that round the Fastnet sweeps," and praises the sure hand and brave heart that can face "an autumn gale." Fastnet Rock is a small, 100-foot-high rocky islet off the coast of southern Ireland. Home to Ireland's tallest lighthouse, the outcrop owes its fame mainly to the Admiral's Cup, one of the world's oldest and most renowned ocean regattas. This last leg of the Admiral's Cup is called the Fastnet Race, the Indianapolis 500 of the ocean sailing world.

A rescuer ties a line to a survivor so he can be winched into a helicopter.

The Admiral's Cup

The Royal Ocean Racing Club (RORC) of Cowes, based on the Isle of Wight off the coast of southern England, has organized the biennial Admiral's Cup ever since 1957. Participants enter as national regatta teams of three yachts each. The competition consists of five separate races, of which the final and most dangerous leg includes the rounding of Fastnet Rock. Before becoming part of the Admiral's Cup regatta, the Fastnet Race had been famous in its own right since 1925. Today, the regatta sets out from Cowes for a 608-mile journey to the rock, a trip that takes several days. After rounding the rocky outcrop, the regatta heads back to the harbor city of Plymouth on the southwest coast of England.

"Y"

The atmosphere in Cowes on August 11, 1979, was upbeat and festive, as is always the case at the start of the Fastnet. A record number of 303 yachts from twenty-two countries had assembled in the harbor awaiting the start signal. At 14:00 hours, the boats and their total of 2,500 crew members sailed out of the harbor aided by moderate winds. A force 4 or 5 wind posed no challenge to the experienced yachtsmen. When a

mist began to rise on the horizon the following day, many feared that wind speeds would wane further.

At this point in the race, the yachtsmen knew nothing whatsoever about "Y," as the still distant low pressure system that had hovered over North America for the past few days had been dubbed. The low was a raging storm over Halifax, Canada at the time the race began.

Most storms of this kind break up while still over the North American mainland; very few are strong enough to make it across the Atlantic Ocean. The system was, therefore, not considered a threat to the race and no one involved was following its progress.

On August 12, with the yachts still sailing slowly through the mist, the low pressure system suddenly began to pick up speed, racing across the Atlantic toward Europe. On Monday, the third day of the race, European meteorologists began to track the storm in an effort to predict its direction. They assumed the storm

A navy helicopter rescues the crew of the Carmargue. *The crew had to jump into the water because the wildly swinging mast had prevented rescue aircraft from approaching the boat. All nine members of the crew were saved.*

A crew member celebrates his rescue with his wife and friends.

The lighthouse on Fastnet Rock is the tallest in Ireland.

day afternoon a strong wind whipped up, allowing the crews to unfurl their colorful spinnakers—large, curved foresails—to achieve maximum speed. At the same time, "Y" began setting a dangerously different course than had been predicted. Swinging around to the northeast instead of following the expected easterly course, it headed toward the southern tip of Ireland, and Fastnet Rock. The first warning that a severe storm with force 10 winds was on the way came during a French evening news broadcast at 20:00 hours. Despite the new predictions, the British broadcaster, the BBC, stuck to its original forecast of force 8 winds. The coastguard chose to trust the British forecast over the more dire predictions of the French. The yachtsmen, unsettled by the sudden appearance of deep-black clouds on the horizon, were reassured by radio. Nevertheless, the difference between force 8 and force 10 winds is considerable. Whereas force 8 winds snap the occasional tree branch, force 10 winds can uproot the entire tree.

would pass to the south of the regatta route. The storm's proximity would not necessarily be a bad thing for the race; the yachts could look forward to wind speeds up to force 7, a big improvement on the slight winds they had encountered on the first two days of the event.

Rounding Fastnet by night

The regatta route is traditionally timed so that the dangerous rounding of the Fastnet Rock takes place during the night and early morning hours between Monday and Tuesday. On Mon-

20 hours of hell

Chaos descended in the darkness of August 13, 1979 when "Y" thundered over the yachts at hurricane strength. Fifty-foot waves broke over the lightweight racing boats. The 40-foot yachts were completely at the mercy of the wind and water. The coastline was too far away to make sailing for shelter a possibility. The first boats struck by the storm were pressed flat against

the ocean surface by wind and waves. Some capsized at once. Sails not yet furled were torn to shreds. Masts were snapped and torn out of their sockets. The crews of twenty-five yachts were forced to abandon their boats and seek safety in life rafts. Seventy-five of the 303 yachts participating were sunk by the storm, including five of the most technologically advanced racing yachts ever built. Miraculously, the storm, which would endure until noon the following day, claimed only fifteen lives. It is nevertheless the worst disaster in the history of the Fastnet Race. Although ocean regattas are not without their dangers, prior to the disaster of 1979, only two sailors had lost their lives in the Fastnet. Many yachtsmen praised the heroic actions of the crews of the emergency sea-rescue boats and Royal Navy helicopters that saved them from certain death. No level of admiration is too great for those who ventured out into a force 10 storm to rescue hundreds of sailors shipwrecked by a hurricane.

The Beaufort scale

The Beaufort scale is named after its inventor, Sir Francis Beaufort (1774–1857). It began as a largely subjective scale used to categorize wind strength based on visible effects (such as flags and sails). In the meantime it has been modified to reference wind speed and other measurable factors, as well. It ranges from force 0 (calm) to force 12 (hurricane).

WIND FORCE	DESCRIPTION	WIND SPEED		INLAND EFFECTS	SEA CONDITIONS
		MPH	KM/H		
0	Calm	0 mph	< 1	Smoke rises vertically	Flat
1	Light	1–3	1–5	Wind motion visible in smoke	Ripples, no crests
2	Light breeze	4–7	6–12	Leaves rustle	Small wavelets
3	Gentle breeze	8–12	13–19	Leaves and twigs in constant motion	Large wavelets
4	Moderate breeze	13–18	20–27	Loose paper moves	Small waves
5	Fresh breeze	19–24	28–37	Smaller trees sway	Some foam, spray
6	Strong breeze	25–30	38–48	Large branches in motion. Difficult to use umbrella	Large waves with foam and spray
7	Near gale	31–38	49–62	Whole trees sway, walking difficult	Seas heap up
8	Gale	39–45	63–73	Branches break, cars swerve	High waves
9	Strong Gale	46–54	74–87	Light structural damage	High waves, dense foam and spray
10	Storm	55–63	88–102	Trees uprooted	Very high waves
11	Violent storm	64–73	103–117	Widespread damage	Exceptional waves
12	Hurricane	74–95	> 118	Considerable widespread damage	Sea white with foam & spray, poor visibility

A HUNDRED-YEAR FLOOD IN EAST GERMANY

EXTREME HIGH WATER ON THE ODER AND ELBE RIVERS

During the summers of 1997 and 2002, heavy rains fell in south-eastern Europe, leading to exceptionally high water levels in the Oder and Elbe Rivers. The events in both of these years were categorized as "hundred-year floods," since the water reached flood levels that would commonly be reached just once in the course of a century. In 1997, the town of Oderbruch was close to being completely flooded, but could miraculously be saved at the last moment. In 2002, floods struck the cultural metropolis of Dresden. An ancient and familiar combination of weather conditions was responsible. Rainfall of biblical proportions in the Alps caused so much water to flow from the upper reaches of the rivers that catastrophic flooding was inevitable.

The Oderbruch

The border between Germany and Poland is an old polder area—a combination of landfill and reclaimed wetlands protected by dikes—on the lower reaches of the Oder. The Prussian king Frederick the Great had had the former coastal marsh drained between 1747 and 1762, and the Oderbruch polder had been under cultivation for over 250 years. Construction of the polder changed the course of the Oder River, shortening it by 15 miles. The area was then settled with new inhabitants recruited from all over Europe with offers of land and special privileges. The polder lay only a few feet above sea level, making it subject to frequent flooding. Its inhabitants had long had to depend on the strength of the dikes and the vagaries of weather.

The 1997 flood

So-called Vb weather conditions (see p. 83) were the story of the summer of 1997, which

In 2006, the Elbe again overran its banks much as it had done four years previously. This time Dresden was spared, but the town of Königstein was flooded.

saw exceptionally heavy rainfall in southeastern Europe, and the resulting high water levels were equally extreme. Long before they reached the Oderbruch, floodwaters had already caused catastrophic flooding in the Czech Republic and Poland. 180,000 people had already been evacuated further up the river, with 114 lives lost. In mid-June, the brunt of the floodwaters reached the Oderbruch. Terrified by reports from the Czech Republic and Poland, the polder's inhabitants expected the worst. One question was on everyone's mind: Would the dikes be strong enough to hold back the water?

Large-scale deployment

The alarm was raised with the Federal Armed Forces, the Technical Public Relief Organization, the fire department, and the German Border Police. All were instructed to stand ready to protect the dikes and rescue the inhabitants in case of emergency. All of Germany looked on anxiously at the developing catastrophe on its eastern border. Should the levees at the south-ern end of the Oderbruch have burst, as many as 19,000 people would have had to be evacuated as quickly as possible, and the personal and economic repercussions would have beeen immense. Thousands of citizens worked day and night to strengthen the dikes. They filled and dragged countless sandbags to the river-banks. Small breaches were frequent, with all the affected areas evacuated at once.

The "Miracle of Hohenwutzen"

Having been spared the worst of the June flood, a second wave began to move toward the Oder-bruch at the end of July. The dike near the small hamlet of Hohenwutzen was the weak spot in the polder's defenses. Experts gave it only a 10 percent chance of withstanding the approaching floodwaters. If it were to burst, an inhabited region of over 193 square miles would disappear under the floodwaters. Heli-copters continually dropped sandbags onto the banks. For the first time ever, vacuum technol-ogy was used to try to suck water out of the

sodden dikes. After a weeklong battle, against all expectations, the Hohenwutzen dike held. The Oderbruch was saved! The saving of the dike has since been acclaimed as the "Miracle of Hohenwutzen." The region escaped with little more than a black eye considering the potential extent of the disaster. Eight million sandbags had been filled with 195,000 tons of sand and gravel to save the Oderbruch polder. The damage caused by the floodwaters totaled more than $500 million.

The next hundred-year flood

Eastern Germany was once again threatened by catastrophic flooding only five years later. The cause was, once again, the dreaded Vb weather pattern. This time it was the Elbe River that was most affected. What had long been feared became reality when the city of Dresden was inundated by floodwater. On August 16, 2002, the Elbe rose well above its previous record flood level of 28 ft 9 in, a record that had been set in 1845. World-famous cultural monuments including the Semper Opera House and fabulously baroque Zwinger were flooded. The following day, the water rose to a new record level of 30 ft 10 in. Whole districts of Dresden were flooded and 33,000 people had to be evacuated. The Elbe flood caused more than $22 billion in damage in Germany alone.

Indicators of climate change?

When two such devastating floodwater disasters strike the same region within five years, it is only natural to look at the bigger picture. Are the catastrophic Oder and Elbe floods indicators of an ongoing climatic catastrophe? Has humankind simply intervened too much, building dikes, straightening rivers, and paving over wetlands that used to provide natural drainage? Experts' opinions vary. It is difficult to deny that extraordinarily high water levels brought on by extreme levels of rainfall have always been a problem in the affected regions. The Vb weather pattern that caused both disasters had already been identified German meteorologist Wilhelm Jacob van Bebber (1841–1909) at the end of the nineteenth century. Comparable con-

During the 1997 Oder flood, rescue workers from a number of different forces worked together in a desperate effort to save the dikes. Helicopters dropped sandbags non-stop on the most the acutely endangered sections.

ditions today can hardly be blamed on climate change. It is also arguable that reducing or even reversing human intervention along the rivers and coastlines would barely affect floodwater levels. A few percentage points difference would not be enough to change the outcome of a Vb season. Flood disasters will always threaten the Oder and Elbe. Concerted, well-planned responses can, however, lessen the impact of the storms and floods that will inevitably occur.

The tireless efforts of volunteers from all over the country reinforced the flood-soaked dikes.

Vb weather systems

At the end of the nineteenth century, German meteorologist Wilhelm Jacob van Bebber (1841–1909) systematically investigated the paths that low pressure weather systems travel over Europe. His resulting classification was published in 1891 in his most important work, Die Wettervorhersage ("The Weather Forecast"). In it, he categorized the paths of low pressure systems, using the Roman numerals I to V, which were further subdivided using lower case Latin letters. Under certain conditions, the low pressure systems that typically move from east to west (weather conditions I to IV) veer sharply to the south. If they are diverted as far south as the Mediterranean, they absorb a great deal of moisture over the sea. These masses of extremely wet air, called "Genua Lows" or "Adria Lows," can then swing slowly northward again, settling over Austria or Slovenia where the lows release the accumulated moisture in the form of heavy rain or snow. This leads directly to a high water spring and summer in the Elbe, the Vistula, or the Oder, depending on exactly where the cloud masses unload their precipitation. Van Bebber called this reoccurring pattern "Vb." In 1997, a Vb weather pattern flooded the Oder, in 2001 the Vistula, and in 2002 the Elbe. This situation also gave rise to the Alpine high water summer of 2005, which caused heavy flooding and landslides in many places in the northern Alps, including yet another hundred-year flood in Switzerland.

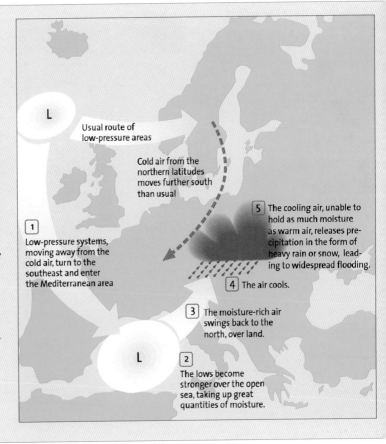

L

Usual route of low-pressure areas

Cold air from the northern latitudes moves further south than usual

1 Low-pressure systems, moving away from the cold air, turn to the southeast and enter the Mediterranean area

L

5 The cooling air, unable to hold as much moisture as warm air, releases precipitation in the form of heavy rain or snow, leading to widespread flooding.

4 The air cools.

3 The moisture-rich air swings back to the north, over land.

2 The lows become stronger over the open sea, taking up great quantities of moisture.

WIPED OUT BY A MONSTER WAVE

THE SUMATRA TSUNAMI

Literally translated, the Japanese word *tsunami* means "harbor wave." They are triggered by an earthquake at sea, spreading in rings from the quake's epicenter and reaching heights of over 100 feet. On December 26, 2004 at 7:58 a. m. local time, a seaquake of category 9.0 on the Richter scale hit the Indian Ocean off the northwest coast of Sumatra. Due to special circumstances, it triggered a flood wave that struck the coastal regions of Indonesia, Thailand, Sri Lanka, and even East Africa, causing devastating damage. More than 230,000 people lost their lives in this horrific catastrophe.

The tsunami's third and largest wave surged over the promenade of Ao Nang Beach in Thailand.

A deadly wall of water crashes on land

It is in the Indian Ocean off the coast of Sumatra that the Indo-Australian and Eurasian continental plates lie alongside one another, and subterranean movement of the plates creates intense pressure and friction. This has always made the western coastal region of Indonesia an area prone to earthquakes. Along a rupture zone of about 600 miles, the Indio-Australian continental plate slides underneath the Eurasian plate by about 7 cm (2¾ inches) a year. There is no slow, constant build-up of pressure; it happens suddenly with a jolt. Every jolt of this kind is registered as an earthquake by seismographs and recorded.

In the morning of December 26, 2004, a fateful disaster occured in the Indian Ocean as about 300 miles of sea floor broke open. Within seconds, unable to withstand the pressure created by the constant friction of the continental plates any longer, the tectonic plates thrust themselves upward anywhere from 30–100 feet, releasing energy of an unimaginable magnitude. The underwater earthquake reached 9.0 on the Richter scale, making it the third most powerful earthquake ever recorded. The energy released was the equivalent of the total energy consumption of the USA for a whole year. However, this energy was not released at a single spot, as happens with an atomic bomb, for example. It was spread over a wide area, as an immense surface rose within seconds and pushed the water above it upward. This created a wave whose height varied with the water depth – the deeper the water, the higher the wave. The sea off the coast of Sumatra is about 16,500 feet deep, and the flood wave generated on December 26, 2004 attained enormous height and sped toward the shore at almost 450 miles per hour, equivalent to the cruising speed of a plane.

On January 2, 2005, rescuers were still finding tsunami victims in a river in Banda Aceh, in northern Sumatra. The water retreated very slowly, revealing the full extent of the destruction.

Eyewitness report

"We felt a blow as if the boat had run aground at high speed or rammed a massive piece of driftwood or a wreck. A few seconds later, the boat was hit by a second blow and around 8:01 a. m. by a third. The instruments went haywire, the data on the GPS navigator was chaotic, and the plotter, sonar, and radio were all dead. About 10 minutes after the first hit, it seemed to us that the sea level had sunk by 10 or 15 meters (32–50 ft). Without a sound and over a huge area the water simply sank away. Then we caught sight of gigantic waves on the southwest horizon that reached the boat around 8:14 a. m. Seconds later, the boat, submerged in water up to the railing, was lifted up 30 meters (98 ft). Three of these waves hit the boat all together, lifting it 50 meters (165 ft) above the previous height, that is, 35 meters (115 ft) above the normal water level."

Sofyan Anziba, captain of the fishing boat *Bintang Purnama*, which was at sea on the Straits of Malacca on December 26, 2004.

The Wave of Death was hardly noticed on the open sea; the sea level rose only slightly. It only became dangerous in shallower water as the wave approached the coast. Its speed was reduced, and the nearer the wave came to land the higher it piled up until it became a giant, deadly wall of water that crashed onto the shore, tearing up and engulfing everything in its path.

The appalling aftermath

The tsunami caused devastating destruction along the Bay of Bengal, the Andaman Sea, and the west coasts of the Indian Ocean, even reaching Somalia on the East African coast some 3,200 miles away. It claimed more than 230,000 lives in eight Asian countries, among which Indonesia alone was left mourning 170,000 victims. Hundreds of thousands were injured, and an unimaginable 1.7 billion people lost their homes. The true number of victims is presumably much higher, since many regions beyond the tourist areas are practically un-mapped. In addition, fear of disease led to mass burials and the cremation of corpses, making an accurate body count impossible. The immediate

A couple whose lives have been left in ruins by the terrible tsunami. Countless people lost literally everything they had.

In Banda Aceh alone, there were many more victims than originally thought: 122,000 are counted as dead and 114,000 as missing.

fear of disease and epidemics spread everywhere, as almost all sources of drinking water in the afflicted regions were contaminated. As a result of the hot climate and the many corpses, which were often only discovered and retrieved many days later, mosquitoes multiplied in masses and the outbreak of epidemic diseases such as cholera and typhus was feared likely. In India, the populace is inoculated against both, but these diseases were not the only anxiety. Contaminated water that infiltrates the respiratory tract can cause lung infections. Blood poisoning posed another widespread danger, as it can easily occur when wounds are exposed to dirty water. The humid climate, with temperatures continuously around 86 °F, coupled with inadequate hygiene, is obviously highly conducive to such conditions.

Aftershocks shake the region

During the remaining days of 2004, the region experienced an average of twenty-five aftershocks each day, typically reaching a magnitude of 5.5 on the Richter scale.

On March 28, 2005, a quake of 8.7 magnitude, the last severe aftershock for the time being, rattled the west coast of Sumatra. It affected the Banyak Islands, Nias and Simeulue. As a result, 80 percent of the buildings on Nias collapsed, and fatalities are estimated at around 2,000. Additional thousands of people were made homeless by this renewed assault.

Eyewitness report from Sri Lanka
All of a sudden, I found myself being swept out to sea with startling speed. Although I am a fairly strong swimmer, I was unable to withstand the current ... I swam in the direction of a loose catamaran, grabbed the hull and pulled myself to safety. My weight must have slowed the boat down, and soon I was stranded on the sand ... As the water rushed out of the bay, I scrambled onto the main road. Screams were coming from the houses beyond the road, many of which were still half full of water that had trapped the inhabitants inside. Villagers were walking, stunned, along the road, unable to comprehend what had taken place.

I was worried about my wife, who was on the beach when I went for my swim. I eventually found her walking along the road, dazed but happy to be alive. She had been trying to wade back to our island when the water carried her across the road and into someone's back yard. At one point she was underwater, struggling for breath. She finally grabbed onto a rope and climbed into a tree, escaping the waters that raged beneath her. Our children were still asleep when the tsunami struck at 9:15. They woke up to find the bay practically drained of water and their parents walking back across the narrow channel to safety."

Michael Dobbs,
journalist for the *Washington Post*, December 27, 2004

Geological after-effects, economic and cultural damage

As a geological after-effect, fifteen of the 572 islands that comprise the Andaman and Nicobar Islands, situated in the Indian Ocean southeast of the Bay of Bengal, sank below sea level. In addition, both the Nicobar Islands and the Island of Simeulue that lies off the coast of

Nothing is left of the exclusive Laguna resort in Khao Lag (southern Thailand) but a pile of rubble.

In April 2005, under a psychologist's supervision, children were brought to the beach to try and overcome their trauma.

Sumatra and is nearest to the epicenter of the quake, have shifted approximately 50 feet to the southwest.

In addition to the human tragedies, the tsunami also caused enormous and lasting cultural and ecological damage. For example, approximately 10 percent of the coral reefs off the coast of Thailand were either damaged or eradicated. It will take decades for this natural protection from high waves to recover to its pre-2004 condition. Further natural coastal protection is provided by the mangrove swamps, which were also detroyed by the flood wave. The native fauna was also badly affected. On the island of Nicarugo, for example, the last living turtles of a rare species were killed, and the nesting areas of the Leatherback and Sea Turtles were badly disrupted. The humus has been washed away by the mass of water that hit the land with such great force and only retreated after some time; the areas affected have thus become relatively barren. Along coastal strips between 800 feet and 2 miles in width, the fertile soil layer, often no deeper than 12 inches, has been washed away and the plants ripped out. The harvests of the coming years therefore can be expected to be extremely poor. In several regions, historic buildings such as museums and historic monuments have been completely obliterated. According to UNESCO, treasures belonging to the world's cultural heritage are in ruins, including the Old Town

Foreshocks and aftershocks: what does the magnitude tell us about the energy released?

The magnitude of the foreshocks and aftershocks off the coast of Sumatra around December 26, 2004 ranged between 5.0 and 9.1 (the main quake) on the Richter scale. An increase of one point on the Richter scale entails a 32-fold increase in the energy released. The main earthquake with a magnitude of 9.1 thus released thirty-two times more energy than an aftershock of a magnitude of 8.1. Compared to a quake of 5.1, the main earthquake released 1,048,576 times more energy.

Natural phenomenon tsunami: FAQs

WHAT CAUSES A TSUNAMI?
Tsunamis are most often caused by underwater earthquakes or volcanic eruptions. However, they can also be caused by a meteorite impact.

WHERE ARE TSUNAMIS MOST FREQUENT?
Around 90 percent occur in the Pacific Ocean and in Southeast Asia. However, they can also occur elsewhere. Following the Lisbon earthquake of 1755, for example, 60,000 people were killed by a tidal wave that swallowed up everything along the course of the River Tejo, thus doing due justice to its name of "harbor wave."

HOW HIGH CAN A TSUNAMI GET?
An earthquake off the coast of Alaska in 1964 triggered a monster wave that reached a height 100 feet when it struck Hilo, Hawaii's largest city. When Krakatoa erupted in 1883, a 130-foot wave engulfed coastal regions. It is said that a tidal wave off the Japanese island of Ishigaki reached a height of 280 feet in 1971. When tsunamis force their way into narrow bays or fjords (such as the mouth of the Tejo in Lisbon, for example) they can grow much higher. According to legend, the eruption at Santorini over 3,000 years ago is said to have triggered a wave of 800 feet.

In all this, it should be remembered that a tsunami is not a mass of flowing water like a river. Rather, it is a transfer of energy in which one water molecule hits the next and so on. The deeper the sea where the wave is triggered, the higher the wall of water becomes when it reaches land.

HOW FAR CAN A TSUNAMI WAVE TRAVEL?
A tsunami can travel halfway around the globe. The tidal wave of the 1964 quake off Alaska caused considerable damage in New Zealand. Tsunamis can easily travel more than 6,000 miles without losing force.

WHAT SPEED CAN A TSUNAMI REACH?
Here, too, the water depth is the decisive factor. Speeds of up to 600 miles per hour are not unusual. At this speed, it takes no more than a day for a wave to reach every conceivable point in the Pacific region.

WHICH TSUNAMI CAUSED THE GREATEST DAMAGE AND INFLICTED THE GREATEST LOSS OF LIFE TO DATE?
The tragic record in both is held by the Sumatra tsunami of 2004, followed by the Alaskan tsunami of 1964, the tsunami following the Sanriku earthquake of 1896 in Japan, and the monster caused by the Krakatoa eruption of 1883.

---

and fortifications of Galle in Sri Lanka, the ancient monuments at Mahabalipuram in India, and the Sun Temple of Konarak.

Tourism has inevitably suffered, as many tourists avoid places that have been visited by such disasters. As a result, the surviving inhabitants who had depended on tourism for their livelihood become poorer still. Women, in particular, struggle with the social aftermath of the disaster. In many of the affected regions, a woman cannot marry if there is no dowry for her. Many young women therefore suffer, disgraced by their poverty, and suicide rates among young women in some areas have escalated.

How can the magnitude of a disaster be measured?

In an age replete with disasters, every calamity becomes the "greatest disaster of the century" or even the "greatest disaster of all time." Such superlatives are not always appropriate. It is true that the extent of the area affected by the Sumatra tsunami is unequaled in history. Also unparalleled is the fact that, owing to mass tourism, the victims included people from almost every country in the world. There are other disasters, however, either restricted to a particular region or occurring in countries intolerant of politically negative media attention, that claim yet more lives than the tsunami of 2004. China, for example, has regularly suffered from devastating floods such as the one in the Henan province in 1887 that took more than 900,000 lives. At the other extreme, the disastrous drought in India between 1965 and 1967 claimed the lives of some 1,500,000,000 people. The question of how to measure the magnitude of a disaster must remain a matter of debate.

Arial photography gives an impression of the devastation in Sumatra in the wake of the 2004 tsunami.

A Storm's Terrifying Trail of Destruction

KATRINA: ONE OF THE WORLD'S DEADLIEST HURRICANES

Between August 25 and 31, 2005, Hurricane Katrina first hit the southeast coast and then the Gulf States of the United States. Growing from a category 3 to a category 5 hurricane, it laid waste to the entire infrastructure of about 125 miles of coastline, destroying everything in its path and changing the face of one of America's most distinctive cities, New Orleans, forever. Katrina proved to be one of the most devastating hurricanes of all time.

This parking lot in Fort Lauderdale, north of Miami, was hit by Katrina on August 25, 2005. The immense force of the hurricane is clearly visible.

Hurtling energy over the Gulf of Mexico

With wind gusts of 80 miles per hour, a hurricane newly dubbed Katrina struck the densely inhabited southeast coast of Florida on August 25, 2005. Though it was "only" a category 1 hurricane at the time, it caused substantial property damage and several people lost their lives. Damage attributed to the flooding caused by the heavy rainfall that accompanied the

storm ran into millions of dollars. The population along the south coast, so often plagued by hurricanes, breathed a sigh of relief as Katrina turned away from them and moved over the Gulf of Mexico.

Unfortunately, this was premature. By late summer the waters of the gulf had warmed to about 86 °F, and fueled by this heat from below Katrina gained enormously in strength and especially in size. Within a short time it grew to become a category 5 hurricane with top wind speeds of more than 155 miles per hour. It also changed direction again and began to approach the south-central coast of the United States. A mandatory evacuation of the 480,000 inhabitants of the city of New Orleans was issued on August 28th. People barricaded their houses, nailing planks and boards over doors and windows before moving to safety (often against their will). Tens of thousands of the city's inhabitants, however, slipped through the net and remained in their city.

On August 29th, Katrina slammed into southern Louisiana and Mississippi with stunning force, devastating a coastal strip almost 125 miles wide. The destruction was so extensive that the entire infrastructure was demol-

ished. Hurricanes lose strength relatively quickly over land, however, and, luckily for New Orleans, Katrina hit the city as a category 3 hurricane with winds of "only" 125 miles per hour. The damage it wreaked was nevertheless immense. Whole sections of New Orleans were razed and almost the entire city was flooded after a series of critical levies were breached. Katrina weakened to a tropical storm over the state of Mississippi, and continued to lose strength as it made its way through Alabama, Tennessee, Kentucky, and Ohio. Fortunately, although accompanied by heavy rainfall and the occasional tornado, Katrina had lost much of its enormous destructive force, and its journey finally ended on August 31st.

The devastating aftermath

During this natural disaster, which plunged the United States into a deep domestic political crisis, more than 1,500 people lost their lives. Thousands were still missing afterwards. Millions were homeless for many days and weeks, and even today, many are still unable to return to their homes. Whole suburbs of New Orleans lie in ruins and may never be restored to their former glory. Almost one year

Long lines of people in New Orleans wait for a bus to take them to the Houston Astrodome and out of the danger zone.

after Katrina, some 100,000 people in Mississippi and the neighboring state of Louisiana continue to live in trailers instead of houses, because their homes are still uninhabitable. Many thousands more have left for other parts of the country and may never return. The immediate damage caused by the tragedy amounted to $150 billion, while the medium- and long-term damage is estimated at more than $600 billion. This almost unimaginable sum makes Katrina the most destructive hurricane of all time; in terms of material loss, its wreckage exceeds even that of the Indian Ocean tsunami disaster in late 2004 (see pp. 84–89). Katrina has therefore been categorized as one of the world's worst natural disasters, and one of the three deadliest hurricanes in the history of the United States. We can be extremely grateful that it did not claim the same unspeakably high toll in human life as the 2004 tsunami and other disasters, but resulted primarily in material damage.

The 7th Ward in New Orleans was especially badly hit by Katrina. Helpers had great difficulty controlling the situation.

Post-disaster chaos

The tally immediately after Katrina showed that almost one million people had lost their homes and at least 350,000 houses had been rendered uninhabitable. The grand city of New Orleans, which lies at or below sea level and is thus highly prone to flooding, was under water, in places as much as 20 feet deep. Days after the disaster, the supply situation remained chaotic and people were still waiting on rooftops to be rescued. There was a shortage of drinking water, the water supply was cut off, there was no food, no electricity, and no telephone service.

Prior to August 25th, New Orleans held the dismal record of being the city with the second highest rate of murder and violent crime in America (no. 1 is Camden, New Jersey). Looting began soon after the hurricane subsided, with people carrying off anything of value they could find. Violence escalated. One looter even gunned down a police officer standing in his way. Martial law was declared in the city, and still thousands of national guard troops and police officers were unable to stem the violence that broke out in the aftermath of Katrina. Even aid and rescue operations had to be halted in some cases. As a result, tens of thousands of people were trapped in New Orleans for days without medical care. Corpses drifted through the flood waters, toxic substances leaked into the water, and an unbearable stench hovered

Emergency shelter for the residents of the city's poorest districts was provided in the New Orleans Convention Center.

over the city. The threat of disease was acute. In addition to all the damage on land, US coastguards announce that twenty oil platforms were missing in the Gulf of Mexico.

After several days, food, drinking water, and medical supplies finally began to reach the people in the city. President George W. Bush admitted that he had failed to assess the situation adequately and made $60 billion in aid available. His first response had cost far less: he had asked Americans to pray for their suffering fellow citizens.

Criticism of preparations for the emergency

It was the breach of the levies of the higher-lying Lake Pontchartrain that flooded the city with water until it reached the same level as the lake. Today, many American experts criticize the government for taking inadequate precautions in the 1960s against a possible disaster; they had prepared for far less powerful storms than Katrina.

Recent studies show that when planning the levies built to protect New Orleans, the worst

---

Hurricanes

The average hurricane has a diameter of 340 miles and releases more energy in one day than all the power plants on earth combined. The year 2005 saw all previous world records for measured hurricanes broken: in that year, Wilma and Katrina became the strongest storms ever measured. But it was not only in North America that such storms occurred. In Asia, fierce typhoons (the local name for hurricanes) also raged in 2005. Europe has been spared such storms up to now, because European waters do not have the necessary surface temperatures for the creation of hurricanes. However, scientists warn that warming of the Mediterranean could in the future lead to the formation of hurricanes in Europe, as well.

The strongest hurricanes since 1900:
1900: USA—Galveston Hurricane
1935: USA—Labor Day Hurricane
1961: Central America—Hattie

1969: USA—Camille
1979: Japan—Tip
1988: Caribbean—Gilbert
1992: USA—Andrew
1996: Taiwan and China—Herb
1998: Caribbean—Mitch
2000: China—Saomai
2001: Taiwan—Nari
2004: Japan—Tokage
2004: Grenada, Jamaica, Cuba, and USA—Ivan
2005: Cuba and USA—Dennis, Katrina and Rita
2005: Central America—Stan
2005: Mexico and USA—Wilma
2005: Azores, Canary Islands, and Spain—Vince
2005: Taiwan—Haitang
2005: China—Matsa, Talim, Khanun and Damrey
2005: China and Taiwan—Longwang
2005: Japan—Nabi

The damage caused by Katrina was immense. Little of this McDonald's in Biloxi, Mississippi was left standing apart from Ronald.

Eyewitness report

"It was one of the most awesome experiences of my life, as I was in New Orleans at the end of 2005. I was overwhelmed on several levels. Everywhere, I found strange scenes and bizarre objects—overturned automobiles resting on roofs, boats in living rooms. Whole precincts of the city looked as if they had been bombed, toilets and beds and dishes lay everywhere in ironic and biting contradiction. I could have shot a series on the unbelievable force of nature alone, but I had traveled there to occupy myself with something other than just the destruction. It took a quite a lot of discipline to remain true to my intention and concentrate on the more subtle signs of human tragedy. I experienced a deep feeling of mourning and loss there; not commiseration for the damage and loss the victims have suffered, but much more a feeling for that which was happening to me myself, the feeling everyone suffers when a disaster of this immensity hits his own countrymen. Over the past few years the USA has lost something holy, and Katrina is the visible evidence for this. It has to do with our community, with compassion and solidarity that has been sacrificed to our materialistic society. I, as a person, am willing to face up to this damage, and perhaps, through my work, I can persuade others to do likewise."

Chris Jordan, photographer, on the lasting consequences of Katrina

This satellite picture shows Katrina approaching the
Gulf States of Louisiana and Mississippi.

possible disaster had not been considered. Due to prohibitive cost, much weaker storms had been assumed, and the dimensions of the levies set accordingly. The engineers had simply not included the worst possible storm in their calculations. It should be asked, however: are we ever fully prepared for a disaster?

Global warming

Climatic researchers have demonstrated that global temperatures have risen and will continue to rise as a result of the greenhouse effect. First and foremost, it is the surface temperature of the seas that has risen by an average of 0.9 °F (0.5 °C). Hurricane research has shown that the surface temperature of the oceans plays one of the most significant roles in their physical creation. Enough water evaporates at a surface temperature of 79 °F or more to generate and fuel a hurricane. But the warming of the air over the oceans is also decisive. The higher the air temperature rises, the greater the quantity of moisture it can absorb, and this results in increased energy and intensity of a hurricane. In Katrina's case, the high temperature of the water in the Gulf of Mexico is one of the factors that fed its energy and intensity until it reached the highest hurricane category.

As additional bodies of water exceed the critical threshold of 79 °F and become warmer, more and more hurricanes will develop. Some researchers also consider it likely that the future has hurricanes in store for the Mediterranean region. Not only has the number of tropical hurricanes increased over the last twenty years, but their intensity and duration are on the rise, as well.

FAMINE
AND DROUGHT

Drought has been the main cause of famine since time immemorial, but crops can also be destroyed in other ways. Plant diseases and insects can decimate fields, and war frequently leaves infertile earth behind. Although there is enough food in the world to nourish all its inhabitants, not everyone has access to the fruits of the earth's abundance. All over our planet, millions of people still suffer the effects of catastrophic famine.

THE DARK SIDE OF THE MIDDLE AGES

RECURRING FAMINE

Tree bark, ferns, acorns, berries, grass: during the medieval period in Europe, people regularly turned to these dubious food sources in a desperate attempt to stay alive. Families cast out children and neglected the sick and elderly in order to survive the seemingly endless cycles of drought and famine. Even kings were not always spared. During one particularly extended drought in the fourteenth century, millions of people starved in just a few years, a disaster on a scale that is virtually incomprehensible today.

The situation in the Middle Ages was so desperate that the starving were ready to eat the corpses of hanged thieves.

Vita brevis—Life is short!

Between 1315 and 1317 Europe experienced one of the most severe and widespread famines the world has known. The hunger zone reached from Scandinavia to the Alps and the Pyrenees, from the Russian steppes to the Irish coast. Seen by contemporaries as evidence of God's displeasure, the great medieval famine is now understood as one link in a whole chain of disasters.

The average lifespan for a man was between 25 and 32 years, and most women died even younger. With a high infant mortality rate and the constant threat of disease, famine, and war, early death was the rule in Europe at the time,

Famine in the fourteenth century
Famine was a regularly event in the fourteenth century. Between 1315 and 1351 there were five famine years in England, and French sources noted an astounding 14 famine years in the same period, with a further 9 years of starvation in the second half of the century. 1306 and 1312 were famine years in Bohemia and Austria, where records are not as complete. In light of accompanying waves of epidemic disease, it is hardly surprising that medieval Europeans were acutely aware of death's proximity.

other infectious diseases. Once recovered, the population began to grow steadily, slowly at first, then speeding up between 850 and 1050. This was possible in part due to increasing reliance on agriculture as opposed to animal husbandry. Agriculture improves living conditions by providing more food, promoting permanent settlement, and because newly cleared fields provide sources of winter fuel for heat. The growth of cities and towns transformed a subsistence level rural society into a flourishing, market-oriented economy. All these developments provided alternatives to utter reliance on the whims of nature, at least for while.

When people are weakened by hunger they become highly susceptible to all kinds of illnesses.

Starvation and mass death in 1315

Dramatic change came in spring and summer of 1315. Cool temperatures were accompanied by

for aristocracy and commoners alike. In 1276, the English royal family had an average lifespan of only 35 years.

A steadily increasing population

Several demographic trends have been detected in medieval Europe. Population declined significantly in the mid-sixth century following the Justinian plague, a devastating epidemic that was likely a combination of bubonic plague and

Population in medieval Europe (in millions)

	Year				
	300	600	1000	1340	1440
Spain/Portugal	4 m.	3.6 m.	7 m.	9 m.	7 m.
France	5 m.	3 m.	6 m.	19 m.	12 m.
Italy	4 m.	2.4 m.	5 m.	9.3 m.	7.5 m.
British Isles	0.3 m.	0.8 m.	1.7 m.	5 m.	3 m.
Holy Roman Emp. & Scandinavia	3.5 m.	2.1 m.	4 m.	11.6 m.	7.5 m.

constant rain all over central Europe. The grain crop could not sprout in the chilly, wet fields, and anticipation of a failed harvest caused the price of staple foods like bread to skyrocket. In England alone, many foods cost twice as much in June as they did in March. Stores of grain, if they existed at all, were quickly exhausted. Many farmers were driven to make a fatal decision. They could eat their remaining grain seed themselves, or feed it to their starving animals. In desperation, people began to dig out roots, tear bark from trees, collect nuts and berries, and eat ferns and grass. Even the nobility was not safe from hunger. When King Edward II of England stopped in St. Albans on August 10, 1315, there was no food available for him and his court. The mighty lord had to go hungry!

The famine that does not end

The spring of 1316 brought no improvement, with bad weather continuing unabated. By then all remaining grain seed had been consumed and the livestock had been slaughtered. The people did not know where to turn. Food stocks

This fresco by Fra Angelico (1447–1449) shows St. Laurentius distributing alms to the poor and hungry.

The medieval menu

In comparison to today, there were relatively few agricultural plants culti-vated in the Middle Ages. Potatoes and corn, high yielding and nutritious, were native to the yet undiscovered New World. Vegetables in general played a minor role in the diet. Cabbage, kale, beets, peas, carrots, and beans were grown, but the system of three-field crop rotation made these less important than rye, barley, wheat, oats, millet, and spelt used to make the porridge that sustained most of the population. Oil was pressed from linseed, rapeseed, or beets. Sugar from sugar beets, native to India and the Middle East, was still little known, although the plant was cultivated in tenth-century Sicily and Spain by the Arabs. Sugar beets did not spread to Western Europe until the Crusades; honey was the primary sweetener.

The dangerous fungus Claviceps purpurea *infected stored grain, leading to dangerous ergot poisoning, which was widespread in medieval times.*

were exhausted everywhere. The church often helped with handouts, but just as often had to turn the starving away. In those desperate times, small children were frequently left to their fate. The fairy tale of Hansel and Gretel suggests as much when the father leaves his children behind in the forest because of the family's bitter poverty. The crisis reached its climax in 1317. The winter was icy cold and the rain never stopped. The undernourished populace easily fell to disease, dying by the thousands of respiratory infections and tuberculosis.

Mortal fear and apathy

The worsening climate, the famine of 1315–1317, and finally the Black Death reduced the population of Europe by 70 percent. The constant misery influenced thoughts and emotions. Churches were decorated with depictions of the dance of death, visual reminders that everyone should prepare for their imminent end, regardless of rank or station. Many people were uprooted and wandered the country as vagrants. Morals declined and behavior became more brutal. Some turned their backs on the Roman Catholic Church. Most, however, clung more firmly to religion than ever, finding their only refuge in the hope of life after death.

Dangerous ergot

Even in good times, most medieval farmers survived on a diet of porridge, bread, peas, lentils, chestnuts, and cabbage. Crop failures often forced them to eat moldy bread or make porridge from grain infected with ergot, a toxic fungus. In times of famine, the rural population suffered badly from ergot poisoning. With nothing left in storage, they would eat freshly harvested green grain kernels that contained high levels of the toxin. The purple-colored "ergot" (*Claviceps purpurea*) caused a condition known as *Ergotismus gangraenosus*, more popularly known as St. Anthony's fire. The disease caused skin sores and gangrene of the toes and fingers, which eventually fell off. A variant of the disease produced convulsions and hallucinations. A monk from Cluny described the course of the illness as a fire searing through the limbs.

An illness of the poor

In the cool, wet famine periods, St. Anthony's fire was rampant. As early as 993/994, 40,000

deaths from the disease were reported in Limousin and Périgord in France. There were 14,000 deaths in Paris in 1128/29. France was often hardest hit, as were Russia, Germany, and Sweden. Into the early nineteenth century, the rural poor were still dying from this mutilating illness brought on, in the end, by hunger.

A marker in the Camposanto Monumentale in Pisa marks the grave of a wealthy person. Few traces remain of the poor who starved to death.

DEPARTURE OF THE "NIMROD" AND "ATHLONE" STEAMERS, WITH EMIGRANTS ON BOARD, FOR LIVERPOOL.

In Cork, Irish emigrants board a steamer for Liverpool, from where they will emigrate to America.

IRELAND STARVES

CROP FAILURE CAUSES "THE GREAT IRISH POTATO FAMINE"

From 1845 to 1849, Ireland was struck by a series of devastating crop failures. The annihilator of the potato harvest was a fungus that caused a disease called potato blight. More than one million Irish men, women, and children starved, froze to death, or fell victim to the epidemics that followed in the famine's wake. A further two million people fled Ireland in a wave of emigration to North America.

British newspaper report from summer 1845

"A terrible disease has appeared among the potato plants. We hear of ruin from all sides. It is said that the fields in Belgium are totally devastated."

Gardener's Chronicle and Agricultural Gazette, 1845

The Irish population explosion

Irish smallholders were doing comparatively well at the turn of the nineteenth century. The warm water of the Gulf Stream kept the climate mild and Irish soils were generally fertile. The environment provided ample raw material for housing, and a small peat fire was sufficient heat most of the year for a small rural cottage. A small parcel of land was all that was required for cultivating potatoes, a crop that produced yields generous enough to feed an extended peasant family.

The effects of this prosperity were everywhere to be seen. Young people were able to start their own families at a younger age, leading to a massive increase in population over a relatively short period of time. In 1801, the population of Ireland was somewhere between 4 and 5 million; within only forty years it doubled to just over 9 million. This population explosion meant that individual tenant families' parcels of land became smaller and smaller, because in Ireland, land was traditionally divided between the all the sons in a family. Inevitably, the individual parcels of land became too small to feed a family.

SEARCHING FOR POTATOES IN A STUBBLE FIELD.

A poor Irish family digs for any potatoes that might remain in a stubble field.

The fungus from America

Circumstances outside of Ireland would soon turn the problem of incipient overpopulation into a catastrophic burden. In 1842, the *Phytophthora infestans* fungus, popularly known as the potato blight, destroyed the entire potato harvest of North America. The fungus crossed the Atlantic from America in the damp holds of ships, and quickly began to spread throughout Europe. In September 1845, potatoes on the Isle of Wight in the English Channel showed widespread signs of the blight, but at the time no one was particularly alarmed. Bad news about rotting potato harvests in the Netherlands and France were also ignored. Farmers were used to suffering setbacks from time to time. No one knew quite how bad this particular blight would be, but most nineteenth-century farmers were diversified enough to give the matter little thought. In Ireland, however, the situation was different. The Irish climate was so mild that the fungus could spread exceptionally quickly in a country where potato cultivation was omnipresent. Irish smallholders and their many children

The starving relied on handouts.

were not in the least diversified. They lived almost entirely on the nutritious and quick-growing potatoes. Powerful landowners controlled the larger parcels of land devoted to the cultivation of wheat. Irish tenant farmers had long been forced to export any wheat they grew to England so as to be able to pay the high rents demanded by their wealthy landlords.

The famine takes hold of Ireland

There was still hope in the fall of 1845 that the Irish potato harvest would not be too badly affected. These were dashed when it became clear within a few days of the harvest that a large portion of the crop was already blighted. The government in London stepped in with financial subsidies to

A woman sprinkles holy water over young potato plants to help them grow.

keep the price of bread low, but the rural population, with no savings at all, could not afford to buy it. 1846 was even worse. The weather was so bad that the wheat and oat harvests were also very poor, and the potato harvest was again completely destroyed. An exceptionally bitter winter followed. Frightening reports of children starving and freezing to death reached the British government, but had little effect. The attitude of the conservative Liberal government to the problems of the poor in Ireland was cynical at best. The ministers refused to provide financial help based on the argument that government handouts demoralized the starving population, robbing them of the will to rise above the disaster by their own efforts. The British government was willing to support charity workhouses and municipal labor forces, but would do no more than that.

Evidence of this state-supported program of public works can still be seen in the west of Ireland, where the countryside is crisscrossed by the so-called bread walls lining every road. Meanwhile, the starving people grew ever weaker. Infectious diseases such as typhus began to take hold.

THE EJECTMENT.

Soon, many people were no longer capable of doing the strenuous manual labor required of them for support by the government.

Coffin ships depart from Ireland

Jobs in commerce or industrial production were rare in nineteenth-century Ireland. It became clear that the only alternative to starvation was to emigrate. As early as 1846, impoverished smallholders began to flee the country. In the famine years, which continued until 1849, around one million people died of starvation, cold or disease, and more than two million Irish fled their country. Of the 1841 population of 9 million, only 6 million remained ten years later. Almost 25 percent of the population died or emigrated. The immigrant ships leaving Ireland were mostly bound for the United States and Canada. Conditions onboard these "coffin ships" were terrible; they were no more than freighters with passengers stuffed into the leaking holds; crews treated the emigrants no better than cheap cargo. Typhus and other diseases raged onboard and in the quarantine camps on the other side of the Atlantic. More than 10 percent of the passengers did not survive the trip.

Irish not welcome

The survivors were often faced with rejection and hatred in their new countries. The Catholic Irish were rejected in the USA, which was dominated by Protestantism. Even the underclass rejected the Irish, seeing the starving newcomers as unwelcome competition in a tight labor market. Advertisements for jobs often included the phrase "Irish need not apply." Too often, all that remained were the worst jobs in railroad and canal construction, or in the mines. Jobs like these were not only unpleasant, but also very dangerous. The saying "an Irishman under every tie" was common among American railroad workers. The Irish emigrants nevertheless won their place in their adopted countries through their tenacity and distinctive sense of community. Just over one hundred years after the great Irish potato famine, John F. Kennedy, the grandson of an 1847 Irish immigrant, became president of the United States.

Starving tenant farmers were evicted when they were no longer able to pay their rent.

From 1845 onward, the fungus Phytophthora infestans, known as potato blight, destroyed most of the Irish potato harvest.

A Black Cloud of Dust from Canada to Texas

THE DUST BOWL DROUGHT OF 1932–1940

During the Great Depression years of the 1930s, the Great Plains, a vast swathe of semi-arid grassland running north to south through the middle of the United States, was transformed into a desolate, dust-choked hell. The culprits were poor soil management and severe, ongoing drought. Thousands began to starve after several years of failed harvests, and many more died from lung diseases caused by inhaling the dust.

The Great Plains needs people

"Dust bowl" was the term used to describe large areas of the plains states plagued by massive, drought-induced dust storms.

By the beginning of the twentieth century the coastal regions of the USA had been settled, but the Plains states of North Dakota, South Dakota, Montana, Nebraska, Oklahoma, Arkansas, and Texas were still rather sparsely populated. Settlers for these areas were sought in the

major urban centers of Europe, and people were coaxed to immigrate to the prairie with enticing offers of 640 acres of free land. All that potential settlers had to do was to show up, stake their claim, pay a small registration fee, and live on

Sand dunes pile up in 1936 on what is left of a small farm in Cimarron County, Oklahoma.

the land and improve it for five years. After that, the land was theirs free and clear, and what they made of it was up to them.

The United States needed people to fill the underpopulated towns founded by the railroad companies. People were also needed to use the railroad, and to transport goods by railway. In short, without a sufficient population living in the Great Plains states, there was little justification for the construction of the railroad in the first place. For people living in the tenements of London, Paris or Berlin, 640 acres represented an unimaginable amount of land for one family—and all of it was free!

The Great Plains was subject to extremes of temperature and had long been affected by recurring periods of drought. The American government was well aware that the land they were offering would always be threatened by lack of rain.

The balance of nature is destroyed

During World War I, the American economy boomed. The 1920s were characterized by continual agricultural overproduction. Soils were overexploited, beyond their natural limits. Land that under normal conditions would have been considered barren was forced into cultivation. All the natural growth was cleared, destroying the ecological balance of the unique Great Plains biosphere. Indigenous grasses, for example, were ploughed up to make way for wheat fields, leaving nothing in place to retain the thin layer of topsoil. The native herds of buffalo, whose manure had sustained the land's fertility, were mindlessly exterminated, sometimes simply to provide entertainment for the railroad passengers on their long journey from coast to coast.

The rural population of large parts of the Plains states was reduced to abject poverty. Many starved or died of disease. This famous photo by Dorothea Lange shows a mother who had fled the dust storms with her children.

Dorothea Lange
The American documentary photographer Dorothea Lange (1895–1965) was commissioned by the Farm Security Administration (FSA) to record the impoverishment of the rural population following the Great Depression. Her photographs are primary documentation of the devastating sand storms of the 1930s. Her "Dust Bowl" series, full of human tragedy, earned her international fame. She captured the United States of that period better than anyone else.

These circumstances set the stage for the disaster that ensued when, at the beginning of the 1930s, little or no rain fell for several years. Strong winds swept across the prairie, ushering in an ecological disaster that would continue for years. The wind caught the fertile upper layer of topsoil, which had been turned to dust by the drought, and blew it away in immense black clouds. In the years 1934 and 1935, 650,000 farmers from the states of Texas, Oklahoma, Arkansas, and the Dakotas lost their land. This was the era of the Great Depression, and money was scarce. Already heavily in debt, most small farmers finally gave up, leaving the Plains in a mass exodus. More than 500,000 people left behind the land they had only recently won through their own hard work. The pejorative term "Okie," originally used to describe dirt farmers from Oklahoma, became more widely used to describe the scores of homeless rural refugees who moved westward in search of work and a new home. Many traveled along Route 66, the legendary highway leading to California, that was celebrated again and again in folk songs and popular music.

Houses collapse under the weight of the dust

The most severe dust storms occurred in 1934 and 1935. In May 1934, a "black blizzard" rolled its way from Canada down to Texas, carrying off billions of tons of fertile soil. In March of the following year, tens of thousands of cattle suffocated in a marathon dust storm that lasted an incredible twenty-seven days. The dust clouds were blown as far as Chicago, where the topsoil fell from the sky like snow. A few days later, that most powerful storm reached the East Coast cities of Boston, Washington, and New York. There, red-brown snow fell from the sky. The sun was not seen over the Great Plains for a whole month, and many houses collapsed under the weight of the dust. During these two years, a time when the entire country was still in the grip of the Great Depression, thousands of people starved to death, and thousands more died as a result of pneumoconiosis and other respiratory diseases that were caused by inhaling the windblown soil.

Farmers who hadn't abandoned their land tried to limit soil erosion by planting windbreaks. They were only partially successful. It was simply too dry for anything to grow. Reservoirs were empty because it had barely rained in the ten years. As the water shortage became acute, salt began to accumulate in the soils. Of course, it rained occasionally during those years, but usually in the form of short, violent storms that did more harm than good by washing away yet more of the loose, dry topsoil that remained, taking seeds with it. Today, fields are plowed parallel to slopes to limit erosion. Fallow years are observed, with stubble fields left uncultivated for a year or more to give the land a chance to retain moisture and nutrients. While many of these innovations were introduced right away, once the scale of the disaster became clear, for most of the Great Plains it was too little, too late. The land had already been bled dry.

Strangers in their own country

The vast majority of the displaced farmers headed toward California, the "Golden State"

Over-cultivation demanded too much of the parched soils.

and land of promise. They soon found that living conditions there were not much better than those they had left behind, and were frequently even worse. In the 1930s, many of the farms in California were corporate, larger and more modern that those in the Plains states. Many Californians were not happy to see the Okies streaming in, and took advantage of them or made their lives difficult. The Los Angeles Police Department stationed officers on the border to Nevada to prevent the refugees entering their turf. It is estimated that 40 percent of the Plains State immigrants found jobs as agricultural laborers in San Joaquin Valley, working for $1.25 a day on fruit or cotton plantations, often living in huts or tents without sanitation or running water. Mexican farm workers who had replaced by the newcomers, now unemployed, caused new problems for the state. The final chapters of John Steinbeck's famous novel *The Grapes of Wrath* are set in this period in California, where the newly arrived Joad family picks peaches on a corporate farm torn by labor strife and racial unrest.

Women and children were among the hardest hit victims of the Dust Bowl disaster.

THE SUFFERING OF THE POOREST OF THE POOR

FAMINE IN THE SAHEL

Throughout the world generally, and in the Sahel in particular, famine is not always a disaster with a clear cause. Hunger can gradually creep up on a people, starting off mildly before developing into a major human tragedy. *Sahel* means "coast" or "shore" in Arabic, and is a term coined by the French botanist Auguste Chevalier (1873–1956) for the zone bordering the southern edge of the Sahara Desert, a semi-arid zone marking the transition between desert and savannah across the African continent from the Atlantic Ocean to the Red Sea. Severe droughts in arid and semi-arid regions can have terrible repercussions for the people who live there, particularly if the dry periods are accompanied by famine that lasts for many years.

The widespread evil of hunger

Hunger is a widespread malady in modern Africa. Many of the continent's countries are not capable of producing enough food to support their population. Instead, many Africans are dependent on imported food, but there are not enough financial resources to make that a long-term solution. The poorest countries rely to a large extent on the benevolence of the

1.6 million of Mauritania's original stock of 2.1 million cattle died due to drought. The herds have since recovered.

The victims of the Sahel drought were too weak to flee a threatening cholera epidemic.

wealthier industrial nations that support them with development aid. Help of this kind is not entirely altruistic, however. It is also a business, with much of the funding paid out in the form of loans to be repaid, with interest.

Some of the factors, especially in the Sahel, that have led to recurring famine are drought, the infertility of already desiccated soils, climatic fluctuations, erosion, parasitic disease, and swarms of locusts: all of these taken together have made the ongoing Sahel famines disasters of apocalyptic proportions.

In addition to the harsh natural conditions, which people in that region have always had to contend with, further factors that have contributed to scarcity of food are political instability and armed conflicts in the region, particularly when hunger was purposely used as a war tactic by the military in the civil wars that plagued many of the Sahel nations. Corruption and economic mismanagement combined with a trade policy that worked against African agriculture only increased the level of suffering among the population.

In other parts of Africa, the economic effects of the AIDS epidemic have moved to the forefront: the disease has decimated large segments of the workforce, leading to further decline in the labor-intensive enterprise of food production. According to United Nations figures, since 1985, approximately 7 million agricultural workers have died of AIDS in twenty-five African countries, and a further 15 million people are threatened by the disease.

A nomadic woman, with her child on her back, searches through the sand and dust for food.

Between subtropical savannah and the Sahara

The Sahel encompasses an area of 1.2 million square miles and extends into ten countries, including Senegal, Mauritania, Mali, Burkina Faso, Niger, Nigeria, Chad, the Sudan, Ethiopia, and Eritrea. With the exception of Nigeria, which derives some wealth from its deposits of oil, all of the Sahel nations are among the

Diary entry from 1850

"The rains came regularly. The whole of nature breathed with new life and the animal kingdom pursued its sociable side with the full force of its newly awakened desires. The thick canopies of the trees buzzed with the merry twittering of buntings and finches and the cooing of pigeons. Apes descended to the small hollow behind our tents to have a drink of water, while the distant call of a lion echoed intermittently."

Heinrich Barth (1821–1865), German geographer and explorer, whose diary entry reads as if he were describing a tropical rainforest instead of the southern edge of the Sahara.

poorest in the world. The northern reaches of the Sahel consist of thorn-shrub savannah, giving way first to dry savannah, then to fertile savannah, and finally it borders on tropical rainforests located further south. The northern edge of the Sahel, bordering the Sahara desert, has a hot and arid climate. The different regions of the Sahel receive varying amounts of rainfall, ranging from 20 mm (less than an inch) in the north to 19 inches per year in the south, much of which falls during the June to September monsoon.

Rainfall averages in the Sahel have been continually declining since the early 1960s, however, and the Sahara itself is expanding, creeping slowly southward. Because the average temperature is relatively high at 68 °F, much of the rainfall during the few wet months

evaporates before it can do much good. The ground itself retains very little moisture. The result has been severe drought and widespread starvation, particularly in the 1970s and 1980s.

Overpopulation and overgrazing

A growing population and ever-larger herds of livestock grazing already meager vegetation have badly strained an environment already under stress from decades of declining rainfall. Too many animals eat the few plants available, right down to their roots. The already hard, impermeable earth has been trodden firm by the large animals, further reducing its ability to retain moisture. As the soils dry out, they begin to drift like sand, further contributing to the desert's expansion.

Since there were also times of sufficient rainfall in the not-too-distant past, many groups that had originally been nomadic herders settled down in villages to live off the land. They no longer lived according to the rhythm of the natural environment, wandering with their herds in search of the regions that had received the most moisture. Instead, they bored wells that further desiccated the ecosystem by tapping into the groundwater. Farms encroached further and further into the arid north, relying almost entirely on artificial irrigation. The number of wells increased, many dug without adequate study of the local environment or, indeed, any planning at all. Groundwater levels continued to plummet. The sensitive ecological balance of the arid belt was tilted further toward desertification.

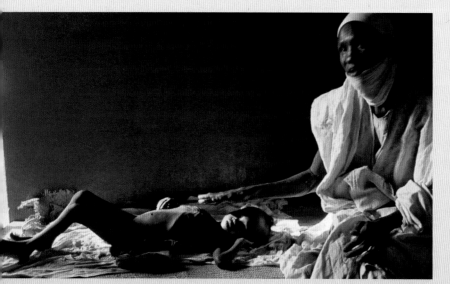

The result of all these many factors and trends has been disaster. Starvation and infectious diseases claimed the lives of hundreds of thousands of people between 1968 and 1973, and again from 1982 to 1984. Having lost their herds of livestock, many of the Tuareg, a proud, pastoralist nomadic people who once roamed throughout the Sahel, can now be found living in the growing slums of cities further south.

No rain, no harvest, no money

The United Nations is the first responder, the organization most often in charge of food programs and the distribution of aid on an international level. Each person is supposed to be provided with food that provides 2,100 calories every day. In time of food shortages, this means that hundreds of tons of food in the form of rice, corn, lentils, beans, oil, and smaller quantities of salt and sugar have to be delivered to the affected areas. The logistical problems in dealing with the Sahel famines were vast. Delivering supplies to war zones is often impossible due to the lack of security, leading to life-threatening shortages of food in what are often the most severely affected areas.

Children and the elderly, especially, suffer from ongoing malnutrition. The current situa-

Emigrants following the mirage of a better life

"The First World feels threatened and under siege from economic refugees who are desperately trying to escape poverty, chaos, and oppression. The way out of sub-Saharan Africa for tens of thousands of people each year is a journey by truck through the Sahara to a relatively prosperous country such as Algeria or Libya, and from there, perhaps to Europe—if they do not die along the way."

Ali Bensaad, an Algerian journalist sentenced to death in his country in 1993, who now lives in exile in Germany

tion is still extremely serious in Niger, but also in Mali, Mauritania and Burkina Faso, with most food stocks exhausted. Few have died directly of starvation in recent decades. Instead, weakened by a lifetime of hunger and malnutrition, hundreds of thousands die of otherwise curable diseases like tuberculosis, typhus, and, most recently, cholera.

The Sahel itself is expanding southward, extending today to include the Cape Verde Islands off the Atlantic coast. Completely deforested by Portuguese colonists, the islands have long been susceptible to wind erosion, the effect of which has increased as the climate becomes drier. The former British colony of Gambia is also becoming an arid steppe; failed harvests are already common.

People suffering from malnutrition are more susceptible to epidemics. In Burkina Faso, the World Health Organization provides immunizations against infectious diseases.

MILLIONS STARVE IN TIGRAY PROVINCE

ETHIOPIA AND ERITREA

In 1984, one million people died of starvation in the Tigray region of Ethiopia, one of Africa's poorest countries. Even today, two-thirds of Ethiopia's 74 million citizens rely entirely on international food aid for their survival. Life expectancy in the worst affected areas is only 46 years for men and 49 for women.

A group of Ethiopian rebels roams the streets of Aksum in June 1998.

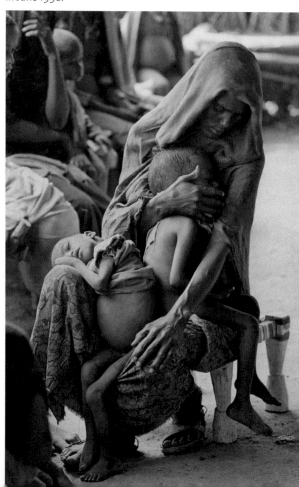

A mother, weakened by hunger and suffering, with her exhausted children

The old agricultural country of Ethiopia

Ethiopia lies to the south of Egypt in East Africa, wedged between Somalia and the Sudan. It is the oldest Christian country in Africa, and unlike most of its African neighbors, has never been colonized. Independence under Emperor Haile Selassie (1892–1975) followed a brief period of occupation by Mussolini's troops (1936–1941) during World War II. A Marxist military regime ruled the country between 1974 and 1991. The present prime minister, Meles Zelawi of the EPRDF (Ethiopian

Famine and Drought

People's Revolutionary Democratic Front), a former Marxist, is today a supporter of a free economy. To the north of Ethiopia lies the now independent nation of Eritrea, a former Italian colony and Ethiopian province. Eritrea finally gained its independence in 1993, but border conflicts with Ethiopia are still a problem. The only constants in the region are famine and drought. The region was hit particularly hard in 1973, 1981–1984, and again in the 1990s.

The mass deaths of 1984

The first portent of the 1984 crisis came in 1981, when crops failed due to drought. At the time, international aid was only intermittent. When rain failed to arrive in the spring of 1984, herds of livestock in the agriculturally important region of Sidamo began to fall prey to disease. In March of 1984, the government announced that famine was imminent. Economists estimated that the country would only be able to harvest 6.2 million tons of grain, one million tons short of what would be needed. Many countries were still reluctant to commit to major programs of food aid, in part because they were unwilling to support the head of Ethiopia's Marxist government, Mengistu Haile

The stony road to independence
Briefly under Italian sovereignty, occupied by the British in 1941, and ultimately annexed by King Haile Selassie of Ethiopia, Eritrea has failed to find peace since gaining its independence in 1993. Although it signed a peace treaty with Ethiopia in 2000, United Nations troops are still on hand to keep conflicting parties apart. The constant flow of refugees and military conscription of nearly all young men keeps Eritrea's economy weak. The one-party state of President Isaias Afewerki is, like Ethiopia, split into factions of Christians and Moslems. The country's infrastructure, devastated by decades of conflict with Ethiopia and Yemen, is badly in need of rebuilding, but the necessary funds are simply not available.

Mariam. Mengistu was well known for seizing funding sent for food and using it to purchase military hardware for his civil war against the rebel provinces of Eritrea and Tigray instead. If donating countries sent food instead of money, he seized it to feed his soldiers and other supporters. Western nations were less than enthusiastic about contributing to a bitter cycle that, in the end, could end up costing more lives than it would save.

By the summer of 1984, thousands were starving. The international aid organization Oxfam took the initiative and provided aid in the

Ethiopia is not always dominated by drought. Fertility returns to large parts of the country every year following the monsoon season.

The farmers' situation

Land is nationalized in Eritrea, and modern irrigation is scarce. Wooden plows are still used much as they were 3,000 years ago, and an average farmer cultivates just 2 acres of land. Grain delivered to Eritrea and Ethiopia as aid often won't germinate because it is too old, has been heat-treated, or is unsuitable for the climate. Farmers rejected tons of hybrid grain sent by an American firm because hybrids cannot self-propagate, meaning new seed has to be purchased each year. Imports of grain better suited to the climate have long been blocked by the government, which seeks to establish a monopoly. With so much going against them, farmers cannot survive without falling ever further into debt.

The refugees in this camp near Addis Ababa depend on the support of international aid organizations.

Armed with Kalashnikovs, members of the Hamer tribe patrol their area. Tribal conflict contributes to hunger crises in the region.

amount of 500,000 pounds sterling, but problems distributing the aid and criticism by the Ethiopian government led to further delays. There had been a record harvest in Europe that summer, in stark contrast to images of emaciated Ethiopians on television and in the newspapers. Memories of the Biafra famine of the 1960s were reawakened, and food aid began to arrive. In part thanks to initiatives of musicians

such as Bob Geldorf's "Band Aid" and events such as the "Live Aid" concerts, the public was spurred into action, contributing huge sums in donations. The situation in Africa deteriorated further when people fleeing the civil war entered the Sudan, however, creating a desperate situation in overcrowded refugee camps. For many of them, aid came too late. Tens of thousands of Ethiopians died of starvation and diseases that prey on the malnourished.

Eritrea: Africa's youngest country

In an effort to legitimize its independence, the young country of Eritrea taxes all food aid, stops the distribution of grain to the starving, and confiscates the trucks of aid organizations. Foreigners can only move around outside the capital of Asmara with special permission. This mistrust, based on bad experiences with the United States and the Soviet Union, among others, both supporters of the enemy Ethiopia, means that people continue to die of hunger. Eritrea still produces only about a third of the grain it needs. It survives, among other things, on money sent by Eritreans living abroad and through loans from China.

Instead of encouraging sustained development through targeted support and aid for rebuilding Eritrea's damaged infrastructure, aid organizations are often reduced to merely distributing handouts, even in years following record harvests. Approximately 800,000 tons of grain is imported each year, of which at least 30 percent ends up on the open market. This cripples the local pricing structure by overwhelming the markets with foreign grain. Unable to sell their crop, many farmers have switched to growing the mildly hallucinogenic drug khat instead, for which there is a brisk market in Yemen and neighboring Somalia. The state trading companies make a good profit off the resale of international donations. What is not sold on the open market is often be redistributed to tribal members and political supporters.

Why do millions have to starve?

Are climatic factors the sole cause of recurring famines? For Eritrea and Ethiopia, the answer to that question is decidedly "no." Economic underdevelopment, antiquated methods of cultivation, territorial conflicts, and tensions between tribal and religious groups are the prime causes, as well as the manipulation of hunger by the military. AIDS, a disease that has infected two million people in Ethiopia, is a contributing factor, as are the restrictions on the kinds of international aid acceptable to corrupt and self-interested leaders. These problems are not restricted to Ethiopia and Eritrea. More than 200 million people in Africa suffer from undernourishment, with drought only seldom the primary cause. Civil wars play a major role, contributing to social and political instability. Corruption, years of insufficient investment in agriculture and uncontrolled population growth are all home-made problems. External factors play a role, as well. When industrialized nations treat Africa solely as a market for products of the industrialized world, the developing economies of the continent's poorer nations are further diminished. Until these issues are dealt with, people will continue to starve, despite the best efforts of international aid agencies.

Like many other women during the famine crisis of 1984, this mother is seeking food for herself and her child.

PLAGUES
AND EPIDEMICS

"Plague" has long been used as a generic word for all epidemics. Apart from the Black Death, there were other plagues, such as smallpox, that killed whole peoples. It was not until the nineteenth century that their causes and cures were discoverd, making it possible to stop their spread. Today, old epidemics return and new ones, such as AIDS, arise. Science is often powerless. No one knows what other diseases lie in ambush, waiting to afflict humankind.

THE BLACK DEATH—STILL A THREAT

THE PLAGUE PAST AND PRESENT

The plague is the epitome of the deadly epidemic—it has killed millions upon millions of people. As recently as between 1896 and 1930, over 12 million people fell victim to the plague, and even today WHO (World Health Organization) estimates that it claims a world-wide death toll of some 2,000 people every year. The Congo is currently a plague hot spot; Algeria, Malawi, and India have not been spared in recent years either. Even in North America, people still occasionally contract the plague through contact with infected housecats.

From flea to rat to human

The plague is caused by gut bacteria of the *Yersinia pestis* family, which can hardly be eliminated among rodents living in the wild. Sick rats can transmit the disease to humans via fleas or other parasites, and human-to-human infection is also possible. There are two main types of plague. Bubonic plague announces itself with a swelling of the lymph nodes, and pneumonic plague is frequently accompanied by pneumonia, dark sputum and subdermal hemorrhages—hence the name "Black Death." In the case of septicemic plague, which is a consequence of pneumonic plague, the blood is infected. Without medical treatment, the mortality rate for bubonic plague is 60–80 percent, and almost 100 percent for pneumonic plague.

In 14th-century Florence, Italy, the Black Death led to piles of corpses, mass misery and barbarization—all depicted here by Giovanni Boccaccio.

Mephitic air

In the past, any occurrence of widespread deaths was likely to be called "pestilence." Before an Italian physician, Girolamo Fracastoro (1448–1553), showed that some diseases can be transmitted from person to person, through infected objects or through air, conventional wisdom held that epidemics were caused by contaminated air and harmful vapors (miasma). It was only with Louis Pasteur (1822–1895) and Robert Koch (1843–1910), both microbiologists, that the spreading of infectious diseases was well understood. Studies by French-Swiss physician and bacteriologist Alexander Yersin (1863–1943) and Shibasaburo Kitasato (1853–1931) of Japan, who conducted relevant research in Hong Kong in 1894, led to the discovery of the cause of the plague.

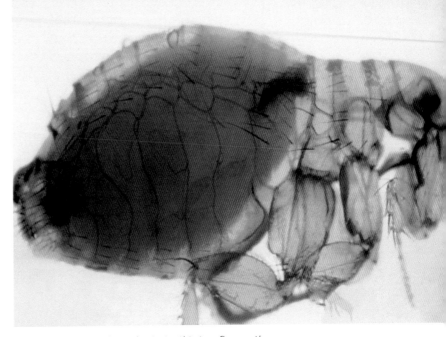

Rat fleas transmit plague bacteria; this is a flea on the third day of infection. The dark spot in its blood-filled stomach is a sign of the infection.

Early mass mortality

Early references to the plague include the Bible, which mentions the "diseases of Egypt" as a punishment meted out by God, and the Greek poet Homer, who described the rapid transmission of the plague (Greek *nosos* or *loimos*) metaphorically: Apollo and Artemis shoot Niobe's children with plague-tainted arrows (*The Iliad*, Book 24). Ancient physicians would often take to their heels when confronted with epidemics, knowing that there was nothing they could do.

The first well-documented major plague epidemic occurred in Constantinople under Emperor Justinian (527–565). Probably introduced in 542 by ships coming from Egypt, it spread rapidly and claimed thousands of lives in many countries. Gregory of Tours (538/539–

Protection against the plague

Doctors protected themselves with oilcloth gowns and beak-shaped masks filled with vinegar or herbs. Legend also tells that 4711, the original Eau de Cologne marketed by the Farina brothers in Cologne, Germany, originated as a "plague water." In 1634, the people of Oberammergau in Bavaria pledged that if God would spare them from the plague, they would stage a Passion play every ten years. They did, and the tradition is still alive today.

A physician, protecting himself from the plague with an oilcloth gown and face mask. Sponges drenched in vinegar were also thought to prevent infection.

594), a well-known bishop and historian, was one of several who chronicled the disastrous consequences for France.

The Crusades add to the spreading

The epidemic flared up time and again, and the great armies regularly traveling across the European continent during the Crusades only added to the problem. When the Seljuk Turks occupied Jerusalem, Christian pilgrims were no longer safe, and this led to Pope Urban II's call on Christendom to free Palestine. Urban offered the crusaders remission for their sins and eternal life. Of the 200,000 crusaders who set out on the First Crusade, only about 15,000 arrived in Jerusalem in 1099; the rest died on their way through infested areas; 50,000 are reported to have died in Antioch alone. The hospital ships that accompanied the knightly orders were a significant stimulus to the development of hospitals ashore.

The Black Death of 1347–1352

From 1325 to 1351, the plague ravaged China. The bacteria that cause it multiplied in the fur of rats on ships and in fur clothing, in particular. Originating from the Caspian Sea and Black Sea, the epidemic came to Venice and Messina via Constantinople and quickly spread to every seaport town in the eastern Mediterranean: the *mortalega grande* (Great Mortality) had arrived. The consequences are described, for example, in Giovanni Boccaccio's famous collection of stories, *The Decameron*, written from 1348 to 1353. In his tales Boccaccio described how red-clad members of the *Compagnia della Misericordia* (Confraternity of Mercy) gathered up corpses with their long crooks, also scooping up the sick and dying to

Patron saints
Many of the sick prayed to patron saints, notably to St. Sebastian (died ca. 288), whose legend states that God brought him back from death after he was shot to death with arrows, and to St. Roch of Montpellier (ca. 1295–1327), who contracted the plague while caring for the sick, but was saved by an angel and a dog who brought him bread.

This medieval representation of a plague victim from Anne of Britanny's Book of Hours shows the boils that are characteristic of the disease.

Who is to blame?

For religious Christians, the epidemic was first and foremost a punishment from God. People also believed that the planets had some influence on the course of the epidemic. Apart from that, they sought out scapegoats: Jews were thus accused of poisoning wells to help the plague spread further. In Spain, France, Italy, Switzerland, and Germany, persecutions on a massive scale ensued, often in connection with the flagellant movement. In some towns Jews were burnt at the stake; in one town—even though the plague had never broken out there—the king guaranteed impunity for killing Jews in exchange for payment of a fee. Many Jewish communities were annihilated, and Jews were evicted from their home towns everywhere. Venice, the busy seaport town, offered them refuge, but soon afterward created the first ghetto. Jews had to wear yellow hats, and their freedom was severely constrained.

avoid having to come back for them later. According to Boccaccio, from March 1348 until June 1349, over 100,000 people died in Florence alone. That same year, Siena lost half its population within just a few months. Ships packed with people suffering from the plague were set adrift on the oceans. Some ships were driven out of Messina and landed in Marseille, France. From there the plague spread to Avignon, the seat of the pope. Most of the 60,000 dead were thrown into the Rhône River because there were too few undertakers. While most physicians fled, the monastic orders, especially the Franciscans, did care for the sick. Those monks not infrequently paid with their lives for practicing *caritas* (charity).

Moving north from Marseille in 1348, the Black Death reached Paris, then Calais, then England, whose population shrank from 4 million to 2.5 million. Almost all of Europe was in the clutch of the Black Death; only Poland and Russia had relatively large areas that remained unaffected. About a quarter of Europe's population, some 25 million people, perished of the plague. As a further consequence, the epidemic caused a mass emigration from the countryside to the cities; farm lands degenerated into steppe and resulted in food shortages.

After the end of the Black Death in 1679, the populace of Vienna erected an ornate column, called a plague cross, as a sign of their gratitude and a reminder to posterity.

Early quarantine measures

Though the mode of infection was not known, the idea that the plague was contagious caught on, and hospitals were more often built outside city walls. Hygienic conditions (which were at times terrible) improved a little, and livestock breeding and muckheaps were restricted within cities. Traditional treatment consisted of blood-letting, giving herbs, and lancing the plague boils. Baths were avoided to prevent opening pores, which would make it easy for the disease to enter the body. The sick were quarantined, and rooms and belongings were fumigated with sulphur, saltpeter or camphor. Faces and hands were washed with vinegar and corpses covered with lime. Many trading towns, especially Ragusa (now Dubrovnik) and Venice, forced potentially infected travelers to spend thirty days, and later forty (*quaranta*), in quarantine. In Venice they had to stay in the Isola di S. Lazaro (St. Lazarus' Isle), where lepers traditionally had been quarantined—hence the term "to isolate." The *quaranta giorni*, on the other hand, have given their name to "quarantine."

DDT is sprayed to kill off fleas, which spread plague, in northern Namibia. While the pesticide is itself a health risk, it is less dangerous than the plague.

Faith or prophylaxis?

In early modern times Constantinople (Istanbul) was a constant hotbed of the plague. The Turks trusted Allah with their lives and closed their quarantines. Many Christians subscribed to this fatalistic view as well and accepted their fate.

At the same time, provisions against the plague improved. People started burning plague victims' furniture and clothing, and the first attempt to study the "little worms" under a microscope was undertaken by the Jesuit priest Athanasius Kircher in 1656.

Although the *cordon sanitaire*, a military border 1,200 miles long established by Austria to defend itself against Turkey, went a long way toward preventing further spreading of the plague by land, there were continued outbreaks. One was the Great Plague in London 1665–1666. The Great Plague of Marseille (1720–1722) was the last significant outbreak of plague in the Western world. The third pandemic, which originated in China during the second half of the nineteenth century, did not reach Europe.

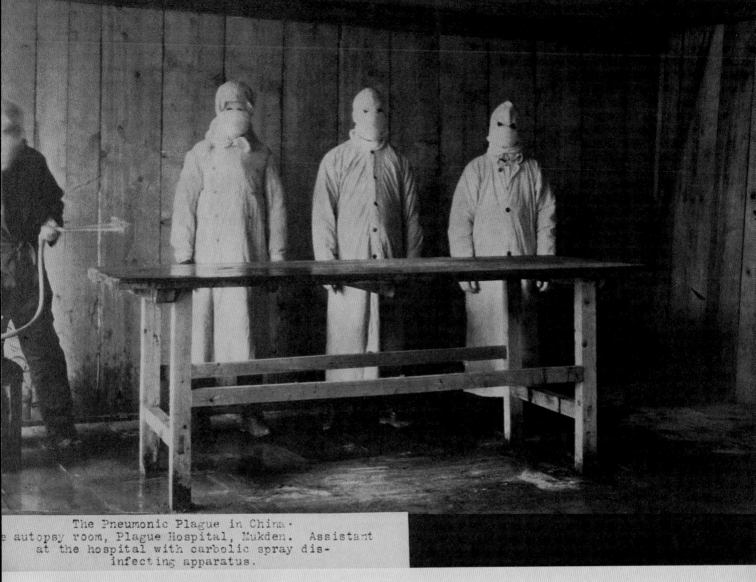

The Pneumonic Plague in China.
e autopsy room, Plague Hospital, Mukden. Assistant
at the hospital with carbolic spray dis-
infecting apparatus.

When the plague broke out near Antananarivo, Mada-
gascar in May 1983, all children had to stay indoors.

Today, the plague can be effectively treated with streptomycin, tetracycline, and chloramphenicol. Nonetheless, further outbreaks cannot be avoided entirely, and sometimes there is no intention of avoiding them—on the contrary! Like the anthrax, smallpox, and Ebola viruses, plague agents could be used for biological warfare, thus bringing back the horrors of medieval times.

An apparently sinister scene is actually an autopsy table being sprayed with the disinfectant phenol at the Mukden Plague Hospital in China during the winter of 1910/1911.

Covering the mouth with a hand

On August 29, 590, a city-wide church procession against the plague took place in Rome. Seven choirs marched simultaneously from seven points of origin toward the church of Santa Maria Maggiore. It is said that eighty victims died of the plague en route, and this inevitably led to the infection of other participants. Since "pestilent" air was thought to be the cause of the disease at the time, this—according to legend—is the origin our habit of covering our mouth with a hand whenever we yawn or sneeze. But this had nothing to do with protection from airborne infection: it was intended to prevent demons from entering the body.

DEMENTIA FROM SEX

SYPHILIS

Syphilis attacks the genital organs, leaving little doubt as to how the illness is contracted. Since sexual activity is subject to some level of taboo in most cultures, the afflicted readily assigned its origin to an unloved neighboring country. The French called it the *mal de Naples*, while the Germans, including the physician and alchemist Paracelsus (1493–1541), referred to it as the French disease. To the Poles it was the German disease, and to the Russians, the Polish disease. The Italian physician and poet Girolamo Fracastoro (1478–1553) coined its modern name in his poem *Syphilis sive morbus gallicus* ("Syphilis, or the French disease"). Loosely translated from ancient Greek, the name means both "one who likes pigs" and "one who makes love."

The four stages

Syphilis progresses in four stages. Three weeks after exposure to the *Treponema pallidum* bacterium, hard sores called chancres develop on the genitalia. About eight weeks later fever and lymph node swelling occur, along with a highly contagious rash on the torso, back, hands, and feet. This secondary stage can also be accompanied by hair loss. After an asymptomatic phase that can last several years (latent syphilis), the tertiary stage of the disease begins, characterized by chronic inflammation of the skin and internal organs and soft tumors throughout the body. The heart, bones, and joints can be severely affected. During the fourth and

Poverty is often accompanied by a higher susceptibility to infectious diseases. In this family, the mother of two children has both syphilis and tuberculosis.

From Naples to the rest of Europe
The first massive outbreak of this highly infectious disease occurred in 1494. After Naples had been besieged by the army of French king Charles VIII for three months, 32,000 soldiers are reported to have contracted the disease. This first outbreak was particularly virulent. Infection was followed by fever, intense joint pain, and early, agonizing death. The siege of Naples was abandoned because of syphilis. Of the regiment of 8,000 Swiss soldiers, only 148 survived to make the journey home. The city of Bern shut its gates as the limping, cadaverous men approached, covered with fetid ulcers. Rather than possibly becoming ill themselves, the citizens of Bern left them to die outside the city walls. Bathhouses, which were frequently ersatz brothels, were shut down all over Europe in response to the crisis.

Did Cristopher Columbus, Vasco da Gama, and other explorers of the early modern era bring the disease back to Europe from their expeditions? Some scholars believe so.

final stage, about 20 percent of syphilis patients suffer from severe neurological degeneration, often leading to dementia. If the unborn child of a syphilitic mother is infected, the disease is called congenital syphilis. If syphilitic children are born alive, they are often blind, deaf, and have a number of developmental disabilities.

A disease comes back with the booty

There are several theories about how syphilis suddenly became a disease of epidemic proportions. Some scientists claim it existed in antiquity and was recognized in the early medieval period, for instance in England, where it was called by many names. However, many other researchers have studied the historical records and reached an entirely different conclusion.

In 1493, Christopher Columbus boldly returned to Europe from the New World. Although he had not found the passage to India as planned, he had discovered America. He may have brought more back from these distant lands than gold trinkets and tales of glory. Immediately after Columbus landed in Palos in the south of Spain, his crew began leaving a deadly trail behind them in the harbor city's brothels. According to some experts, syphilis was not native to Europe, but arrived from the New World, where it had long been endemic.

Syphilis and fashion
Syphilitic ulcers and the frequent loss of hair that accompanied the disease had a decided influence on fashion. Scholars believe that the rise of wigs and the popularity of high-necked jabot shirts and thick layers of powder during the rococo era were related to a desire to hide syphilitic symptoms. The court of King Louis XIV in France, where most of these fashions were popularized, was a hotbed of syphilis and other STDs at the time.

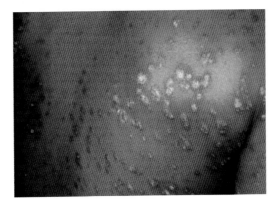

During the secondary stage, the syphilitic ulcers found on the back, torso, hands, and feet are highly contagious.

POVR VN
PLAISIR MIL
DOVLEVR
IL SVE LA
VEROLE

Chaut ce
braise

The sweatbox cure was a typical 17th-century remedy for syphilis. Patients were expected to spend several weeks like this.

Sweat bath treatments

There are many indications that syphilis was new to Europe. As is typical for an imported infectious agent and an unexposed group, the earliest syphilis epidemics in Europe were much more devastating than the effect of the disease today. The Naples outbreak ran through its four stages much more quickly, often killing its victims within weeks. At the same time, the native peoples of the New World were familiar enough with the disease to have devised remedies. South American tribes treated it with the bark of the guaiacum tree, and the tree's wood was soon exported to Europe in quantity. More commonly, however, syphilis was treated with sweat baths in combination with a mercury ointment. Paracelsus, the well-known physician, advocated use of this strong poison in his essay *On the French Disease* (1530). It was thought that mercury removed harmful matter from the body by stimulating the secretion of saliva, but many patients found the treatment so horrible that they preferred to die.

Penicillin works

Mercury treatment was the only remedy available until the early 20th century, when it was replaced by arsenic. Only with the large-scale production of penicillin after World War II could syphilis be cured. The road to that cure, however, was horrific. One long-term experiment involving some 400 poor African Americans from Tuskegee has become notorious. From 1932 until 1972, the infected men did not receive penicillin so that doctors could study the long-term effects of the disease. The experiment was conducted with the patients completely in the dark about why they were being observed, and they had no idea that a treatment for the disease existed. The Tuskegee experiment only ceased in 1972 after details were leaked to the public. Today, syphilis is on the rise in many industrial countries, in part due to the susceptibility of those whose immune systems are weakened by AIDS.

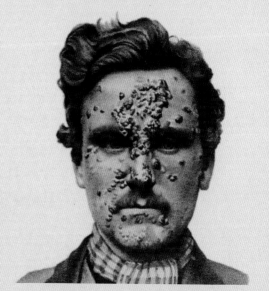

In his Atlas of Clinical Medicine (circa 1893), *Byrom Brawell included this detailed illustration of the disfiguring sores characteristic of syphilis.*

A patient's account

Ulrich von Hutten (1488–1523), a famous philosopher, was himself a syphilis patient. In 1519, he described the mercury and sweating cure that he had endured eleven times.

"From three, four or more of these drugs they would produce an ointment that was rubbed on the joints of the arms and legs. Patients were then locked in a sweatbox that was permanently heated and kept at a very high temperature, for twenty, thirty or even more days. This caused the disease to flow from the throat and the mouth so violently that the teeth fell out. The gums swelled, teeth loosened, and saliva gushed from the mouth incessantly."

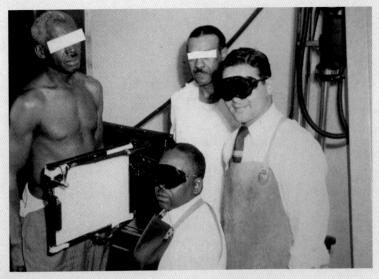

Some patients involved in a blind experiment in the United States did not receive treatment well into the penicillin age so that the progress of the disease could be studied.

Syphilis is common in Australia as well. These two south-Australian aboriginal women are suffering from the disease.

Syphilis does not recognize social class

Sometimes the skin ulcers would disappear after sweat baths, leaving the patients with an often deadly case of mercury poisoning instead. Those not left out on the streets were committed to what were once leper houses. These were much less than hospitals and more like penitentiaries, a fitting place for those infected by a disease associated with the indulgence of forbidden lusts. In the end, however, it was not just the laborers and prostitutes who were infected. Syphilis also attacked emperors, kings, popes, and bishops. The illustrious list of famous syphilis sufferers includes, among others, Popes Julius II (1503–1513) and Leo X (1513–1521), the French king, Francis I (1515–1547), his successor Henry II (1547–1559), and King Henry VIII of England (1509–1561). More recent famous victims include the German poet Heinrich Heine (1797–1856), who spent his last years suffering from syphilitic dementia on his "mattress grave." Philosopher Friedrich Nietzsche died of it, both blind and paralyzed (1844–1900).

Old and young alike beg in front of Mother Teresa's leper hospital in Kolkata, a haven for many desperate people seeking help.

DISFIGURED AND DETESTED

LEPROSY—THE DISEASE OF THE POOR

No disease is more disfiguring than leprosy. According to the World Health Organization (WHO), the ancient disease, which is already mentioned in the Bible, still afflicts approximately 15 million people today, most of them in Southeast Asia, Africa, and Central and Latin America. Infection with the *Mycobacterium leprae* pathogen results in 400,000 new cases every year. The leprosy bacteria is transmitted through sustained, close contact with an infected population. This makes it primarily an illness of the poor, and one to which children are particularly susceptible.

A disease that eats away identity

There are two kinds of leprosy: lepromatous leprosy, also known as Hansen's disease, and tuberculoid leprosy. Lepromatous leprosy is an insidious disease that starts with ulcers on the nose and forehead. Lesions and skin growths soon make the face completely unrecognizable; age and gender can often no longer be determined. The mucous membranes of the mouth and nose are destroyed, teeth fall out, and the voice becomes hoarse and nasal. Tuberculoid leprosy brings skin numbness and paralysis, often leading to loss of toes, fingers, and even the hands and feet. Contrary to popular belief, the disease does not cause limbs and skin to rot. Numbness is what causes problems: due to nerve damage, people with tuberculoid leprosy cannot tell when they have cuts or wounds. Not realizing they are injured, a leper's sores become infected and the tissue around them deteriorates, accompanied by a characteristic foul odor.

Washing is a sin

Leprosy was already well known in Mediterranean regions in antiquity. It reached central Europe somewhat later, probably in the fourth century. Its spread was perhaps accelerated by the decline of the bathing culture enjoyed during the period of the Roman Empire. In its wake, many Christians, who considered touching and washing the body a sin, limited bathing to once a year, if at all. Bodily hygiene was frowned upon for nearly a thousand years. It was only in the fourteenth century, when the last crusaders returned to Europe from the Near East, that bathing briefly became popular again.

Isolating the sick

Many considered the repulsive appearance of those afflicted with leprosy to be a bodily manifestation of sin. The New Testament mentions the need to isolate lepers, and church fathers at the 589 Council of Lyon declared that they should be separated "as if they were already

Infection by tattoo

In addition to close contact and poor hygiene, infection can also occur via the globally widespread practice of tattooing. Many traditional peoples mark their bodies using thorns, needles, knives, or other tools, mixing the pigments with saliva, nasal mucous, urine, or pigeon excrement. This introduces the leprosy pathogen directly into the bloodstream.

Two lepers, a father and son, in Pushkar, India. The cruel disfigurement that accompanies the disease can arouse feelings of disgust rather than compassion.

Molokai, an island in the Hawaiian chain, is a former leper colony once off limits to all non-sufferers except for missionaries and medical personnel.

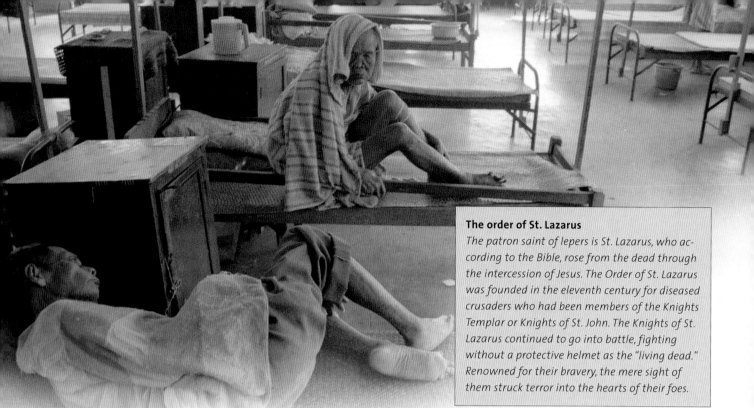

The Western Visayas Sanitarium in the Philippines provides care for 185 lepers with the help of Belgian nuns.

Raymundo Mestidio suffers from leprosy. He is receiving the best treatment possible in the Western Visayas Sanitarium on the Philippines.

dead". Until the eleventh century lepers were pariahs, living in poor huts outside the towns. They were required to carry a clapper or ring a bell, warning anyone approaching of their illness, but also drawing attention to themselves in the hope of receiving charity.

Later lepers were housed in special quarantine hospitals, called "leprosaria." In times of famine, malingerers could be found there as well. Mingling with disfigured, foul-smelling lepers was better than starving outside. Although most leprosaria closed in the eighteenth century, there is still one at Fontilles, near the Costa Blanca in Spain, with around eighty patients.

Social death

In medieval times, priests and physicians would examine the populace for signs of leprosy. After examining the whole body, if the diagnosis was leprosy, the afflicted person was led in procession to church and dressed like a corpse in what were called "Lazarus robes." The leper lay in front of the altar while funeral hymns were sung. Still wearing the distinctive robes and gloves that would mark them as a sufferer, the leper was then given a clapper or bell with which to warn people not to come too close. Married people diagnosed with leprosy received an immediate annulment, and their possessions reverted either to relatives or the Church.

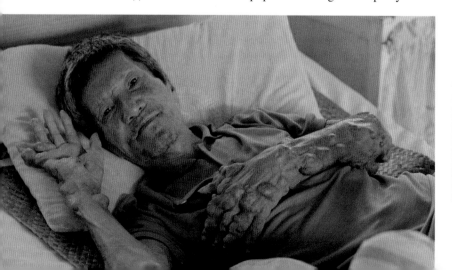

Spread by colonization and slave trade

Leprosy has not been endemic in Europe since the sixteenth century. No one is quite sure why its incidence declined, but part of the answer may be the arrival of a more virulent disease that killed impoverished members of society before they could contract and spread leprosy. Tuberculosis is a likely candidate. Before that, however, leprosy traveled with the conquistadors from the Iberian peninsular to Central and South America. Spanish conquistador Fernando Cortez (1485–1547) built the first leprosaria in the New World in Mexico. To this day, Latin America and the Philippines, the latter also a Spanish colony, are hard hit by the disease.

Buried alive on Molokai

Once James Cook (1728–1779) put the Hawaiian Islands on the map in 1778, European sailors arrived, bringing new infectious diseases. Within eighty years, Hawaii's native population declined by four-fifths, from 330,000 to around 60,000 inhabitants. Hawaii's first case of leprosy dates to 1845. For fear of spreading the infection, anyone with clear symptoms was marooned on the island of Molokai. The Hawaiian lepers remained there, abandoned to their fate, for the rest of their lives, living on the island's craggy cliffs with only the sea in front of them. At

first, there were no medicines or doctors, or even housing for them to live in. Then, in 1873, the Belgian priest Damien de Veuster (1840–1889) arrived. Nauseated by the appalling condition of the reeking lepers with maggots eating their rotting flesh, he had himself taken to Molokai so that he could organize shelter and distribute donations of clothing and medicine. Father Damien shared the lives and deaths of the lepers until he himself was infected and died of the disease, on Molokai. He was beatified in 1995.

It can be cured today

In 1873, Norwegian scientist Gerhard Hansen (1841–1912) succeeded in isolating the pathogen, thereby proving that the disease was infectious rather than inherited or caused by bad air. Today Hansen's Disease is the preferred name for leprosy because it lacks the overwhelmingly negative historical connotations of the older term. Hansen's discovery led to the first treatments for the disease and later to combination therapies utilizing antibiotics. Today, if diagnosed in time, it is possible to stop the disease from progressing. The danger of infection is relatively low, and most of those treated are not contagious. Nevertheless, rehabilitation of the healed into society can be difficult depending on the degree of disfiguration.

The grave of the Belgian priest Damien, who devoted his life to lepers, is located on the island of Molokai, Hawaii.

THE CHILD STRANGLER

THE RETURN OF DIPHTHERIA

Diphtheria is again on the advance in the states of the former Soviet Union, where large-scale epidemics claimed at least 5,000 lives during the 1990s. Indonesia, India, Nepal, and Papua New Guinea were also affected. Diphtheria is so virulent that all cases must be reported immediately to the WHO (World Health Organization). Travelers to affected lands should get a booster vaccination against diphtheria before their departure.

An agonizing death

This terrible disease is caused by the bacteria *Corynebacterium diphtheriae*. The agony of the disease, however, is due to the toxins released by the bacteria rather than the bacteria itself. Passed on directly from person to person via airborne transmission (sneezing, coughing, spitting), diphtheria has a short incubation period, with symptoms appearing after just two to five days. The first sign is usually a sore throat and fever. The mucous membranes at the points of infection—the mouth, throat, and nose—change color and give off a foul, sweet smell, hence the disease's earlier name of "brown mouth" or "brown throat." Diphtheria becomes life threatening when the toxins spread throughout the body, causing either a neural inflammation with accompanying paralysis or an inflammation of the heart, bringing on sudden cardiac arrest and death. If the larynx is affected, a dangerous croup develops, with swelling, coughing, hoarseness, and shortness of breath. Patients repeatedly grab at their throats, trying in vain to free themselves from the stranglehold of the disease before suffocating in agony. Only a quick incision to the windpipe, a tracheotomy, can then save their lives.

The disease swept through Europe repeatedly, with a particularly virulent outbreak occur-

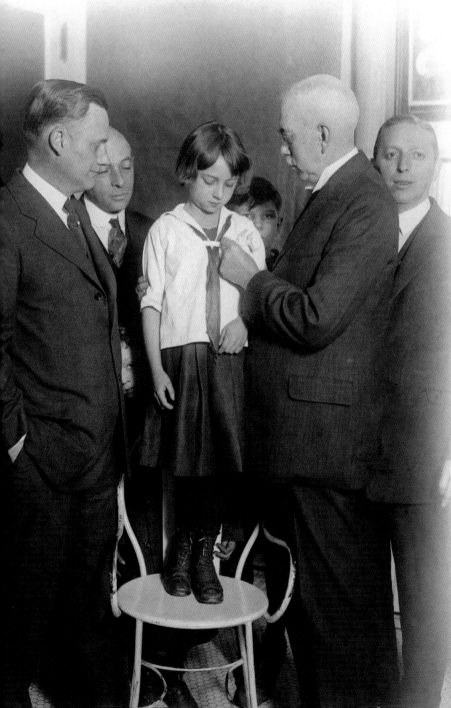

> **Magic and excrement against diphtheria**
> *Diphtheria was already known in ancient Greece and Rome, where it was called the "Egyptian illness." According to Pliny the Elder (ca. 23–79 CE), it was treated with ground swallows' nests, crushed millipedes, or compresses of pigeon excrement steeped in wine. During the medieval period, people sought help from St. Blaise, the patron saint of throat diseases, or from a barber, who would make an incision in the windpipe when the danger of suffocation was acute. After treatment by a "cut-throat," the patients didn't suffocate, but often bled to death instead. Physicians refused to perform such operations, leaving such drastic measures to their much-maligned and despised colleagues, the barbers, or surgeons.*

The fight against the disease began following the discovery of the antitoxin and continued with the development of a vaccination in 1923. Here, a young girl is vaccinated.

In 1925, sled dogs transported antitoxin to Nome, Alaska to stop a diphtheria epidemic.

ring at the time of the Reformation. In Spain the disease was known as *garrotillo* after the *garrote*, the executioner's wire used to strangle condemned prisoners. According to records, 60,000 children in the Kingdom of Naples died of the disease in 1617. In the mid-nineteenth

> ### Balto's statue in Central Park
> *In New York's Central Park there stands a statue of a black husky named Balto. Balto was the lead sled dog that headed a pack of 150 huskies who pulled sleds carrying the diphtheria antitoxin to Nome, Alaska in 1925. Amazingly, the dogs and their twenty human mushers covered made the 600-mile journey through inhospitable terrain in just five and a half days. They were celebrated throughout America for their feat.*

century it claimed almost as many young victims in Russia, Greece, and Turkey.

The war against diphtheria in Paris and Berlin

In 1821, a French physician from Tours, Paul Bretonneau (1771–1862), gave the disease its name based on the changes it causes in the larynx: diphtheria is derived from the Greek word

for "membrane." The pathogen was identified in 1884 by Friedrich Loeffler (1852–1915) of the Prussian Imperial Health Authority and, almost simultaneously, by Emil Roux (1853–1933) and Alexander Yersin (1863–1943) at the Pasteur Institute in Paris. A serum for treatment and the discovery of the antitoxin in 1890 by Emil von Behrings and Shibasaburo Kitasato (1853–1931) were major steps in the battle against the disease. In 1901, Behring was awarded the Nobel Prize for Medicine for his work. Guinea pigs were used initially, and later horses, to produce the antitoxin in quantity. Although the mortality rates fell, large epidemics were still a regular event until a vaccine was developed in 1923. Vulnerable, under-vaccinated populations, however, remained susceptible to major outbreaks, as an epidemic striking war-ravaged Russia and Berlin at the end of World War II illustrated very well.

Although diphtheria is seldom encountered in Europe today, action must be taken at the slightest suspicion of infection. The antitoxin, an antidote against the poison released by the bacteria, must be administered as soon as possible. The disease still has a mortality rate of 10 percent, rising up to 20 percent among the young children who have always been diphtheria's most vulnerable victims.

Emil von Behring (1854–1917) was awarded the Nobel Prize for Medicine for his discovery of the diphtheria antitoxin.

Delirium and high fever

The cause of typhoid fever is the bacterium *Salmonella typhi*. It can only be passed on via the ingestion of contaminated urine or feces. The first symptoms of the illness follow an incubation period of one to two weeks. Weakness and muscle aches are accompanied by a spiking rising fever of up to 105 °F. The high fever, which can last for weeks, is usually accompanied by delirium, diarrhea, skin rashes, intestinal bleeding, and frequently cardiac and circulatory problems. In 2–5 percent of cases, a patient can be chronically infected, capable of passing the bacterium on to others for several years, but show no symptoms of it themselves. The presence of these so-called carriers may be due to a genetic mutation.

A history of death by diarrhea

Well into the early twentieth century there were still places in North America and Europe that lacked sanitary sewage disposal systems and secure drinking water supplies. As long as humans have lived in cities, excrement and urine have been simply tipped from chamber pots into the street. Where drains existed, sewage flowed from the houses into streams and rivers, or down open gutters in the street. The gutters and cesspits in medieval cities would be

A patient and an infant waiting for treatment in a Vietnamese hospital. Typhoid fever is far from eradicated.

FLIES AND EXCREMENT

TYPHOID FEVER IS STILL RAMPANT

From September 2004 through January 2005, the Republic of the Congo reported 42,564 cases of typhoid fever. Throughout the world, many countries, most of them impoverished, are similarly affected, with recent major outbreaks in Haiti and South Africa. According to the World Health Organization (WHO), around 16 million people fall victim to this severe diarrheic disease every year, and some 600,000 of them die as a result. Typhoid is spread by drinking water that has been contaminated by excrement, often spread by the common fly.

> ### The infamous Typhoid Mary
> *In 1906, a New York banker named Charles Henry Warren rented a vacation house on Long Island. His Irish cook, Mary Mallon, prepared the food for his large family. Six of the eleven people in the house came down with typhoid fever. Mary continued to work in the New York area, setting off a local epidemic in which three people died. After tests it became clear that Mary Mallon was the source. She promised to stop working as a cook, but continued to do so using a false name. When she was tracked down again she was summarily incarcerated against her will in the quarantine hospital on North Brother Island in the East River between Manhattan and Queens. She died there of a stroke in 1938. She had been in quarantine for twenty-three years.*

cleaned out about once every fifteen years. The sanitations systems in place on battlefields were especially inadequate. Throughout human history, many more soldiers have died from dysentery than through enemy action.

Prevention is the best therapy

Although there is a vaccination against typhoid fever, there is none against the related disease of paratyphoid, caused by a similar, though distinct, bacterium. The only defense is good personal hygiene, including thoroughly washing one's hands, and, in typhoid-threatened regions, avoiding un-bottled water, ice, raw fruit, vegetables, and salad. A bit of advice for travelers: "Peel it, cook it, or forget it!" Cases of typhoid have to be reported, and patients are treated in hospitals in rigorously enforced isolation.

**Typhoid fever
in modern Europe**

Typhoid fever can still break out in Europe today, usually brought in by persons who have been traveling in regions where the disease is common. In January 2006, the Robert Koch Institute recorded the case of a 54-year-old man who had been in India for three weeks and died within a month of his return. He had dragged himself to work despite having a fever and had refused admission to the hospital. Luckily, he had not infected his friends or coworkers.

Background: Countless people died of typhoid fever in Nazi concentration camps such as Bergen-Belsen, shown here.

Below: Health workers wear protective clothing when spraying disinfectants to kill the Salmonella typhi bacterium.

DEATH IN THE DRINKING WATER

THE HISTORY OF CHOLERA

"While carrying out my official duties, I have ... visited many places in which the excrement lay heaped around the houses, cellars, and yards, in such amounts and to such heights that one could only move with great difficulty," reports a member of the Metropolitan Commission of Sewers in 1841. "I met people who lived and slept in rooms where the walls were oozing dung. The effects of the stinking dung heaps exhaling their poisonous gases can be gathered from the haggard, pale and unhealthy faces and shivering limbs of the people who have to live in such pools of filth and misery."

A deadly illness

Refugees from Rwanda file past an endless row of cholera victims at the Goma camp.

The origins of cholera lie in the densely inhabited marshy delta of the Indian Ganges and Brahmaputra Rivers. Long ago, it spread from here throughout Asia, and it continues to rage in epidemics around the globe: several thousand people were killed by a 2006 outbreak in Angola and the Sudan. Cholera has a short incubation period, with symptoms appearing two to five days after infection with the water-borne *Vibrio cholerae* bacterium. An illness that attacks the intestinal mucous membranes, severe diarrhea and vomiting may follow only a few hours after ingestion of contaminated water. If saline transfusions are not administered immediately, the body quickly loses water and mineral salt, leading to a catastrophic fall in blood pressure and death.

The bacterium is excreted with the feces, and items contaminated with feces, such as clothing, can also transmit the disease. Once it enters the water supply the number and rate of infections rises dramatically. Approximately half of all untreated patients will die, and for children, the elderly, and anyone with a compromised immune system, such as the malnourished, the mortality rate can be as high as 90 percent.

Religion and hygiene

That cholera still claims so many victims today in Asian and African countries is in part due to religious customs. In India, Hindus believe the waters of the Ganges River are sacred, capable

of purifying the soul and washing away sins. Many sick and dying people are brought to the river's banks. After they die, their ashes are deposited in the holy river, as are the often only slightly singed bodies of the very poor, whose families could not afford enough wood for a complete cremation. The pilgrims then drink the sacred water, which is also contaminated by raw sewage, and fill their flasks to take it home to their villages. In this way, infectious diseases are carried to even the most remote locations.

The first cholera pandemic, 1815–1824

Widespread outbreaks of cholera were once confined to the Indian subcontinent. Following the eighteenth-century British conquest of what is now Bangladesh and northeast India, a land and sea route linking India with the coast of the Arabian Peninsula was opened up to international trade. This brought the disease to the Islamic pilgrimage sites of Mecca and Medina, where tens of thousands of pilgrims from all over the world gathered each year. The sanitary conditions in the pilgrims' camps were atrocious. Cholera spread so rapidly that the Arabic name for it is *el hawa* ("the storm"). Pilgrims returning home carried it as far as North Africa, from whence it spread throughout the Mediterranean region.

In 1815, following several years of severe floods and crop failure, a particularly virulent cholera epidemic broke out along the Ganges. Within a few years, the disease reached pandemic proportions in the Philippines, Bombay, Arabia, Persia, and Russia. A cold wave beginning in the winter of 1823/24 finally halted the spread of the bacteria, which cannot survive sustained periods of freezing temperatures.

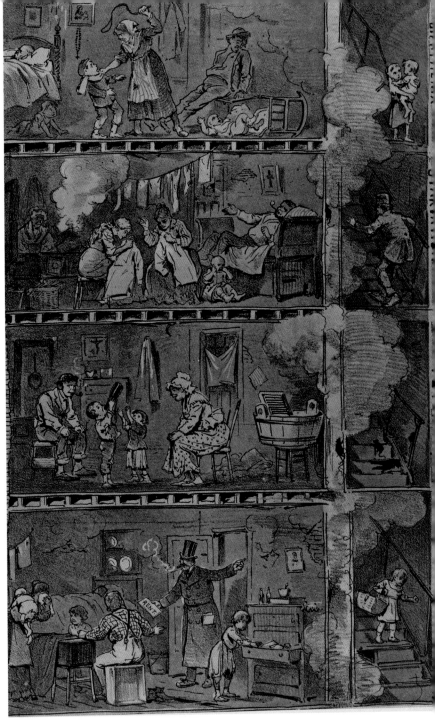

In 1884, fumigation was used to disinfect French railroad passengers and their luggage in an attempt to prevent the disease from spreading.

The second pandemic, 1826–1836, Moscow – Warsaw – Berlin – London – Paris – New York

The second pandemic followed in 1826. Like the first, it spread from the Ganges westward, with particular rapacity along the Volga River. At the time it was believed that cholera was caused by what was called *miasma*, essentially bad air and foul smells; no connection was made with contaminated water. The 200,000 victims along the Volga, many of them boatmen and washerwomen, were quickly buried in

In 1880 the economy was booming in New York City, but the poor continued to live in deplorable conditions. Cholera took a heavy toll here, too.

Renowned Berlin doctor Robert Koch (1843–1910) identified the bacillus of both cholera and tuberculosis.

mass graves. It was impossible to provide individual burial in cemeteries for so many dead.

The second pandemic continued westward to Poland and Berlin. Prussian General Field Marshal von Gneisenau (1760–1831) and his chief of staff Carl von Clausewitz (1780–1831) were put in command of an observation army on the Polish frontier. In order to stop the spread of the "Oriental dysentery," most of the Polish border had been shut down. Only twelve crossings, each with a quarantine station, were open to travelers. Travelers were required to spend between ten and twenty days in quarantine before being allowed to proceed on their journeys. All mail and imported goods were fumigated in smoke infused with sulfur, saltpeter, and wheat chaff. As they had during the plague, doctors wore protective coats of oilcloth when treating patients. Nevertheless, too often, all their precautionary measures were in vain. Both Clausewitz and Gneisenau died of cholera in 1831.

In spite of all efforts, the pandemic forged ahead to Berlin. City leaders immediately cordoned off all infected areas, and a fumigation chamber for visitors was set up beside Charlottenburg Palace, where the Prussian court had fled from the disease. Smoking in the street, previously prosecuted by the police, was now encouraged—it was thought that the smoke might cleanse the bad air! More than 1,400 resients of Berlin lost their lives, including the philosopher Georg Wilhelm Friedrich Hegel (1770–1831).

Europe's great cities in the grip of cholera

The cholera pandemic then spread to Hamburg, traveling along the Havel and Spree Rivers. Careless implementation of quarantine regulations contributed to a major outbreak in the port. Conditions in Hamburg, which lacked both a central water supply and covered sewers, were much worse than in Berlin. Waste contaminated by the bacterium went directly into the Binnenalster, the lake from which Hamburg drew much of its drinking water. Almost 2,000 of Hamburg's 145,000 residents died.

London was next, with 10,000 victims. Paris follows suit in 1832. The poet Heinrich Heine described the horrific conditions he witnessed on the streets and in Hôtel-Dieu, the hospital near Nôtre-Dame Cathedral: "There is no sewage canalization in Paris either. The overflowing cesspits are emptied by barrel-carts that deliver their loads every night to the Dépotoirs aux Voiries, the sewage depot on the outskirts of the city. When the depot begins to overflow, the sewage is channeled directly into the Seine near Saint-Denis."

Almost 230,000 Frenchmen fell ill, and more than 100,000 lost their lives. In one year, 1832, 19,000 died from cholera in Paris alone.

After hundreds of thousands had lost their lives throughout Europe, cholera reached the USA in 1832 as well, probably brought by infected Irish immigrants. The epidemic raged with special ferocity among the Native American population, which had an exceptionally high mortality rate.

The conditions in Goma refugee camp were horrific. Here, a refugee from Rwanda administers an infusion to a man with cholera.

No end in sight

New pandemics followed with some regularity. The worst, from 1840 to 1861, claimed more than a million victims. The most recent pandemic, the seventh recorded, began in 1936. By then, Europe was largely spared; the cause of the disease had been discovered by then and counteractive measures introduced. As early as 1854, the English physician John Snow (1813–1858) recognized a connection between the high rate of infection in the London district of Soho and the use of a single water pump in Broad Street. He had the handle of the pump removed, and the epidemic died out. The belief in miasma as the cause of cholera was so entrenched, however, that Snow had difficulty publishing a paper stating that contaminated drinking water was the primary factor in the spread of the disease.

In 1854, Max Pettenkofer (1818–1901), a Munich professor of medicine, identified a link between soil contaminated by feces and the spread of cholera. Through his efforts, sewage systems were upgraded and extended. Nevertheless, Pettenkofer was a strong opponent of the theory that water could transmit the disease.

It was only in 1883, after Robert Koch (1843–1910) identified the *Vibrio cholerae* pathogen in drinking water from Alexandria, Egypt, that the method of transmission was widely acknowledged. During an outbreak in 1892, the people of Hamburg were ordered to boil their drinking water. Nevertheless, as doctors at the time pointed out, as long as the poor were stuck in damp quarters, malnourished, and lacking the means to maintain basic hygiene, the disease would continue to recur. The doctors understood, as medical professionals do today, that poverty fuels the spread of cholera. While modern medicine can treat cholera, sadly, it has made few inroads in eradicating the widespread misery that lies behind it.

Orphans lie closely pressed together in a refugee camp. Their parents have died of cholera.

Flu: The Under-estimated Threat

FROM SPANISH FLU TO AVIAN FLU

1918 was the final year of World War I, the war that had drawn in nearly all of Europe and claimed some 9 million lives all over the world. It was early in the year, and no one realized that the great catastrophe of the early twentieth century would not be this devastating war, after all, but a flu epidemic.

Bad news from Spain

The earliest reports of a massive flu epidemic came from Spain in the spring of 1918. Because Spain was not directly involved in World War I, the country censored news less strictly than others. The war-faring countries, by contrast, made every effort not to let terrifying news weaken their people's morale, which explains how this global epidemic came to be called the "Spanish" flu. Today, however, it is clearly understood that the illness did not originate in Spain.

The first cases probably occurred in March 1918 at an American military base in the state of Kansas. The disease spreads rapidly, and within a very short time entire battalions were infected. Its contagiousness was badly underestimated, allowing the flu to spread rapidly among the soldiers' families, and it reached Europe with the arrival of the first American active service troops.

Waves of death

The Spanish flu spread in several waves. The first occurred in the spring of 1918 and abated in August of the same year. But the flu returned in the fall of 1918, originating this time from France. Again the disease was extremely contagious—but this time it was deadlier still. The epidemic mainly affected people between 18 and 35 years old (that is, people in their most productive years). The effects were so dramatic that public life was brought to a standstill in many places. Schools and other public institutions were forced to close, and face masks

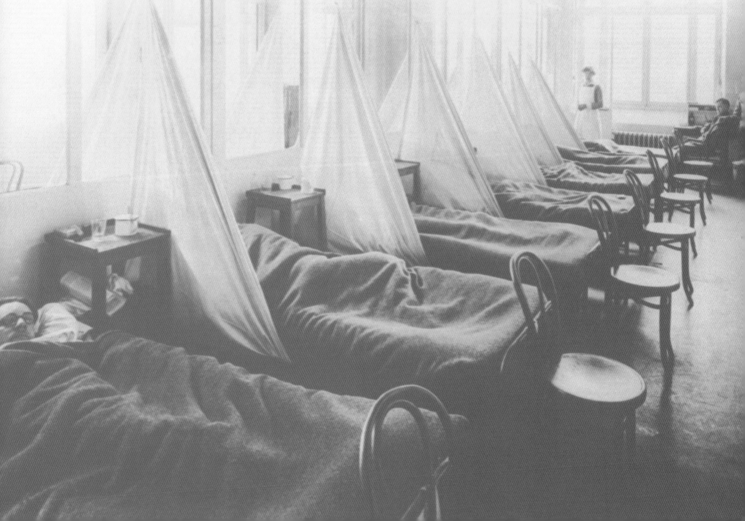

In the fall of 1918, the flu hit France. Huge numbers of US soldiers were treated in this military hospital.

were seen in every street. By early 1919, the worst was over. While there were additional, smaller waves, most of the victims died during the first nine months of the crisis. When the flu finally receded in 1921, it had claimed 25 to 50 million lives worldwide, at least three times as many as World War I (which ended in 1918). The US Army lost more soldiers to the Spanish flu than died in combat.

A virus is the cause

Epidemics of such a catastrophic scale have come to be known as pandemics, a word derived from ancient Greek that literally means "concerning the entire population." Like epidemics, pandemics are also defined as occurring within a certain period of time. Unlike epidemics, however, pandemics are not limited to a particular geographic region; instead, they spread across all the continents. Other pandemics comparable to the Spanish flu include the Black Death (1347–1352), which also claimed over 20 million lives, and AIDS, the immunodeficiency disease that has been rampant since the 1980s.

The powerlessness of medicine in the face of the widespread deaths caused by Spanish flu

was partly due to the fact that the influenza virus was still unknown at that time. Scientists originally assumed that a bacterium caused the disease. There would have been no defense

When avian flu broke out in China, millions of poultry were destroyed.

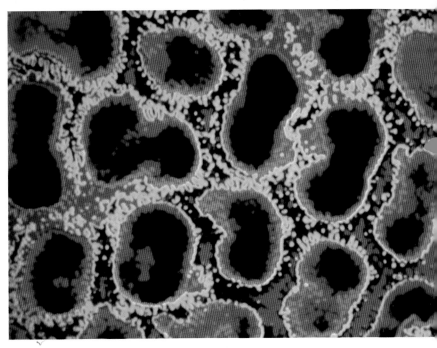

Originally, the disease was thought to be caused by a bacterium. However, in 1933, the virus responsible for the flu was discovered.

against viruses anyway, since there were no methods available to detect them. It was not until 1933 that English researchers successfully isolated the influenza virus in animal experiments, and even then, the subtype that caused

the Spanish flu remained unknown. In 1951, scientists came closer to the cause by studying the bodies of victims of the influenza epidemic that had been conserved in the freeze-up of Alaska. This approach was not successful until 1997, when the American molecular biologist Jeffery Taubenberger finally solved the long-standing mystery. The 1918 killer virus had been of type A/H1N1, an extremely aggressive strain that uses birds as hosts before mutating to affect humans, as well.

The danger of mutations

The Spanish flu remained the most catastrophic virus epidemic of the modern age for some forty years, as the world was spared further epidemics on a global scale. Then, in 1957 and 1958, another epidemic of global proportions occurred: the Asian flu. The disease originated in China and was carried to Hong Kong by refugees from Red China, and from there, it spread throughout the world. This pandemic

Types of influenza virus

The strains of human influenza virus can be divided into three types. Type B and C viruses affect humans almost exclusively and are relatively harmless. Type A, however, is both the most dangerous and the most widespread type of influenza virus. It not only affects humans, but also poultry and pigs. Type A occurs in various subtypes that are distinguished by names such as H1N1 or H5N1. Genetic transfers between avian flu viruses and human influenza

viruses give rise to deadly new subtypes for which humans have no antibodies (specialized cells that fight off infection). The third big influenza epidemic of the twentieth century, the Hong Kong flu of 1968, was also caused by mutations of a type A virus. In this case, a type-A H2N2 virus (which caused the Asian flu, below) recombined with an avian flu virus to form a new subtype, A/H3N2. This deadly mutation claimed approximately one million lives worldwide.

claimed 1 to 4 million lives within a relatively short period of time.

This particular flu virus descended from the A/H1N1 influenza virus (which had caused the Spanish flu) by recombination with an avian influenza virus. This produced a new virus—type A/H2N2—against which the human immune system had no defense.

After this wave died down, many people had become immune to the virus and, as a result, the Asian flu has not circulated in decades. However, subsequent generations have developed very few antibodies against this particular strain of virus, and this could lead to catastrophic effects in the event of a new A/H2N2 epidemic.

In light of this historical background, the stir caused by a press release issued by the Robert Koch Institute in Berlin in April 2004 is understandable. The research institute stated that it had mistakenly sent samples of this virus to thousands of labs all over the world for routine testing. The World Health Organization immediately called on all of the labs to destroy the samples.

When will the next pandemic take place?

A new virus subtype that could cause the next major pandemic might develop at any moment through a recombination of human and animal influenza viruses. Asia seems especially prone to figure as the originating region of such mutations. The simple methods of animal husbandry practiced in Asia create favorable conditions for simultaneous infections of humans and animals. The H5N1 bird flu virus, which originated in Asia, has been rampant since 2003. Although it apparently has not yet combined with human influenza viruses, there is a real and ever-present danger that it will. It is estimated that a pandemic triggered by the H5N1 virus would claim between 7 and 150 million victims.

Following the outbreak of avian flu, there has been an all-pervasive fear of a new influenza epidemic in Asia. Hardly anyone dares to walk in the streets without wearing a face mask.

A famous victim: Egon Schiele
*Famous victims of the flu include the Austrian painter Egon Schiele (1890–1918). This luminary of the Viennese art scene was 28 years old and had just been a pall bearer for his patron and mentor Gustav Klimt (1862–1918), the most famous representative of Jugendstil, when he and his wife both became victims of the second wave of Spanish flu. At the time, Edith was six months pregnant. She died on October 28, 1918. Egon Schiele, who sketched his dying wife in agony, only survived her by three days.
Today, Schiele's works sell for record prices in international auctions.*

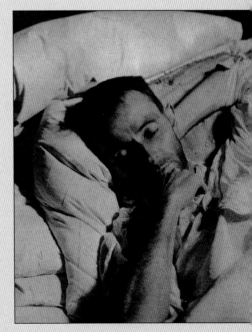

Egon Schiele on his deathbed.

3,000 Deaths Daily

MALARIA CLAIMS COUNTLESS LIVES

Mal'aria ("bad air" in Italian), tertian fever, swamp fever, and marsh fever are some of the many names given to the same dreadful disease. With 300 to 500 million cases every year, malaria is currently the world's worst infectious disease. Of those who contract malaria, more than 2 million will die, and most of the casualties are among children aged 5 and under. Worldwide, malaria is a greater threat than AIDS or tuberculosis. It is common in more than 100 countries, wherever the anopheles mosquitoes that transmit the plasmodia parasites live.

Widespread everywhere but Europe

Europe, North America, and large parts of Russia are free of malaria today, but the disease is still commonplace in Africa, Asia, and Latin America. About 40 percent of the world's population still lives with the constant threat of malaria. There are, of course, exceptions. Every once in a while, Europe will report a case of "airport malaria" caused by the unintentional import of infected mosquitoes.

Malaria remained a serious problem in Europe well into the twentieth century. As late as the end of World War II, a major malarial zone was Italy, where the last recorded cases occurred in 1962. Today, all outbreaks of the disease are required to be reported to the World Health Organization. Countries can only be declared malaria-free zones several years after the last reported case.

The malaria parasite in the human body—cells explode

Malaria parasites are among the oldest pathogens plaguing humankind. It is thought that they originally developed in the intestines of reptiles some 60 million years ago. The parasites breed in two phases, once in the human host, and again in the mosquito. The female mosquito transmits the parasite larvae to humans while drinking our blood. The pathogens travel to the human liver, where they mature. After a few days or months, they return to the bloodstream, where they breed inside the red blood cells, causing them to burst after two to three days. The parasites continue to attack red blood cells, causing more and more of them to explode. Only in this final stage does an infected human realize that something is wrong.

When a mosquito bites an infected person, it passes the parasite on to its next host.

In addition to mosquitoes, there are other means of infection, but most of them rare. The disease can be transmitted by a blood transfusion, a used syringe or from an infected mother to her unborn child via the placenta.

Symptoms of a malicious disease

An infected person at first experiences rather vague symptoms including fever, body aches or diarrhea. After several breeding cycles, the parasite triggers regularly recurring, spiking fevers of up to 105 °F, accompanied by chills, anemia, and an enlarged spleen.

Four varieties of the parasite have been identified. *Plasmodium vivax* and *Plasmodium ovale* lead to malaria tertiana, characterized by a spiking fever every third day. *Plasmodium malariae* causes malaria quartana, which brings a four-day cycle of fever; the days in between are fever-free. Malaria tropica is the most dangerous variant. Caused by the *Plasmodium falciparum* parasite, it exacts by far the highest

Two children watch with great interest as a physician in Indonesia fishes mosquito larvae out of stagnant water.

Different types of malarial infection and their distribution			
Pathogen	Type	% of cases	Distribution
Plasmodium falciparum	Malaria tropica	49 %	*Worldwide, mainly the Sahara, Asia, New Guinea, and Haiti*
Plasmodium vivax	Malaria tertiana	43 %	*In temperate climates, particularly India, Latin America, and Southeast Asia*
Plasmodium ovale	M. tertiana	1 %	*Mostly in West Africa*
Plasmodium malariae	M. quartana	7 %	*Mainly in Africa*

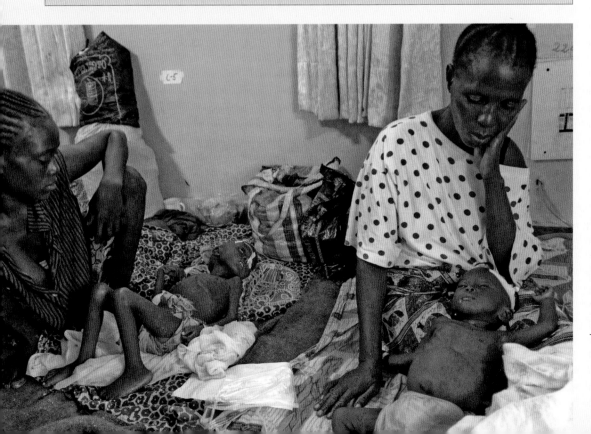

The international humanitarian aid organization Doctors Without Borders provides treatment for these young malaria victims in Monrovia, Liberia.

death toll. If a population has not acquired some level of immunity to the parasite through repeated bouts with the disease, some 20 percent of those infected will die. This type of malaria is characterized by an irregular fever pattern, kidney failure, respiratory arrest, blood clotting disorders and, if it affects the brain, disorientation and coma.

Medical treatment and prophylaxis

The treatment for malaria depends on the type of pathogen causing it. The more benign forms of malaria caused by *Plasmodium vivax*, *ovale* or *malariae* are treated with quinine-based chloroquine tablets. Depending on the region of origin, the more serious *Malaria tropicana* may be treated with the same medication, or with blood transfusions. Travelers on their way to malarial regions are required by health authorities to take drugs before and during their trip, a practice called chemoprophylaxis. While the drugs cannot prevent an infection, they do stop the disease from progressing. Unfortunately, the parasites in many malarial regions have developed a resistance to the most common drugs, reducing their effectiveness. It may be that drugs were administered indiscriminately for too long, with little oversight in place to

determine whether the medication was taken as prescribed. Humans have also developed other means of resistance. Sickle cell anemia, a hereditary disease of the red blood cells that is common among sub-Saharan Africans and their descendants in the Americas, is an acquired biological immunity that prevents the parasite from breeding in the red blood cells.

In addition to proper medical treatment, the risks that lead to infection must be confronted. People living in the tropics and tourists traveling there are strongly advised to heed the following recommendations:
– do not go outside at dawn or dusk,
– wear long sleeves and long pants that cover the maximum area of skin
– thoroughly apply mosquito repellents to any exposed skin,
– use fly screens, mosquito nets, and air conditioning systems. Spray all mosquito nets with insecticide.
It is difficult to comprehend just how many people living in poverty do not have access to protective clothing, screens or mosquito nets.

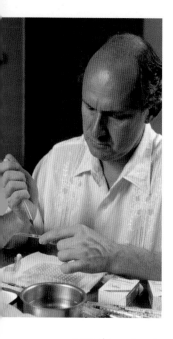

Animal experiments are part of the battle against malaria. Here a scientist tests monkey blood as part of the search for a vaccine.

The 2004 tsunami in Indonesia put the country at high risk for an outbreak of malaria. Chemical insect repellent was sprayed everywhere in an effort to prevent mosquitoes from breeding.

Many of malaria's victims live in slums, where the Anopheles mosquito finds ideal breeding conditions in the stagnant water of dirty puddles, ponds, and open sewers.

The historical battle against malaria

Malaria has been documented for millennia in India, ancient China, and Egypt. Mummies more than 3,000 years old have been found to have the enlarged spleen characteristic of malarial infection. The Chinese have been using sweet wormwood as a remedy since 168 BCE, and today, some 2,000 years later, its active ingredient is the basis of the drug Artemisinin. The ancient Greeks, among them Homer and Herodotus, not only described malaria, but went so far as to warn that swamps are dangerous, even though they had no idea that the danger came from the mosquitoes that thrived there. Most of the ancients assumed that the cause of the disease was the harmful vapors or fetid water.

Increasing populations, as well as trade and travel over long distances, led to the spread of malaria across all of Europe. During the age of exploration, the disease was exported to North and South America, as well. South America is where a remedy for the dreaded disease would eventually be found. Spanish physicians and Jesuit priests noticed that Peruvians laboring in the water-flooded silver mines treated chills and fever with the bark of the Cinchona tree. By the seventeenth century, an extract of this bark called quinine was the standard treatment for malaria throughout Europe.

During the twentieth century, two Nobel prizes were awarded to the researchers who identified malaria's infectious agents. Ronald Ross (1857–1932), a military surgeon working in India, won it in 1902 for his discovery of the mechanism of transmission from mosquitoes to humans. Charles Laveran (1845–1922), a French military surgeon, won his prize in 1907 for work he had completed in 1880, identifying the actual parasite.

The international struggle against malaria

Containing malaria is very difficult. In Italy, Mussolini ordered swamps drained in an attempt to destroy the mosquito's natural habitat. In Spain, a species of mosquito-eating fish called gambusias were imported, with only partial success. In 1956, the World Health Organization (WHO) took up the challenge of worldwide eradication using chloroquine to fight the parasites, together with DDT, a powerful pesticide, to kill the mosquitoes. For decades success seemed within reach, but today, with both the parasites and mosquitoes increasingly resistant, the death toll is again on the rise. The new "Roll Back Malaria" program is trying to reduce the number of new infections by distributing mosquito nets and prophylactic medication. The goal is to significantly lower the number of malarial cases by 2015.

In 2001, a new, relatively inexpensive drug to treat malaria came on the market. However, for most patients living in poor countries, it remains unaffordable. Indeed, ineffective counterfeit drugs are frequently sold to the most impoverished victims. Today, efforts to find a solution are broad-based. WHO cooperates with big pharmaceutical corporations, with additional support for the battle against malaria coming from individuals such as American software billionaire Bill Gates.

The malaria remedy quinine used to be obtained by drying the leaves of the Cinchona tree in the sun and then crushing them into a powder.

AVOID INFECTION AT ALL COSTS

THE AIDS PANDEMIC

"In America you see people living with HIV, like Magic Johnson. In Africa people die of AIDS; it's a death sentence," said two-time Grammy nominated singer India Arie in an interview with Nekesa Mumbi Moody after her visit to Kenya. "It's a very rare person who gets antiviral drugs. Try to understand what that really looks like: a 70-year-old woman doing manual labor to take care of 6-, 7- and 8-year-olds because the whole generation, the middle generation, has been wiped out. I saw that over and over again."

Acquired Immune Deficiency Syndrome

These young people in Lagos, Nigeria are protesting child abuse and the threat of HIV infection from a pedophile living in their neighborhood.

In 2005 alone, more than 3 million people died of this disease and some 5 million became newly infected. AIDS—Acquired Immune Deficiency Syndrome—is truly a global epidemic. It began to emerge about twenty-five years ago and has already claimed more than 25 million

lives. Currently, some 40 million people are living with HIV, the virus that eventually leads to AIDS, among them an ever-growing number of women and children.

Epicenter: Africa
The AIDS epicenter is Africa. According to the organization UNAIDS, only 10 percent of the world's population lives in this region, yet it has 60 percent of all AIDS patients. The following figures provide an overview of the current distribution of AIDS:
– Africa: 25.8 million
– Asia: 8.3 million
– Latin America: 1.8 million
– Eastern Europe and Central Asia: 1.6 million
– North America: 1.2 million
– Western and Central Europe: 720,000
– North Africa/Middle East: 510,000
– Caribbean: 300,000
– Oceania: 74,000
In Eastern Europe and Asia in particular, the number of infected persons has been rising disproportionately rapidly in recent years.

What is the difference between HIV and AIDS? The first causes the latter. "HI" stands for human immunodeficiency. HI viruses destroy human antibodies, thereby weakening the immune system. This prevents the immune system from doing its job, which is to fight off intrusive fungi, bacteria or viruses. An HIV-infected person will become sicker than they should when they contract an illness that their body would be able to fend off easily in a healthy state. AIDS, therefore, is the late stage of an HIV infection.

AIDS viruses have a particularly long incubation period (that is, a long time may pass between infection and when the first symptoms start to appear). During that time, before they even know they carry the virus, HIV-infected people can pass the disease to others.

Children mourning their mother. Given the lack of homes and schools in Africa, most AIDS orphans are entirely on their own.

How does HIV work?

Whenever pathogens enter the body, helper cells (also known as CD4 cells, T4 cells or T4 helper cells) fight them off. Helper cells are a specialized kind of white blood cells (leukocytes). HI viruses attack precisely these helper cells before they start spreading. The human body tries to counter-attack the viruses with antibodies, but fails. The viruses proliferate, and this is frequently followed by an immunological overreaction. The immune system is working flat out and may start attacking the body's own cells (autoimmune diseases). Patients are also more likely to suffer from allergies.

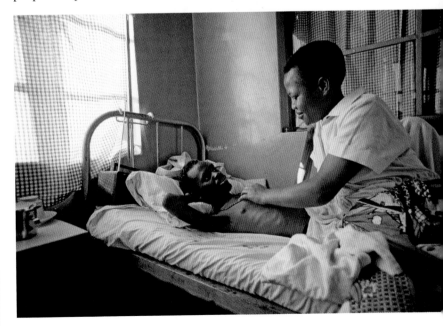

A woman tends her husband, who is suffering from AIDS, in a hospital in Rubwe (Tanzania).

Plagues and Epidemics

How Is AIDS transmitted?

Contrary to popular belief, HI viruses cannot be transmitted by mosquito bites, coughs or sneezes. About 80 percent of all infections are caused by vaginal, anal or oral sexual intercourse with an infected partner and without protection. The virus is found in semen and in vaginal secretions. From there, it can enter the body through the mucous membranes or through small scratches in the skin. Immediately after infection, the patient is a particularly high infection risk to others because the number of viruses in their body is extremely high at this point. People already suffering from an STD are particularly vulnerable.

The fact that viruses can be transmitted via blood transfusions was realized relatively late. In fact, the risk of infection is especially high in this case. Since 1985, blood donors in many countries have been tested for AIDS, but these tests are often not performed in developing countries due to their cost. Drug addicts sharing needles or syringes are also at very high risk. About 15 percent of AIDS patients in the USA and Europe have been infected this way.

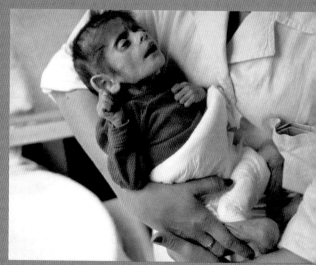

In the 1980s and 1990s, Romania saw a big increase in children contracting AIDS. This baby in a Bucharest hospital is ravaged by the disease.

People working in the medical field can contract infections when handling syringes or insufficiently sterilized surgical instruments; fortunately, however, such infections are rare. Organ transplants are another potential source

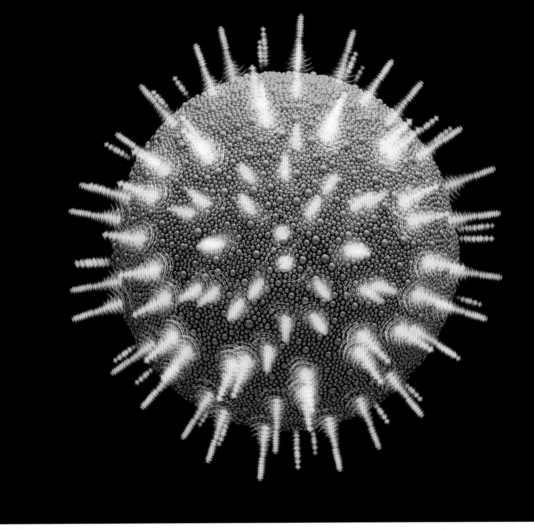

of infection, and infected mothers may pass the virus to their unborn babies. If treatment is begun during pregnancy, however, the risk of infection can be lowered by about two-thirds; C-section birth can reduce the risk even further.

First test, then get treatment

Tests can determine whether an HI infection is present. At least twelve weeks after infection, these tests deliver very sound results. An HIV antibody test determines whether a person's body has developed antibodies against the HIV proteins. Further tests can identify antibodies against the virus, as well as the virus itself. "HIV-positive" means that antibodies are present and, by inference, that the virus has entered the body and it has taken measures against the intruder. The course of the disease varies widely, ranging from an almost complete lack of symptoms to fully developed AIDS syndrome including fever, diarrhoea, pneumonia, toxoplasmosis, herpes, Kaposi's sarcoma (a type of skin cancer), changes in the blood count, tuberculosis, carcinomas, etc. The num-

ber of helper cells per microlitre of blood indicates the severity of the disease (500–1200 = normal, less than 250 = problematic). Whether and how soon these symptoms manifest varies greatly depending on a patient's overall health, their living conditions, the time elapsed since infection, and the kind of medical treatment received. In the industrial countries, there are AIDS patients who have been living with the disease for as long as fifteen years without suffering many symptoms.

A greatly enlarged HI virus. It was first identified by scientists in Paris in 1983.

Combined therapy helps

In the past, an AIDS diagnosis amounted to a death sentence. Now, however, there are improved therapies and combination drugs that enable many patients to experience a long symptom-free phase. The situation in developing countries is entirely different: the high prices of the drugs make it impossible to take them regularly.

This has led to great criticism and protests of pharmaceutical companies and their price policies. A critical problem consists in super-infections (that is, when an AIDS patient is re-infected with a second AIDS virus from a different virus group). This tends to occur among people who have a large number of sexual partners, such as prostitutes.

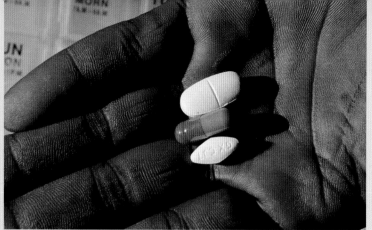

A South African AIDS patient's medication. Many people in Africa cannot afford the medication; they are treated irregularly, if at all.

Advertising for condoms in Abidjan on the Côte d'Ivoire. Used correctly and consistently, condoms considerably reduce the risk of an AIDS infection.

A complicated story

It is not known exactly when AIDS developed. It probably originated in Africa, when the virus jumped from chimpanzees to people. The earliest cases occurred in the late 1970s, and by 1980 it was present on a global scale. In 1981, an aggressive form of Kaposi's sarcoma was diagnosed in a young homosexual man in New York. Two cases of exceptionally rare types of pneumonia were diagnosed in New York and in California the same year. The occurrence of such unusual diseases attracted doctors' attention. At first the symptoms seem to be restricted to homosexuals, but soon drug addicts and hemophiliacs were among those infected with the disease, which was named AIDS in 1982 (SIDA in French and Spanish).

In 1983, researchers at the Parisian Pasteur Institute identified the virus. This led to panic: police officers started wearing masks and gloves when arresting potentially infected suspects, and social workers refused to meet with their clients, talking to them by phone instead. AIDS patients seemed to have contracted their infection mostly in contact with Americans or Africans, many of them from Zambia or Zaire, and especially in homosexual circles. In 1983, WHO listed 3,064 cases in the USA, 40 percent of whom had died. In 1984, the American doctor Robert Gallo isolated the virus (called HTLV-III) and announced a test for determining its presence, which came on the market soon after.

Fear and discrimination

AIDS patients and representatives of the gay emancipation movement struggled against discrimination. Some parents, for instance, would not let their children go to school with young AIDS patients. The first famous person to die from AIDS was actor and ladies' man Rock Hudson, who died on October 3, 1985. The fear of AIDS continued to grow in spite of public campaigns supported by the likes of Princess Diana, who shocked the public in 1987 when she shook an AIDS patient's hand without pro-

tective gloves. In San Francisco, the gay community created a giant quilt made from patches bearing victims' names, and groups such as ACT UP or Gran Fury work toward improving knowledge about and treatment of AIDS all over America. AIDS patients are no longer allowed to enter the USA, and doctors have discussed whether medical secrecy applies if there is a risk of an infected person communicating the disease to a sexual partner. As late as 1998, an AIDS activist was beaten to death in South Africa by her neighbors when she publicly announced that she had been infected.

Setbacks and progress

In 1990, many people in France were infected through contaminated blood transfusions, even though tests had theoretically been available for a long time. Some of those responsible were later sentenced to prison terms, including Michel Garretta, former director of the French National Blood Transfusion Center. In 1998, even the French prime minister, Laurent Fabius, had to appear before the court. In Romania, almost 100,000 orphans have been infected by blood transfusions. In Asia and Eastern Europe, the disease spreads implacably. Ever since 1994, anyone traveling to Russia has to undergo an AIDS test. By 1995, AIDS had become the most significant cause of death in the USA among the 25–44 age group. In its struggle against AIDS, the UN established UNAIDS, a joint program of WHO, the UNDP, UNICEF, the UNFPA, UNESCO, and the World Bank.

The search for a vaccine, financially supported by former US president Bill Clinton and the Bill and Melinda Gates Foundation, turns out to be more complicated than expected. Condoms, special microbicide-based "condoms" for women, diaphragms, and circumcision for men provide varying levels of protection against AIDS, as do education and abstinence.

The giant San Francisco quilt, shown here during an exhibition in commemoration of AIDS victims in Washington, makes a lasting impression on many visitors.

Robert Mapplethorpe: defeated by AIDS

New York photographer Robert Mapplethorpe, born in 1946, made photographic portraits of his friend Patti Smith (the cover of her first album, Horses, features a photo by Mapplethorpe), as well as Richard Gere, Peter Gabriel, Grace Jones, and Andy Warhol. He won his greatest fame, though, with controversial black-and-white photos portraying the gay community. These images triggered a heated debate about pornography in America. Mapplethorpe allegedly maintained sexual relations with 75 percent of his male models, and was known for his excessive drug consumption. After he contracted AIDS in 1986, he fought the disease with all his might. He was shocked to see so many of his friends die of GRID (Gay Related Immune Deficiency)—

the term AIDS was not common back then. In his devastating 1988 self-portrait, he has the mark of death already on him. With medical treatment not resulting in the hoped-for effects, he was confined to a wheelchair by that time. Moreover, he was mourning his partner, the art collector Sam Wagstaff. In May 1988, ten months before his death, he decided to establish a foundation with the proceeds of a sale of his works. Apart from promoting photography, the purpose of this foundation is the fight against AIDS, with a focus on nursing long-term patients. Robert Mapplethorpe died of AIDS at the age of 42 on March 9, 1989. Patricia Morrisroe has recounted his life in a biography entitled This Charming Man.

Deaf, Blind, and Disfigured

Smallpox

In 1950, approximately one million people in India alone died of smallpox. Officially eradicated today, the disease had for centuries left its mark on the history of humankind. As late as 1967, when the World Health Organization (WHO) first announced its vaccination program, there were still some 15 million cases reported worldwide. Nearly 60 percent of the world's population was considered to be in danger of contracting *variola*, better known as smallpox.

Macules and pustules

Edward Jenner (1749–1823) giving 8-year-old James Phipps a cowpox vaccination on May 14, 1796. The cowpox vaccine made James resistant to smallpox.

Two kinds of smallpox, a viral disease, can be distinguished. *Variola minor*, caused by *Orthopoxvirus alastrim*, is relatively harmless. True smallpox is caused by *Orthopoxvirus variola*. Initial symptoms include fever, pain in the limbs, and inflamed airways, followed by smallpox's most characteristic sign: macules, or pimples. These fill with fluid, and later with pus (pustules). As the pustules dry and scab over,

they are unbearably itchy. Constant scratching reopens the pustules, leading to the scarring and pockmarks that mar anyone who has had the disease. Those who came away with nothing worse than scars were relieved to have been spared smallpox's worst effects. The fever accompanying smallpox can lead to delirium, and deafness, blindness, and paralysis were not uncommon. Mortality was at least 15 percent.

Fulminating smallpox

Fulminating smallpox (*variola haemorrhagica*) is a particularly severe form of smallpox that is nearly always fatal. The course of the disease is very rapid and involves severe bleeding of the skin, gums, and internal organs. Death can result within as few as forty-eight hours.

Highly contagious

The incubation period between infection and outbreak of the disease is eight to fourteen days, a relatively long time in which people who do not know they are infected can spread the disease. Well before the pustules break out, smallpox is readily transmitted via airborne infection. Sneezing, speaking or coughing do

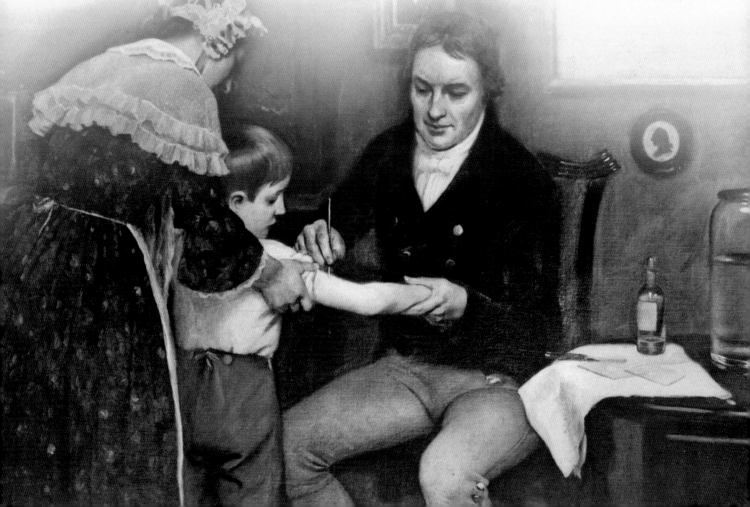

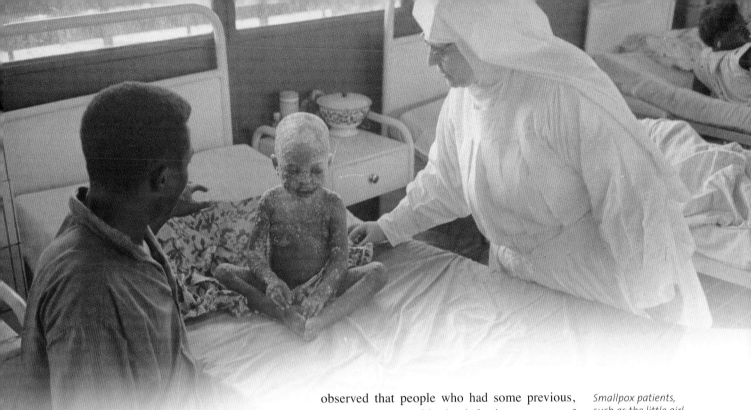

the job, carrying as far as 60 feet. Smallpox can also spread via contact with infected clothing and objects, such as doorknobs. Even dust can carry the contagion. Pus from the pustules sticks to clothes and bedding, making everything the patient has come into contact with contagious for several months. Flies that settle on the infected pus also help spread the disease.

Ancient Chinese wisdom

In China, precise descriptions of the symptoms of smallpox were recorded as early as 340 BCE. By the tenth century at the latest, the Chinese were inoculating against the disease. They had observed that people who had some previous, limited contact with the infectious matter of human smallpox victims developed less severe cases of the disease. Inoculation is the process whereby healthy people are deliberately infected with tiny doses of viruses to build immunity. In China, small quantities of powdered,

Smallpox patients, such as the little girl in this picture, suffer from extremely itchy pustules.

In 1939, mobile vaccination stations were set up, such as this one in Visalia, CA.

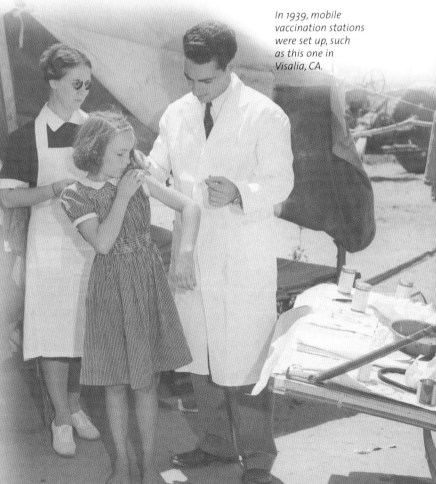

Chronology of a success story

Thanks to WHO's 1967 decision to make vaccination mandatory on a global scale, smallpox is no longer a threat. 1970 saw the eradication of smallpox in western and central Africa. South America and Southeast Asia followed in 1971 and 1975 respectively. In 1977, the world's last case of smallpox was registered in Somalia. On May 8, 1980, WHO officially declared that smallpox had been eradicated worldwide. Since then, the only institutions that still have smallpox viruses are the Center for Disease Control in Atlanta and the Vector Labs in Koltsovo/Novosibirsk, Russia, where they are locked away, stored in liquid nitrogen.

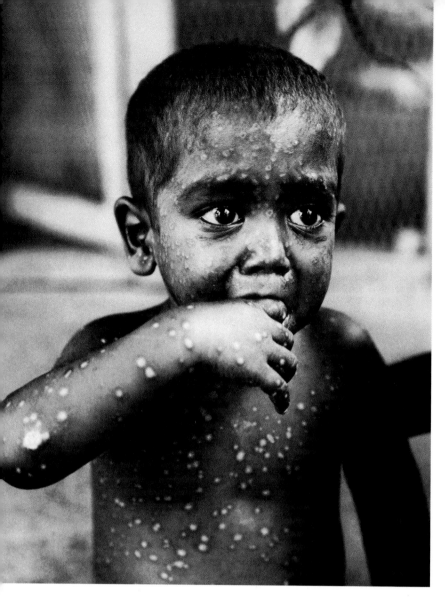

In 1962, India, supported by WHO and UNICEF, began smallpox vaccination on a massive scale. For this disfigured child in a Madras hospital, it came too late.

ders from the Western world to the Orient and back again contributed to the spread of *variola* viruses, leading to an endless cycle of epidemics large and small. In a typical "smallpox year" in medieval times, 10 percent of all mortality was due to smallpox alone. One in five smallpox patients died, and 60 to 80 percent of the survivors were disfigured for life by pockmarks.

Bacteriological genocide

During the fifteenth and sixteenth centuries, smallpox was common in Europe. Anyone who survived the disease was immune. Smallpox arrived on the American continent with conquistadors like Hernán Cortés (1485–1547). Haiti, Cuba, and Mexico were the first areas affected, followed by South and North America. The slave trade spread the disease further. The conquistadors also brought measles and other maladies to which inhabitants of the New World had no immunity whatsoever; at least 2 million died. By 1700, the Native Americans living in the Caribbean and the coastal areas were almost completely extinct. Epidemic plagues are also thought to be responsible for the downfall of the Inca and Aztec empires. The rest of the North American natives would suffer a similar fate.

Native Americans ravaged by smallpox

The viruses spread freely among the New World populations, particularly in the early years of European contact when there was no native immunity to slow their spread. The figures speak volumes. In 1508, some 60,000 Native Americans are thought to have lived in Hispaniola (present-day Haiti and the Dominican Republic). In 1510, there were 46,000 and by 1512, there are a mere 20,000. By 1514, their number had fallen to 13,000, and by 1547 all had perished. Colonial expansion in other parts of the globe had similar consequences. The arrival of the Dutch in Africa in 1652 killed a large proportion of the native population of the Cape of Good Hope. World trade carried the disease to the remotest corners of the earth.

Vaccination to the rescue

There was no hope of eradicating smallpox before the invention of vaccination. Inoculation could grant immunity, but required a live smallpox virus to do so. The method developed by Edward Jenner (1749–1832), an English country

infected pus were used with some success. This knowledge would not reach Europe until the early eighteenth century.

The first recorded European smallpox epidemic occurred in the sixth century. The disease is thought to have entered Europe with invading Huns, who then transmitted it to the Teutons and Gauls. The migration of armies of Crusa-

The pharaoh who died of smallpox

Pharaoh Rameses V (1145–1142 BCE), whose mummy is preserved in the Egyptian Museum in Cairo, probably suffered from smallpox, as indicated by the great number of scars covering his body. China and India, in particular, were hotbeds of infection. Smallpox goddesses have existed in India since at least 1500 BCE. The scars left by the disease were thought to be signs that the goddess had conversed with the afflicted person.

doctor, surpassed inoculation. Instead of using
human smallpox, he exposed healthy people to
the similar, but less virulent, cowpox virus. On
May 14, 1796 he vaccinated young James
Phipps, the son of his gardener. James came
down with a very mild case of cowpox. A few

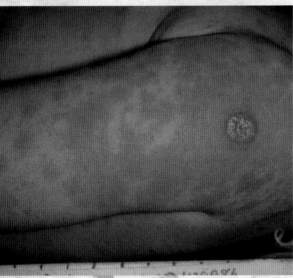

*Some patients are allergic to the smallpox vaccination,
but this is a risk that had to be taken in order to defeat
the disease forever.*

*Long lines of people in front of a New York hospital,
waiting for smallpox vaccination.*

months later, Jenner tried to infect James with
human smallpox virus, without success: he was
immune. Vaccination eventually led to successful elimination of smallpox around the world.

WAR AND TERROR

Wars have been with us since the dawn of human history. No matter how long or short the duration of a war, there are always casualties. As warfare has become more modern, more people have been impacted; increasingly, this also includes civilians. The invention of the atomic bomb has given humankind the theoretical possibility of instantaneous self-annihilation. In recent years, a new, unfathomable aspect has been added to war: terrorism.

Sunk in only Eighteen Minutes

THE SINKING OF THE LUSITANIA

In 1915, the *Lusitania*, at 31,500 gross tons, was the largest and fastest ocean liner operated by the British Cunard Line. On May 7th of that year, eight years after its maiden voyage and one year after outbreak of World War I, the ship sank after being hit by a German torpedo. Of the 1,959 passengers aboard, 1,198 were killed. The sinking of the *Lusitania* remains one of the worst disasters at sea to this day.

The world's fastest ship

The *Lusitania* was the first steamer of her class to be powered by turbines instead of piston engines. Construction began in September 1904 and was completed in 1906. On September 7, 1907, the ship set out on its maiden voyage. At the time there was fierce competition between England and Germany in all matters technological, a rivalry enhanced during the arms race that presaged the outbreak of World War I in 1914. Since 1900, the *Deutschland* had been defending the title of world's fastest ship. The German ocean liner's average speed of 22.84 knots on transatlantic crossings had won the so-called Blue Riband, an award given to the

The Lusitania *set out on her maiden voyage in 1907. She was the fastest ship of her time.*

fastest ship on that route. The *Lusitania* beat the *Deutschland*'s record on her second crossing with a record speed of 24 knots. It was later the first ship to achieve an average speed of 25 knots, corresponding to about 29 miles per hour. The *Lusitania* also carried mail, a source of additional revenue for the Cunard Line shipping company.

When the war broke out, the *Lusitania* was not taken out of service. Her funnels, name, and the British flag were blacked out to minimize the risk of being attacked.

Passengers in shock. In an attempt to illustrate the dramatic events that occurred on Lusitania, *survivors posed in a lifeboat on the Irish coast for the benefit of photographers.*

The starvation blockade

Soon after the outbreak of war in 1914 England began enforcing an embargo against Germany via naval blockade. The blockade was designed not only to protect the British coastline, but also to cut off supplies headed to Germany. Mines were laid and ships patrolled the seas from the Shetland Islands to the south of Norway and the English Channel. In theory, this meant that freighters headed for German ports would be intercepted by British patrol ships, which could then confiscate any suspect goods. In reality, too many ships made it through the inspections by carefully disguising and concealing their cargo. In response, England declared the North Sea a war zone, setting routes for neutral shipping that forced all liners and freighters into English ports for more thorough inspection. These more stringent measures led to great suffering in Germany, and shortages of raw materials and especially food were a major blow to morale. The actions of the British navy became known as the "starvation blockade." In February 1915, Germany reacted by declaring an unrestricted

This German propaganda illustration shows the Lusitania with two guns on each side of the bow to demonstrate that the ship had not been a neutral passenger steamer, but a British admiralty vessel used to transport weapons and ammunition.

submarine war, claiming that England's shipping blockade was in violation of international law. The German submarines quickly became a threat to shipping traffic throughout the Atlantic. Woodrow Wilson (1856–1924), president of the United States from 1913 to 1921, warned Germany of serious consequences should American lives be lost.

The Lusitania sinks in just eighteen minutes

On April 30, 1915, the *Lusitania* made ready for its 201st transatlantic crossing. The captain,

William Thomas Turner, set course for the southwestern coast of Ireland, where the cruiser *Juno* would meet the ship just west of Fastnet Rock and escort it into harbor at Liverpool. 1,257 passengers were on board, 218 of them Americans. The *Lusitania* also carried an unusually large number of children and infants, the highest number since the war broke out.

Germany had already accused England of having converted the *Lusitania* into a merchant warship early on in the war. Indeed, *Brassey's Naval Annual*, the official British naval register, did list both the *Lusitania* and her sister ship, the *Mauretania*, as "armed merchant cruisers." Germany also claimed that the British were using the *Lusitania* to ship weapons and ammunition under the neutral US flag. Moreover, the German navy had information that the *Lusitania* had been equipped with weapons. On April 22, 1915, the German embassy to the US published a warning to transatlantic travelers in fifty newspapers (see box).

On May 7, shortly before 2 p.m., just fourteen sea miles off the coast of Ireland, the crew of the *Lusitania* spotted a torpedo approaching the ship at great speed. Captain Turner attempted an evasive maneuver, but was unsuccessful. The *Lusitania* was hit across the bow, where the torpedo's warhead exploded. Shortly after

---

The German embassy's warning to passengers

On April 22, 1915, the German embassy published the following warning in fifty American newspapers next to the departure listings of transatlantic liners: "Notice! Travelers intending to embark on the Atlantic voyage are reminded that a state of war exists between Germany and her allies and Great Britain and her allies; that the zone of war

includes the waters adjacent to the British Isles; that, in accordance with formal notice given by the Imperial German Government, vessels flying the flag of Great Britain, or any of her allies, are liable to destruction in those waters and that travelers sailing in the war zone on the ships of Great Britain or her allies do so at their own risk."

John Roper (right), a crewman, was the hero of the Lusitania. He saved Captain William Thomas Turner and another 17 people from certain death by drowning.

There are also allegations that then British Naval Minister and later Prime Minister Winston Churchill (1874–1965) deliberately directed the *Lusitania* into the German line of fire in order to bring the United States into the war.

After the sinking of the *Lusitania*, a war of words broke out in Washington D.C. When US President Wilson demanded, though diplomatic channels, that the sinking of *Lusitania* be acknowledged as a crime, the isolationist Secretary of State William Jennings Bryan (1860–1925) resigned in protest, wanting nothing to do with anything that might lead to direct US involvement in a war with Germany. Bryan claimed that each country had a right to prevent the delivery of war material to their enemies, although he also lamented the fact that passengers on board had unknowingly served as human shields, the presence of which was meant to avert just such an attack. In England, Wilson was criticized for not declaring war on Germany at once.

The Lusitania *departs from New York for the last time. She sank off the coast of Ireland after being attacked by the German submarine U-20.*

this first explosion, there was another, much more powerful one that blew away the front part of the ship. Within the incredibly short span of just 18 minutes, the *Lusitania* sank to the bottom of the sea. Only 764 people could be saved; 1,195 were killed, most within minutes of the second explosion.

What caused the second explosion?

The order to torpedo the *Lusitania* on May 7th was issued by Captain-Lieutenant Walter von Schwieger, commander of the German submarine U-20. The sinking of *Lusitania* would have dramatic consequences. In America, more and more voices were raised demanding that the US enter the war alongside the Allies. The controversy over what caused the second explosion remains unresolved to this day. The official English explanation revolved around a coal-dust explosion, while German and skeptical English voices have long suspected that only an explosion of ammunition and weapons could explain the force of the second detonation. As to moral responsibility, many saw the sinking of a civilian liner as mass murder at sea, while others viewed the attack as a legitimate military action on the part of Germany.

OPERATION CHASTISE

"BOUNCING BOMBS" DESTROY THE MÖHNE DAM

During the night of May 17, 1943, British bombers from a special unit flew a mission that was carefully designed to attack several German dams that supplied energy and water to the industrial and densely populated Ruhr Valley region. When the Möhne dam was hit and destroyed, a 40-foot floodwave was unleashed. This wall of water came crashing down on the numerous farms, houses, churches, and industrial plants downriver from the dam. Approximately 1,300 people were killed during that night of terror, the majority of them in a POW camp located near Himmelpforten monastery.

Operation Chastise

Early in 1943, the British Royal Air Force devised a meticulous plan intended to destroy several large dams in Germany's industrial Ruhr Valley, thereby significantly weakening the economic power of the entire region. The targets included the Möhne, Sorpe, and Eder Dams. The RAF's primary aim was to impact the manufacturing capabilities of this strategically important region, but also to interfere with the local supply of drinking water. The plan was given the code name of Operation Chastise.

British military engineer Barnes Wallis developed a special explosive device specifically designed to blow up these dams. His barrel shaped "bouncing bombs" could be dropped from a relatively low altitude, whereupon the cylindrical shape of the bomb would allow it to skip over the surface of the water, bypassing the torpedo nets the Germans had put in place around the dams to prevent just such an action. This would allow the bombs to detonate close enough to the dams to cause maximum destruction. The Royal Air Force assembled a special squadron with experienced pilots who trained for the difficult maneuver for several months. The raid was scheduled for May, when the water level in the reservoirs would be at its highest.

The Möhne Dam the day after the catastrophe. The flood wave had already engulfed the valley below.

The bouncing bomb

The dam was destroyed according to a meticulously devised plan, tried and tested in England well prior to Operation Chastise. The barrel-shaped bouncing bombs had to be released at an altitude of exactly 60 feet above the water's surface. At airdrop, they were given a quick backward spin by the bombardier. When they hit the water's surface, they were designed to skip over the water toward the dam, much like a stone thrown with a spinning motion will skip on the surface of a *lake. This kept the bombs from sinking below the surface too far from the dam to do damage. It also let the bombs jump over the torpedo nets installed to protect the dam. Once the bombs reached the dam wall, they sank to a depth of about 30 feet, where they were detonated by a hydrostatic (pressure) fuse. The experiment was only a partial success. Most of the bombs were dropped too early or skipped high over the dam's wall. Two, however, struck their targets exactly as planned.*

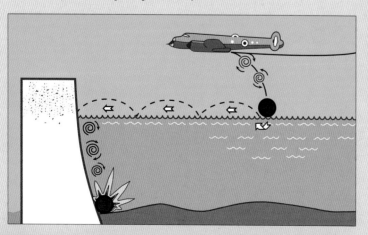

The Lancaster bombers take off

On the evening of May 16, 1943, nineteen Royal Air Force Lancaster bombers took off, each of them with a bouncing bomb on board. They flew over the Ruhr in three groups, each headed toward a different target. The first group of nine planes headed for the Möhne Dam. Eight of the bombers reached the dam in the middle of the night and began their bombing runs. One by one they dropped their bombs from the prescribed altitude and at the designated distance from the dam. Three of the bombs hit their intended target, the first causing what was at first a small leak in the wall; however, this soon widened under the force of the gushing water, eventually causing the dam wall to collapse.

An eyewitness account

"The water kept rising until it was about 10 to 12 meters (30–40 ft) high. Himmelpforten monastery and the old baroque Niederense-Himmelpforten parish church were located right in the middle of the disaster area. One moment, the church's rooftop and tower could still be seen rising out of the floodwaters and spray, the next moment, still more water gushed forth, and the destruction was total. In just a few moments, the Himmelpforten had disappeared in front of our very eyes. The church bell rang out one last time as if screaming in terror before it became yet one more victim of the war. It was the collapse of the abbey church that made the bell ring that one last time. Thus came 700 years of our village history to a tragic end. Our church, our 'Porta coeli,' was no more. Among the many victims was Josef Berkenkopf, our parish priest."

Written by an anonymous eyewitness the day after the catastrophe

The flood wave approaches

People in the village of Niederense, located just below the dam, noticed the anti-aircraft guns being set up at the dam around midnight. From inside the air raid shelters they heard aircraft circling over the dam again and again. Around 12:15 a.m., the air began to tremble with the roaring, crashing noise of the flood wave approaching the village. A 40-foot tidal wave carrying 5 billion cubic feet of water came rushing down the valley. People shouted out to each other in the midst of the rising panic. Suddenly, everything was plunged into darkness: the

Sir Barnes Wallis (1887–1979), inventor of the dam-busting bouncing bomb.

The Eder Dam was also destroyed in the 1943 attacks. This hydroelectric dam was an essential element in the water supply lines running from the Ruhr region to Berlin.

electricity was cut off when the power plant at the foot of the dam was destroyed. The villagers tried to save themselves by running to higher ground. The Himmelpforten monastery, where a forced labor camp for Eastern European prisoners of war was located, sat right in the middle of the disaster area. Locals reported how the monastery church's roof and tower protruded from the water for a short while before being engulfed by the floods and torn from their foundations, at which point, they say, the church bell rang out one last time. More than 700 prisoners in the labor camp drowned. The flood wave only dissipated at the far western end of the Ruhr region, some 60 miles away, leaving a tremendous trail of devestation in its wake.

The next morning, the villagers looked out on a completely altered landscape. The valley was covered with a vast quantity of mud and

debris. The trees at the edge of the woods had been flattened like reeds, with drowned cattle, chicken, and pigs stuck fast in their branches.

A dubious success

Even with the destruction of the Eder Dam in the same night, the effect of Operation Chastise on the course of the war fell well short of British expectations. Reconstruction of the dams began immediately after their destruction, and the work was completed by October 1943. The most enduring, long-term effect was actually as propaganda. Widespread publication of images of the destroyed dams in the British press boosted morale on the home front. The price for this dubious success was paid by 1,300 people in the valley below the Möhne dam who lost their lives that night. Of the 133 men on board the Lancaster bombers, 53 were killed in action during the raid.

Bombing an enormous structure like the Chinese Three Gorges Dam would be inconceivably destructive. In operation since May 20, 2006, it is one of the largest dams in the world.

Twenty-four years after Operation Chastise, a Lancaster bomber flies the route to the German dams once again. The bomber plane was named the Guy Gibson after the commander of the raid.

TORPEDOES STRIKE THE *WILHELM GUSTLOFF*

THE 1945 SINKING OF A GERMAN REFUGEE SHIP

In January 1945, the last year of World War II, the German military forces on the Eastern Front collapsed and began a long retreat to the west. The Soviet Red Army forced the defeated German troops and fleeing civilians back to Baltic Sea coastline. The only remaining escape route for tens of thousands of desperate soldiers and refugees lay across the ice-cold Baltic Sea. Two former cruise ships, the *Wilhelm Gustloff* and the *Hansa*, were their only chance for salvation. Tragically, just a few hours after departure, one of those ships would become a deathtrap.

A cruise ship becomes a troop transport vessel

In spring 1938, the largest passenger steamer of its time set out on its maiden voyage. The *Wilhelm Gustloff* had been commissioned as a recreational cruise ship by the Nazis for the use of the workers' organization *Kraft durch Freude* ("Strength through Joy"). It was luxuriously equipped for its time with hot running water in the cabins, all of which were of equal size, a movie theater, and even an indoor pool. However, the *Wilhelm Gustloff* had little opportunity to fulfill its original purpose, making only a few cruises to Norway and Portugal. Already in September 1939, shortly after the outbreak of World War II, it was reassigned to the German Navy for casualty evacuation. From November 1940 the *Gustloff* was docked near the East Prussian city of Danzig, serving as a barracks

On May 5, 1937, the Wilhelm Gustloff *was first launched in the presence of Adolf Hitler.*

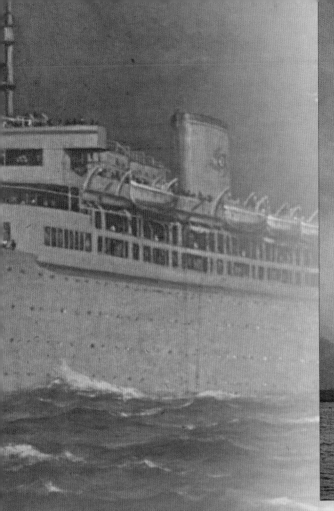

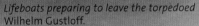

Lifeboats preparing to leave the torpedoed Wilhelm Gustloff.

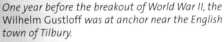

One year before the breakout of World War II, the Wilhelm Gustloff was at anchor near the English town of Tilbury.

and troop transport ship for soldiers of the Second Submarine Training Division.

The desperate situation in the East

At the end of January 1945, the German Eastern Front collapsed. The Soviet army quickly moved to cut off the territory of East Prussia from the rest of Germany. The chaos among the fleeing population and what remained of the devastated German army must have been terrible. In the middle of a bitter winter, with temperatures hovering around −4 °F and with all other escape routes blocked by the oncoming Russian forces, everyone fled northward in utter panic. The refugees had heard terrible tales of Russian soldiers ravaging the countryside. The only remaining escape route was via the Baltic Sea, where the German navy had managed to maintain a few bridgeheads. One of these refugee destinations was the Danzig Bay, where the *Wilhelm Gustloff* and the *Hansa* were anchored in the small port of

Gotenhafen. The German admiral of the fleet was ordered to prepare for departure.

The Wilhelm Gustloff casts off

The *Wilhelm Gustloff* received orders to depart on January 30, 1945, at 12:20 p.m. By that time, the number of people on board could no longer be determined with any accuracy. People

Other refugee ships sunk during the war

Despite the horror of the sinking of the Wilhelm Gustloff, *the escape route over the Baltic Sea remained the only hope for Germans fleeing from the encroaching Russian army. Again and again, convoys set out across the sea with hardly any protection; further disasters were bound to occur. In February 1945, the cruise steamship* Steuben *was sunk by the Soviet submarine S-13. Almost 4,000 people were killed. In April 1945, the passengers on the cargo ship* Goya *met the same fate. The* Goya *sank within 3 minutes beneath the ice-cold Baltic Sea, killing at least 7,000. The sinking of these three refugee ships alone cost more than 20,000 lives.*

were in a state of panic and rushed to get on board at all costs. It is known with certainty that the ship, which had been designed to carry 1,465 tourists, had at least 8,000 people on board, and possibly as many as 10,000, the majority of them women, children, and wounded soldiers. Every nook and cranny below deck was fitted to accommodate as many people as possible, as the frigid temperature on deck was unbearable. The weather was stormy and exceptionally cold, with on deck temperatures of −4 °F. Even the indoor pool area was used to accommodate passengers. Several hundred young women from the naval auxiliary set up camp in the pool; only six of them would live to see the next day. Tension and exhaustion

made the atmosphere on board notably quiet, although the fetid air in the overcrowded halls full of wounded and seasick passengers was almost unbearable.

Death waits in ambush

Two escort ships departed along with the overcrowded *Wilhelm Gustloff* and *Hansa*. The torpedo boat *Löwe* and the torpedo recovery boat *T1* were already insufficient protection against Soviet submarine activity. The situation worsened when the *T1* was forced to abandon the evacuation operation due to heavy seas. Then the *Löwe* discovered that its submarine location device was not working properly in the extreme cold. There was never any chance that the *S-13* submarine would be detected in time to react. Alexander Ivanovich Marinesko, the captain of the *S-13*, had been cruising the Baltic Sea for two weeks. He was on the lookout for prey and needed a spectacular success to avoid being court-martialed for misconduct. On January 30, around 8:00 p.m., he received information that a large troop carrier ship had been sighted. Aided by the poor visibility due to the weather conditions, he began covert pursuit, carefully bringing his vessel into a favorable position. An hour later, Marinesko gave orders to fire four torpedoes. Though one of them stuck and had to be disarmed, three of the weapons launched as intended.

The submarine commander

In 1945, Alexander Ivanovich Marinesko, commander of the Russian submarine S-13, felt himself under great pressure to succeed. Before departing on this mission, he had attracted attention for misconduct and feared being court-martialed. Hoping to avoid a trial, he made a great effort to distinguish himself by sinking enemy ships. After torpedoing the Gustloff *and the* Steuben, *he returned to his home*

region expecting to be celebrated as a hero. However, the high command of the Russian fleet had kept the news secret in order to avoid accusations of atrocities against civilians. Marinesko was dishonorably discharged from the Soviet navy in September 1945. Twenty-seven years after his death, he was officially rehabilitated and posthumously awarded the title of Hero of the Soviet Union.

The sinking

The first torpedo struck the bow of the *Wilhelm Gustloff*. To keep the ship from sinking, the bulkheads were immediately closed, cutting off anyone who survived the direct hit. The second torpedo hit the indoor pool and instantly killed nearly all the naval auxiliary women camped there. The third torpedo hit the engine room, destroying the ship's central power supply. From this point on, the survivors had no more than 50 minutes to leave the ship before it sank below the water's surface. The panic on board was beyond description. Thousands of people who had survived the torpedoe hits rushed to the upper decks in a desperate effort to save their lives. Many who faltered were trampled to death. On deck, everything was covered in slick ice. The refugees slid across the deck of the keeling ship, falling overboard into the ice-cold sea. The lifeboats were designed to accommodate a total of 2,000 people, but there were many times that number on board that day. Moreover, the hooks and winches controlling the lifeboats were iced over, making it difficult to release the boats into the water. Soldiers struggled to keep the terrified crowd in check by firing warning shots. Some lifeboats were lowered into the water only half full of people, while other lifeboats were in danger of sinking because they were so overcrowded. Those who slid or fell or chose to jump into the frigid waters of the Baltic Sea had no chance whatsoever of surviving.

The survivors

After firing its torpedoes, the submarine *S-13* remained submerged nearby, hiding from an attack by the escort ship *Löwe*. The *Löwe* sent out distress calls and immediately went to the rescue of the drowning passengers. Shortly afterward, seven additional ships arrived at the scene of the disaster, but time was too short and the Baltic Sea too cold for anyone to survive for long. Torpedo boat *T-36* picked up some 400 passengers, barely escaping another torpedo attack by the *S-13*. The commander of the *T-36* quickly ordered depth charges to be dropped, managing to severely damage the *S-13*, but not enough to prevent its escape. Around 10:00 p.m., the *Wilhelm Gustloff* disappeared, sinking below the surface of the sea. Some 9,000 people drowned in the waters, many of them children. Due to the chaotic circumstances, the exact number of casualties will always remain unclear. The number saved, however, is known: only 1,239 children, women and men survived what remains the biggest maritime disaster of all time.

Enthusiastic passengers on board Wilhelm Gustloff *wave as the ship casts off.*

Nuclear Holocaust

THE ATOMIC BOMBS OF HIROSHIMA AND NAGASAKI

In August 1945, World War II was over in Europe; in the Far East, however, it was still raging with no end in sight. American squadrons continued to execute air raids on Tokyo and other large cities. Hiroshima, the city on the delta of the Ota River, had thus far been spared the attacks. On the morning of August 6, 1945 that changed dramatically.

The Enola Gay drops its deadly payload

At 8:00 a.m. on that fateful day, a B-29 Superfortress flew high above Hiroshima in the blazing sun. The Japanese assumed the plane was a reconnaissance aircraft—accustomed to attacks from squadrons, no one worried about a single aircraft. While people on the ground went about their daily business, the captain of the *Enola Gay*, Colonel Paul W. Tibbets, and his crew armed an atomic bomb for airdrop. This, the first weapon of mass destruction in human history, was euphemistically christened *Little Boy*. *Little Boy* was 11 feet long and weighed over 8,800 pounds.

The bomb was released over Hiroshima and fell to an altitude of 2,000 feet before a nuclear fission and ensuing chain reaction was triggered that built up an explosive force equivalent to 20,000 tons of TNT. Hiroshima, a city of 390,000, was destroyed in a second, the ground completely flattened. It is estimated that at least 75,000 people were killed instantly, and up to 250,000 more fell victim to the fallout and long-term effects. Never in history has a single instrument of destruction annihilated so many lives and caused so much destruction as the bomb of August 6, 1945.

Metal melts

Any witnesses who survived this catastrophe were necessarily far from ground zero. Everything within a radius of 2 miles was destroyed instantly; within 3 miles, a third of the houses were left standing but went up in flames shortly afterward. Even very distant witnesses felt the bomb's shock wave before they saw the pillar of smoke rising some 11 miles up into the sky. Anything at the center of the explosion was completely destroyed: the extraordinary temperature melted all metal, and everything else was consumed in the fire or blasted away. Any life in this center was effectively pulverized. Around this, a tremendous wind fueled the fires. Only those who found themselves covered by debris or who were protected from the shock wave in some other way escaped immediate death.

Even those who survived, like everything else, were exposed to the penetrating gamma

A mushroom cloud hovered over the city of Hiroshima after the atomic bomb was dropped.

radiation emitted by the bomb (see box). Any living being within a 1.4-mile radius experienced certain death, if not immediately, then shortly after the explosion. Everything was radioactively contaminated. There was no hope for the rescue teams that started arriving soon afterward to do what they could in this most horrific situation: contact with all the contaminated matter meant death for them, too. It was impossible for anyone to take precautions or protect themselves: nobody, including the Americans, knew what terrifying consequences their actions would have.

Unspeakable suffering of the civilian population

For some of the victims, the nightmare came to a quick end, but others continued to suffer un-

In August 1945, under the command of Colonel Paul W. Tibbets, the B-29 bomber plane Enola Gay dropped the first atomic bomb in history on the Japanese city of Hiroshima.

speakably from vomiting, diarrhea, hemorrhages of the skin, lungs, bladder and stomach, recurring fever, hair loss, and the breakdown of their stomach linings for weeks and even months. The victims had hardly any white blood cells left and died in agony. People living in areas surrounding Hiroshima had a 50 percent increased risk of contracting leukemia in the years following the bombing. Many other

The fist weapon of mass destruction in history was named Little Boy. Little Boy was 11 feet long and weighed over 8,800 pounds.

Gamma radiation

Some chemical elements have the property of emitting radiation without an external energy supply; this phenomenon is called radioactivity, and it depends on the instability of the atomic nucleus. Gamma rays, which are highly radioactive, form an extremely high-frequency type of radiation that occurs during nuclear decay and is highly penetrative. Gamma rays are weakened in proportion to the mass of the matter they pass through. An exploding atomic bomb emits a very high level of gamma radiation.
Gamma rays are also used for peaceful purposes, such as in cancer therapy and in tools and material testing.

The attack on Nagasaki

Even following this disastrous strike against its civilian population, Japan appeared to be unwilling to give in or surrender. Moreover, Russia declared war on Japan. The United States administration, under President Harry S. Truman, made a decision in favor of a second nuclear attack: on August 8th the plutonium bomb *Fat Man* was dropped on the industrial city of Nagasaki. *Fat Man* weighed 11,000 pounds and generated an infernal temperature of 540,000 °F that immediately annihilated any life in its path. The shock wave, traveling at a speed of 87,000 miles per hour, wiped out the Nagasaki suburb below the bomb. More than 50,000 people died immediately. For the thousands who survived, again, there was no hope: as in the case of Hiroshima, they died painfully from the long-term effects of the explosion.

That finally brought the Pacific War to an end. On August 15, 1945 Emperor Hirohito announced Japan's surrender.

Hiroshima after the nuclear air attack on August 6, 1945: a scene of utter devastation. The one building that withstood the bombing, the Prefectural Industrial Promotion Hall, has been restored as a memorial.

types of cancer, including lung, stomach, thyroid, ovarian, and laryngeal cancer, occurred much more frequently, as well. Pregnant women experienced miscarriages or gave birth to horribly deformed babies who were barely able or unable to sustain life. To this day, more than sixty years after the attack, people in the region continue to suffer from the long-term health consequences.

Kiyoshi Kikkawa is one of countless burn victims of the Hiroshima atomic bombing. Two years after the bomb fell, he was still ravaged.

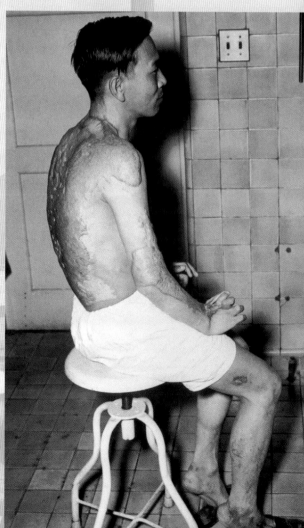

Julius Robert Oppenheimer

J. Robert Oppenheimer (1904–1967) is known as the father of the atomic bomb. From 1943, he was director of the Los Alamos research labs, where the first nuclear bombs were developed and produced. During the McCarthy Era, in 1954, he was dismissed from his position owing to former associations with communists, but was rehabilitated in 1963. Originally, Oppenheimer thought of his invention as the *greatest in the history of mankind, but he later changed his mind. When he saw the extent of destruction caused by his "baby," he is said to have told President Truman in despair: "I have blood on my hands." Truman allegedly replied that he never had any scruples about the affair. With regard to Japan, he is quoted as saying, "When you have to deal with a beast, you have to treat him as a beast."*

Tests in the New Mexico desert

Just a few weeks earlier, on July 16, 1945, the Americans had detonated an atomic bomb for the first time in a test area in the state of New Mexico. Dr. J. Robert Oppenheimer (1904–1967; see box opposite), leader of the scientific team that developed these weapons, spoke of the "birth of a very special baby"—hence the diminutive, euphemistic name for the Hiroshima bomb, *Little Boy*. When he and his fellow scientists at the Los Alamos Laboratories (where atomic bombs were built from 1943, and where research in the maintenance of existing nuclear arms continues today) saw the enormous effects and the destructive potential of their "baby," they experienced a rush of megalomania. They had no way of knowing the long-term damage and effects of the bomb. Edward Teller, one of the physicists working at Los Alamos, told people, "If your mountain is not in the right place, drop us a postcard." Three weeks later, the first atomic bombs were dropped on people.

The balance of terror

In the more than sixty years that have passed since the dropping of these two bombs—fortunately, further atomic bombs have not been used against humans in meantime—a situation emerged in the aftermath of World War II and against the backdrop of the Cold War immediately following it, that became known as the "Balance of Terror". When the Russians developed the capacity to build nuclear weapons themselves, an arms race ensued that was unlike anything the world had ever seen. Nuclear superpowers armed themselves with so many weapons that they could have blown up the world several times over if, on any given day, anything had gone wrong enough to cause one of the world leaders to press the notorious "red button." For a while it seemed that that risk had come under control: the parties approached each other and declared the arms race officially over. Today, however, the danger of nuclear destruction also comes from other nations and institutions, and not only from the former Soviet Union and the USA.

Japanese schoolgirls wearing face masks to help them endure the stench of decay and contamination.

Harry S. Truman

Harry S. Truman (1984–1972), the 33rd president of the USA, served two terms in office from 1945 until 1953. After the end of World War II he increased pressure on the Soviet Union after 1947, which culminated in the founding of NATO in 1949. Truman was known as a political hardliner who extended the Cold War and who stood by his view that the use of the atomic bombs had been necessary. Together with Senator Joseph McCarthy, he got the US embroiled in a witch hunt for communists, who were supposedly undermining the country. Even after his terms as president, he wrote a letter to the Hiroshima City Council in which he stated that given the same circumstances, he would again order a nuclear strike.

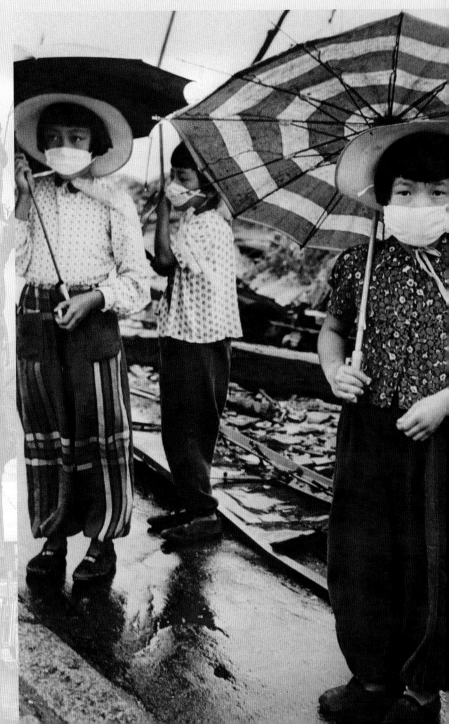

Mass Murder over Scotland

THE 1988 LOCKERBIE AIR DISASTER

On December 21, 1988, a Pan Am Boeing 747 was flying over Scotland at an altitude of 33,000 feet en route from London to New York. Suddenly, air traffic control saw three blips on the radar screen where there should have been just one. Within seconds, the three blips became five. The experienced ground staff knew at once that they did not represent five different aircraft over Scotland, but five parts of one plane, blown apart by an on-board bomb. The 747, with its 259 passengers and crew, fell to earth on the small town of Lockerbie, killing another eleven people on the ground.

The Boeing 747, a symbol of progress

When the Boeing 747 was put into commercial service for the first time in 1970, it was by far the largest commercial passenger aircraft ever built. The enormous, easily recognizable "jumbo jets" could accommodate up to 400 passengers. It soon became a symbol of progress and the flagship of the world's international airlines. Tragically, the 747's early service history corresponded with a period in which terrorists were on the lookout for just such a symbol to exploit for their own purposes. On September 6, 1970, a Boeing 747 was the target of an attack in Cairo, Egypt, only four months after the first jumbo jets began commercial flights. The plane was blown up on the ground, without any pas-

For many people, the Boeing 747 symbolized progress.

sengers on board. In 1972, an aircraft operated by the Japanese airline JAL was hijacked to Libya and blown up after the passengers and crew had been allowed to exit the plane. It was not enough to merely blow up symbols, however. For the purposes of international terrorism, blood had to flow. On June 23, 1985, a bomb blew up an Air India flight while it was airborne over the Atlantic southwest of Ireland, killing everyone on board. Three years later, the Pan Am Flight 103 Lockerbie crash would be the worst commercial air disaster in British history.

Missing from the radar screens

Pan Am 103 was a regularly scheduled flight from Frankfurt via London-Heathrow to New York's John F. Kennedy Airport. An aircraft named *Maid of the Seas*, a Boeing 747, was scheduled to fly the London-New York leg that day. Passengers en route from Frankfurt arrived at London's Heathrow airport to change planes for their flight to New York.

On December 21, Flight 103 was delayed by 25 minutes, taking off at 6:25 p.m. London local time. Jim MacQuarrie, the 55-year-old captain of the aircraft, charted a northwest course over Scotland for the Atlantic crossing. He made contact with the Scottish air traffic control center near Prestwick to request permission to take the northern transatlantic route. Midway through their conversation, Flight PA 103 suddenly broke off all communication. At the same time, air traffic control began to register confusing radar signals. The radar screen showed three blips, then five that quickly disappeared from the screen, one after the

Specialists examining the wreckage of the Boeing 747's cockpit.

An eyewitness account
"There was just a rumble, I thought it was thunder, then came a white flash, and then an orange flash. I saw orange fragments dropping like from a volcano. It was devastating, really devastating. I've never seen anything like it."

Sam Anderson, Lockerbie resident

other. The last blip dropped off the screen at 7:15 p.m. The tower received a flurry of radio messages from other airplanes flying over Scotland, all reporting explosions, airborne debris, and massive fires on the ground.

Seconds later, the wreckage of the Boeing 747 fell down on Lockerbie, a small Scottish town of 2,500 people located 15 miles from the Scottish-English border. One fragment crashed into a gas station, causing an explosion that sent a column of fire more than 300 feet high into the sky. The central fuselage fell in one piece, creating a crater 150 feet long and 30 feet deep. Eleven Lockerbie residents were killed and ano-

ther twelve suffered severe burns. Large areas of the town were completely destroyed.

Suspects in a terrorist attack

From the very beginning of rescue and recovery operations, based on the way the plane had disintegrated, investigators were certain that the accident must have been caused by a bomb placed in the forward luggage compartment. Several terrorist organizations were closely investigated, but no specific group has been implicated to this day. There is, however, widespread agreement that the attack was carried out by Islamic fundamentalists. Two theories emerged following three years of post-disaster investigation.

Libya

According to the first theory proposed by American investigators, Libya was responsible, with Libyan president Muammar Gaddafi the mastermind behind the attack. There was con-

---

No indication of any problems

"There were no mayday signals … no threats, no indication that anything was wrong. There were also no indications prior to the flight that there were any problems on board the aircraft, and no signs that inclement weather was a factor."

Jeff Kriendler, Pan Am Vice President

---

siderable support for this supposition. In 1986, in retaliation for the sinking of three Libyan ships that violated a United Nations-imposed blockade, Gaddafi had ordered the bombing of a Berlin nightclub frequented by American soldiers. Nine people were killed and 230 were wounded, three of them American. In response, American fighter planes attacked the Libyan cities of Tripoli and Benghazi, killing Hanna Gaddafi, adopted daughter of the Libyan president. The American fighter jets had been launched from airbases in England. As a result, Gaddafi had sworn revenge both on the United States and England.

In the wake of the accusations of Libyan involvement in the Lockerbie bombing, the United Nations imposed a series of sanctions with the United States enforcing a complete embargo on trade. With its economy reeling under international pressure, Libya agreed to the extradition of two suspects, both members of the Libyan secret service. Abdel Basset Ali Mohmed al Megrahi and Al Amin Khalifa Fhimah were put on trial by an independent Scottish court in the Netherlands in 1999. Al Megrahi was found guilty and sentenced to twenty-seven years to life in prison. Kalifa Fhimah was acquitted.

Iran/Palestine

On July 3, 1988, the *USS Vincennes*, an American warship on maneuvers in the Persian Gulf, shot down an airliner operated by Iran Air—accidentally, according to the official American version. Almost 300 people from six countries, including sixty-six children, were killed. The

Abdelbaset Ali Mohmed Al Megrahi (left) and Al Amin Khalifa Fhimah, the two Libyans who stood trial for the attack. Al Megrahi was convicted and sentenced to imprisonment. Fhimah was acquitted.

Additional wreckage from the Pan Am aircraft. The bomb broke the plane into five major pieces.

captain of the *Vincennes* claimed the ship's warning systems had misidentified the passenger plane as a military plane flying an attack pattern. The Iran Air disaster is at the heart of the second Lockerbie theory, which claims that Iran ordered a Palestinian terrorist organization to blow up an American passenger plane in retaliation. At issue, particularly in the Islamic world, was how the United States reacted in the immediate aftermath of the disaster. Political commentators around the world were shocked when, the next day, Fourth of July celebrations in the US went on as scheduled despite the tragedy. This was viewed throughout the Middle East as clear evidence of a lack of regret for the incident, leading to the inevitable conclusion that the attack on the passenger jet had been deliberate. On November 14, 1988, just a few weeks before the Lockerbie disaster, then US president George H.W. Bush referred to the shooting down of the unarmed Iran Air passenger jet as an act of self-defense. This continued lack of expression of responsibility may have increased anti-American sentiments within Iran to the point of retaliation.

Investigators arrested a group of Palestinians in Germany and found a bomb with a barometric pressure fuse built into a portable radio. Precisely this type of bomb had been used in the attack on Pan Am Flight 103. There were media reports that the Palestinian Abu

Rescue workers on the scene of the accident in Lockerbie were met with a horrific sight.

According to one theory, Libyan president Muammar Gaddafi was the mastermind of the Lockerbie attack, in retaliation for the American bombing of Libyan cities two years earlier.

Nidal terrorist group had claimed responsibility for the Lockerbie attack. However, most experts considered this unlikely. Relationships between the Palestinian and Iranian groups, like the terrorist organization Hezbollah, were not close at the time. In addition, Hezbollah, along with the Iranian government, regularly opposed attacks on unarmed civilians. Both loudly condemned the September 11, 2001 attacks on the World Trade Center, for example, while applauding the strike at the Pentagon, which was seen as a legitimate military target. The intelligence trail connecting Iran and Palestine with the Lockerbie bombing quickly went cold. No charges or official accusations were filed.

Libya pays compensation

On May 29, 2002, Libya agreed to pay $2.7 billion in compensation to the families of the Lockerbie disaster victims, which amounted to approximately $10 million per person killed in the attack. But there were strings attached. The full amounts were only payable once all UN sanctions against Libya had been withdrawn and the US trade embargo dissolved. The final condition, for remittance of the last 20 percent of the compensation, required that the United States remove Libya from the list of countries that support international terrorism. Uproar from the victims' families ensured that this condition was not met within the time limit set by Libya.

On August 15, 2003, the Libyan UN ambassador delivered a note to the UN Security Council in which Libya officially accepted responsibility for the actions of its secret service agents. The note was accompanied by payments of $8 million to each of the families of the Lockerbie victims. This was the first time in history that a country had paid compensation for a terrorist attack; many politicians and relatives of victims called it "blood money." International observers saw Libya's acceptance of responsibility for the bombing of Pan Am Flight 103 as a business deal rather than a sincere admission of guilt. The point had been to engineer a lifting of the sanctions, rather than to genuinely admit responsibility. In an interview with the BBC on February 4, 2004, Libyan Prime Minister Shukri Ghanem said that Libya had paid the price for peace. He added no new information regarding Libya's role in the Lockerbie disaster, nor did he say that Libya had been behind it.

The aftermath

In part as a direct consequence of the attack of December 21, 1988, the American airline Pan Am ended up filing for bankruptcy. The holding company responsible for the airline's assets has since independently sued Libya for $4.5 billion in compensation for the loss of the Boeing 747 and the economic damage suffered as a result. Syracuse University in New York, which lost thirty-five students in the Lockerbie bombing, founded the Institute for National Security and Counterterrorism (INSCT) in their memory. Every year, the university awards two full scholarships to students from the Lockerbie area. There are Pan Am Flight 103 memorials in Arlington Cemetery in Washington D.C., throughout the town of Lockerbie, and in each of the nineteen other countries whose citizens met death that day over Scotland. Imprisoned in Glasgow, convicted bomber al Megrahi is appealing both his sentence and conviction.

According to one theory, the American attacks on the Libyan cities of Tripoli and Benghazi may have been the triggers for the bombing of Pan Am Flight 103.

After the terrorist attack of March 20, 1995, a unit made up of firefighters and policemen was formed to specialize in emergencies like the sarin gas attack.

A DEADLY GAS ATTACKS COMMUTERS

THE POISON GAS ATTACK ON THE TOKYO SUBWAY

On the morning of March 20, 1995, Tokyo suffered the worst terrorist attack in its history. As it is every day, the subway was jam-packed. Unnoticed, five men boarded three different subway lines. They set down several packages, poking holes in them before leaving them behind on the train. No one expected that the leaking packages held the deadly nerve gas sarin. More than 5,000 people were exposed to the poisonous gas. By the end of morning rush hour, twelve people had died and over 3,000 sickened, many of whom still suffer from the effects of the gas.

Deadly packages on commuter trains

At 7:39 a.m., during Tokyo's early morning rush hour, five people wearing shawls and facemasks boarded the overcrowded cars of Tokyo's subway system. They set down several packages wrapped in plastic and newspaper on the floor of the various subway cars, after which they punctured the packages with the tips of their umbrellas before leaving the trains. Other members of the terrorist group were waiting for them in cars outside the subway stations. Facemasks on the subway are not an unusual sight in Japan, and certainly not in Tokyo, where they are thought to protect against germs. The terrorists had done nothing that would have attracted undue attention.

ness of breath, the early symptoms of sarin poisoning. The next stage can bring muscle spasms and paralysis leading to coma, cardiac arrest, suffocation, and painful death. Around 8 a.m., a passenger kicked one of the packages out of a subway car and onto the platform. Its content leaked out, forming a puddle. Within a short period of time, four people on the platform died from the toxic vapors. Ten minutes later, a passenger on the same train pulled the emergency break, bringing the train to a stop in Tsukiji Station. When the doors opened, several passengers fell out and collapsed on the platform. The authorities reacted quickly, evacuating the train and taking it out of service for inspection. The police did not receive any reports about an attack until 8:17 a.m. A half hour later, the first victim arrived at St. Luke's hospital. The authorities, only now realizing the seriousness of the situation, set up makeshift medical stations outside the subway stations to provide treatment to the ever growing number of victims. Around 11:00 a.m., the police released a public statement that confirmed that the subway had been hit by a poison gas attack. In total, twelve people died, nine of them instantly. More than 1,000 people were severely injured, thirty-seven of them critically, and 5,500 people received emergency treatment at local hospitals.

More than 3,000 people continue to suffer the long-term effects of sarin gas exposure, which can range

Sarin gas is odorless, flavorless, and invisible. Immediate medical treatment is crucial, but most victims only realize that they have been poisoned when it is already too late.

As the departing subway cars picked up speed, the sarin gas started leaking from the packages. This highly toxic nerve gas is almost odorless, flavorless, and invisible. Its victims usually only realize they are in danger when it is too late. Before the passengers in the subway cars could react, they were already wheezing with watering eyes and suffering acute short-

Inexplicable fascination

"We're dealing with the same type of fascination that gets an entire nation to enthusiastically submit themselves to rule by insane dictators, even if it's obvious they will lead them into perdition."
Yokosuna Ide, former follower of AUM, who managed to quit the cult two years before the sarin attack

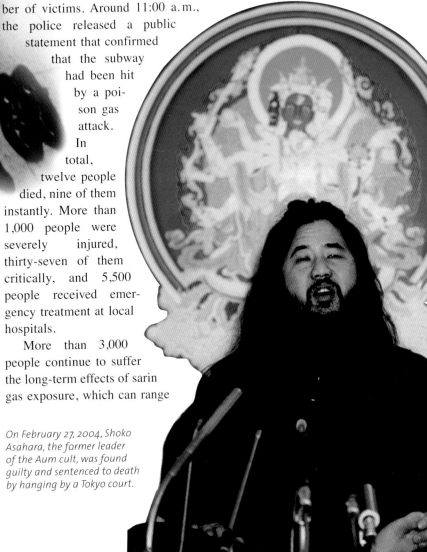

On February 27, 2004, Shoko Asahara, the former leader of the Aum cult, was found guilty and sentenced to death by hanging by a Tokyo court.

Sarin

The nerve gas sarin was discovered in 1938 by German chemist Gerhard Schrader in the course of his research on insecticides for the company IG Farben. The gas is odorless, flavorless, and invisible, with sudden and devastating effects on living organisms. Contact with sarin brings about impaired vision, shortness of breath, muscle spasms, vomiting, involuntary stool loss, respiratory arrest, and death. Sarin gas was employed as a chemical weapon in the Iraq-Iran War as well as against Iraq's Kurdish minority by Saddam Hussein's regime in 1988.

from chronic irritation of mucous membranes to severe depression.

Authorities are in the dark

Initially, the authorities had no idea what to do. Their training had not prepared them for such an emergency. At first, there was even some confusion as to what sarin gas really was. The hospitals were also ill-prepared to deal with a disaster on this scale. Overwhelmed with victims, there was little agreement on just how to treat them, even once the exact type of gas used became known. Back in the subway, many citizens assisted their fellow passengers by dragging them out of the contaminated cars. More than 100 rescue workers became ill because they were not wearing protective clothing. Full-body chemical protection suits would have prevented the gas from getting to any part of the body, but these were not made available.

The five masked men were all members of the cult of Aum Shinrikyo ("Aum the Supreme Truth"). Shortly after the terrorist attack, the sect claimed they had nothing to do with the accident and were instead the victim of a state-controlled conspiracy designed to rid Japan of their unwelcome teachings of the "truth." Eventually, however, they changed their tactics and accepted full responsibility. Ten of the cult's members were tried and sentenced either to death or life in prison.

Blood for enlightenment

Once it was clear that the Aum sect was responsible for the attacks, 2,500 policemen and

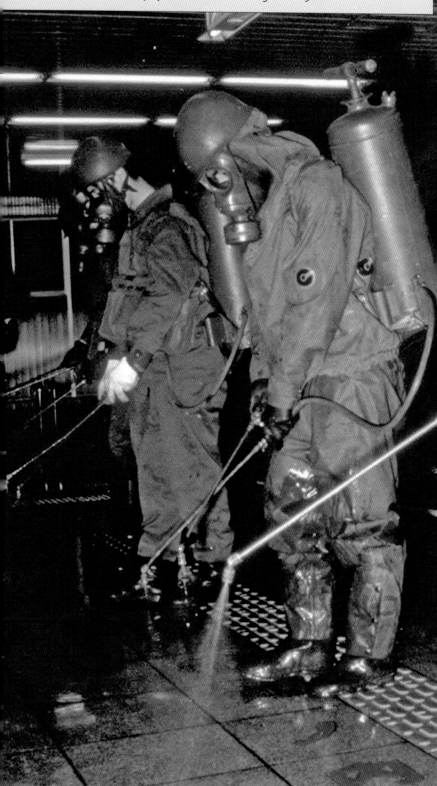

Above: Policemen arrested Shoko Asahara (center), leader of the cult of Aum Shinrikyo.

Left: A chemical weapons unit sanitizes one of the sites of the attacks.

military special forces began searching the many buildings the sect was known to use, both in Tokyo and around the country. While they did find evidence of residues of sarin gas production, they were at first unable to locate Shoko Asahara, the sect's spiritual leader.

Shoko Asahara was a charismatic presence. He claimed to be capable of astral projection and prophesy. In 1990, Asahara, who had political ambitions, even ran for the Japanese parliament. He also masterminded many of the sect's numerous business ventures—the Aum sect owned an entire network of corporations with an annual turnover in the multi-million-dollar range—and had a taste for luxury very much at odds with the asthetic philosophy of the cult. In contrast to his own posh lifestyle, the master dictated the sparsest living conditions to his followers, who were encouraged to disregard their own personal comfort, stop caring for their health, and even engage in self-torture and mutilation. Wealthy disciples were allowed to purchase a flask of his blood at the price of $6,500, which they could then drink in Asahara's presence as a means of attaining enlightenment.

Sect members as guinea pigs

In 1995, the Buddhist Aum sect counted 10,000 followers in Japan with another 30,000 in Germany and Russia. The organization recruited interested people by promising a greater sense of meaning in life and personal fulfillment. The cult's eschatology claimed that living in modern society was comparable to being surrounded by the enemy, which only the Aum sect was prepared to exterminate. Sect members had to completely submit to the cult and its teachings or run the risk of becoming targets of the organization's aggression themselves.

Aum Shinrikyo had long planned an armageddon for Tokyo, but decided to do a test run first. A year before the sarin gas subway disaster, seven people were killed and 600 were injured in a sarin gas incident in the city of Matsumoto. This earlier attack was designed to test the cult members and their resolve more than the sarin gas, the effects of which were well know. The cult's spiritual leaders were not squeamish when it came to dealing with their own. As many as thirty-three members of the sect were murdered, and a further twenty-nine

missing. The police have some evidence that the bodies of the missing cult members were disposed of in a giant microwave incinerator. On March 30, 1995, shortly after the attack on Tokyo's subway, Takaji Kunimatsu, chief of the National Police Agency, was injured in a shooting. Hit by four bullets, he survived to identify the assailant, a member of the Aum sect. On March 30, 1989, anti-Aum lawyer Tsutsumi Sakamoto and his entire family were murdered in Yokohama. Sakamoto had tried to help disillusioned members who wanted to leave the cult but were prevented from doing so.

Aum is also known to have kept death lists that included the names of Japanese politicians as well as that of then US president Bill Clinton. One of the organization's schemes had involved sending packages of sarin to the US. It has also been shown that Asahara used some sect members as guinea pigs in experiments with chemical and biological weapons. In every way imaginable, the Tokyo attacks took terrorism to a new level.

"Oshiyas" are workers on the Tokyo subway who pack people into the cars during rush hour. The five men wearing masks and carrying packages filled with sarin got on the trains in circumstances similar to this. They then dropped the packages and punctured them with umbrellas, allowing the deadly gas to escape.

Assessment of the attack
"The Tokyo attack breaks a taboo and has psychological import. Others will ask whether such tactics should now be adopted. It is now more likely that at least some will say yes."
Brian Jenkins, leading expert on international terrorism, 1995

NINE-ELEVEN

THE 2001 TERRORIST ATTACKS ON THE USA

On September 11, 2001, four commercial airliners were hijacked on the east coast of the USA within a few minutes of each other. Within a little less than 20 minutes, two of the planes crashed into the twin towers of the World Trade Center in New York and a third hit the Pentagon, the US military head-quarters. The fourth plane did not strike its intended target, but crashed in a field in Pennsylvania. This series of catas-trophes claimed 3,056 lives, including the nineteen hijackers, Islamic terrorists aiming a crushing blow against the symbols of Western democracies. Since this disaster, which has gone down in history as "Nine-Eleven," the world is no longer what it used to be. The chasm between the fundamentalist states of the Middle East and the secular democracies of the Western world has become deeper.

A plane, United Airlines Flight 175, approached the south tower of the World Trade Center at 9:03 a.m. local time. Thick smoke was already pouring from the north tower, which had been hit moments earlier. The second plane hit the south tower, triggering an enormous explosion.

International Peace Day

On September 7, 2001 the United Nations General Assembly in New York passed a resolution that declared September 21st the annual International Day of Peace. Only four days later, the city of New York itself was the target of a terrorist attack on a scale that the world had until then deemed unthinkable. September 11th 2001 would become a symbol of horror, re-minding all the world's citizens that mindless terror may befall innocent, unsuspecting people at any time. "9–11" has become shorthand for the worst catastrophe of the very young twenty-first century. Is it mere coincidence that the very same sequence of numbers, 911, is also the nationwide emergency telephone number in the USA?

American Airlines Flight 11

At 7:59 a.m. local time, five terrorists boarded American Airlines Flight 11 in Boston. Their leader was Mohamed Atta, who had been living an apparently ordinary life as a university student in Hamburg, Germany for many years. He is a textbook example of a "sleeper," a covert operative who lives in a foreign environment as an unremarkable and law-abiding citizen until called to action. Only 30 minutes after take-off, flight attendant Betty Ong informed her airline's control center that the plane was being hijacked. By 8:40 a.m. the terrorists, who had undergone pilot training in the USA specifically in preparation for this attack, were in control of the jet.

The Boeing 767 took a turn and headed toward New York, descending to a lower altitude. Five minutes later, the plane crashed into the north tower of the World Trade Center, whose twin towers used to dominate New York's skyline. The plane crashed into the building on the 96th story, penetrating into the center of the tower. Some 10,500 gallons of fuel in the plane's almost full tank exploded,

The Pentagon was also a target of the terrorist attack. The collapsed section of the west wing is shown below.

The terrorists
On September 27, 2001, the US Department of Justice published a poster listing the alleged terrorists' names and photos. Eleven of the nineteen terrorists were from Saudi Arabia, the same country as terrorist mastermind Osama bin Laden.

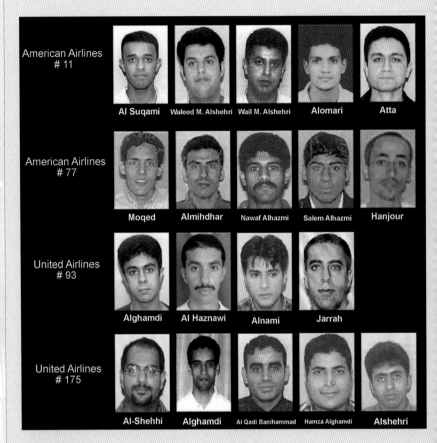

People crowded at the windows of the burning north tower of the World Trade Center in despair. There was little hope of saving them.

creating a fire of incredible intensity and temperatures of 1800 °F. The force of the plane's impact and the resulting explosion was so tremendous that part of the opposite side of the building was blown out. With all downward-leading escape routes completely destroyed, there was no hope of rescue for anyone who was located on the 96th floor or higher.

United Airlines Flight 175

Only 15 minutes after the first aircraft departed, the next plane to be hijacked took off from Boston's Logan International Airport. The Boeing jet, United Airlines Flight 175, was standing in the take-off line just a few hundred yards behind the American airlines plane with Atta and other terrorists on board. Immediately prior to take-off, Atta made a call from his cell

Jumper

In the documentary film 9/11 by the brothers Jules and Gedeon Naudet, the sound of bodies thudding on the ground can be heard in the background again and again: people are jumping out of the windows of the burning World Trade Center in desparation. One of these jumpers landed on a firefighter, killing him. The exact number of jumpers who tried to

escape death by suffocation or burning by this means is unknown; it is estimated that about 200 people died in this gruesome way. In consideration for the victims, the international media largely refrained from publishing such pictures. Only internet sites that specialize in publishing violent material—"snuff" videos—show these horrific pictures.

phone to talk to another student from Hamburg, Marwan al-Shehhi, who was in charge of flying the second plane. The aircraft was carrying fifty-six passengers and nine crew members. Half an hour after take-off, the terrorists tried to force their way into the cockpit. In order to force the pilots to open the doors, they stabbed several flight attendants.

Meanwhile, the first aircraft crashed into the north tower of the World Trade Center. CNN almost immediately began to broadcast footage of the burning building. During the broadcast, stunned viewers all around the world watched, uncomprehending, as the second aircraft approached the towers, banked a sharp turn, and flew into the (until that point) undamaged south tower at 9:03 a.m. The pilot of this plane is presumed to have been Al-Shehhi.

Panic in New York

Live footage of the catastrophe was viewed by millions of people around the globe, and the entire world watched in horror and amazement. The towers were ablaze. All firefighting and ambulance units in New York were called to the scene and, despite the chaos, tried to evacuate the buildings and make their way to the upper storys. Some of the people who found themselves on the floors above the points of impact even jumped to certain death in their desperation, hoping to escape the agony of death by suffocation or burning.

Meanwhile, the US government had begun to grasp the scope of the threat and addressed the possibility of further hijacked aircraft above American cities. At this point in time, about 2,200 planes were airborne in US airspace. All

The World Trade Center collapsed in a massive cloud of dust and debris. The catastrophe was witnessed on TV by millions all over the world.

of those aircraft received instructions to divert immediately to the nearest airport. Interceptors took off in order to shoot down any airplanes that did not follow these instructions. As people around the world sat before their TVs in shock, the horrific scale of the New York catastrophe became increasingly apparent. At 9:59 a.m., the south tower collapsed and grey clouds of dust billowed through the canyons between skyscrapers on the streets of New York City. People in panic ran for their lives in the streets. The north tower, which had been hit a few minutes earlier than the south tower but higher up, withstood the fires half an hour longer. Then, at 10:28 a.m., it too collapsed. The steel frame construction near the point of impact was too weakened by the destructive force of the impact and the ensuing fires to carry the weight of the

upper storys. The floors below were crushed as if by an avalanche. In total, 2,823 people died in this catastrophe, among them 343 rescue workers, who gave their lives to help others.

American Airlines Flight 77

While the images of the New York catastrophe were spreading around the world, two further death planes were already airborne. With five additional terrorists on board, American Airlines Flight 77 took off from Dulles International Airport just outside Washington, D.C. at 8:21 a.m. Its scheduled destination was Los Angeles. With the interceptors already airborne, American Airlines Flight 77 had been brought under the terrorists' control and turned around to head toward the US military headquarters in Alexandria, Virginia, just outside

Exhaustion and horror are written on the faces of these fire fighters sitting on the ruins of what used to be the World Trade Center.

the capital. Around 9:40 a.m. the aircraft, with fifty-three passengers and six crew on board, crashed into the west wing of the Pentagon, a section that had recently been renovated and contained the Naval Command Center. The interceptors were too late to avert further tragedy: 125 military and government officials died in the building.

United Airlines Flight 93

By the time the fourth plane involved in the attacks took off from Newark, New Jersey at 8:42 a.m., after considerable delay, Mohamed Atta, leader of the terrorist group, was close to completing the plan to crash into the WTC. There were four terrorists on board United Airlines Flight 93; their leader, Ziad Jarrah, was the third member of the Hamburg terrorist cell. After studying in Hamburg, he too took a short pilot training course in the USA. By 9:28 a.m. the terrorists were in control of the Boeing 757. The few passengers on board this aircraft managed to contact friends and relatives by phone, and thus learned about the events taking place in New York only a few minutes after their plane was taken over by the terrorists. The passengers instantly realized that a similar fate awaited them, too. The greater number of phone calls made from this plane

A crowd of rescue workers stands aghast amidst the ruins of the collapsed twin towers.

Last words
"Don't do anything foolish! You're not going to get hurt. We have more planes, we have other planes. Just stay quiet and you'll be okay."
8:29 a.m., a voice with a strong accent from American Airline Flight 11 cockpit to passengers

"I see the water. I see buildings. Oh, my God!"
8:44 a.m., American Airlines Flight 11, flight attendant Sweeney immediately before the crash into the north tower of the WTC

"It's up to us. I think we can do it... Don't worry. We're going to do something."
9:54 a.m., passenger on board United Airlines Flight 93 during a phone call with his wife shortly before the attempt to subdue the hijackers

has allowed experts to gain a clearer picture of what took place, and clearly, some of the passengers, facing certain death, decided to defeat the terrorists. Shortly before 10:00 a.m. a shout was heard—"Let's roll!"—the call for the determined passengers to subdue the hijackers.

The cockpit voice recorder found later captured sounds of the passengers' attempt to overwhelm the terrorists, who seem to be in distress. One of them shouted to the pilot, "Pull it down! Pull it down!" just before the aircraft ploughed into a field near Shanksville, Pennsylvania. There were no survivors. It remains unclear what this fourth plane's intended target was. Monuments of symbolic importance that were in the aircraft's path include the White House and the Capitol in Washington D.C., as well as Camp David.

Ground Zero

After September 11, 2001, the site of the New York catastrophe came to be known as "Ground Zero." The term originated in the time of nuclear weapons tests and refers to the point of most severe destruction, the site of a nuclear bomb detonation. The World Trade Center, the US economy's central nervous system, was reduced to a pile of rubble after the attack. Clean-up operations took almost a year, and the planning process for future use of the area took even longer. As of April 2006, construction work at this particularly valuable area in the middle of Manhattan had still not begun. There were architectural competitions, and there are specific plans for a "Freedom Tower," but the funding of this enormous project is not secure. Finally, the many victims' surviving dependants are making legitimate claims for a memorial site in remembrance of the catastrophe that shook America. The terror and fear associated with Nine-Eleven and Ground Zero run deep: to this day, more than half of all New Yorkers would refuse to work at this place of horror.

New York firefighters amidst the debris that used to be the World Trade Center. In the course of rescue efforts, 343 firefighters lost their lives.

Only Time

"Only Time," a song by the Irish singer Enya, unexpectedly turned into an anthem for the victims of September 11th. The singer donated the proceeds from sales of the US version of the song to a fund for the victims' families.

Victims of the train bombing received immediate first aid treatment outside the train on the railways.

DEATH ON A COMMUTER TRAIN

TERRORIST ATTACKS SHAKE MADRID

On March 11, 2004, Madrid was struck by a series of terrorist bombings. A total of ten bombs had been placed on four commuter trains, killing 191 people on their way to work in downtown Madrid. After an initial period of confusion, authorities concluded that the perpetrators were members of a Muslim terrorist group. When the police tried to arrest the suspected terrorists, seven of them blew themselves up, killing a police officer in the process.

A series of attacks

At 7:30 a.m. Madrid's suburban light rail commuter trains were crowded with workers headed for downtown Madrid. For many of them, the Atocha Station in the city center would be the last stop on the line. All the regional commuter trains stopped there. On March 11, 2004, in just a few moments between 7:39 a.m. and 7:42 a.m., a series of seven explosions rocked the central train station. Two trains were blasted open by the explosions; one of them exploded inside the station, while the other, running slightly behind schedule, blew up about 1,600 feet further up the line. Three additional explosions hit trains pulling into the Santa Eugenia and El Pozo del Tio Raimundo stations in the city's southeastern quarter. In total, 191 people died in this series of attacks, and another 2,000 were injured. Apparently, those behind the attacks had planned an even greater catastrophe. Three additional bombs were intended to go off inside the crowded Atocha Station, with timers set so that the rescue teams rushing to the scene of the first explosions would be killed. Just one of these bombs alone would have been strong enough to destroy the entire Atocha Station building. Fortunately, they were found and defused before that could happen.

A false accusation

As soon as the first shock of the attacks wore off, speculation regarding the identity of the perpetrators abounded. The precise planning and the scale of the attacks immediately triggered memories of the 2001 September 11th attacks on New York. The fact that Spain had supported the United States' subsequent military intervention in Iraq added to the suspicion that Islamic terrorist groups must have been involved. The Spanish government, however, at first acccused the Basque underground move-

ment ETA, which had been responsible for repeated terrorist attacks in periods leading up to elections in Spain in the past (The Spanish parliamentary elections were scheduled three days after the Atocha bombings.) From the government's point of view, ETA was the group most likely to be involved. Millions of Spanish citizens gathered in commemoration of the victims on the very next day after the bombings, but there were anti-government protests in

The explosion blasted a giant hole in this commuter train, seen here standing on a railway at Atocha Station, Madrid.

The Atocha Station is in the center of Spain's capital, Madrid.

addition that cast serious doubt on ETA's involvement. The supporters of the opposition Socialist party, in particular, demanded proper investigations into the attacks.

Terrorists choose death by their own hand

The parliamentary elections that took place on March 14 resulted in a landslide victory of the Socialist opposition party. Meanwhile, suspicion that the terrorists might have had links to Al Qaeda had been substantiated. The former government had to face allegations that they had only accused ETA in order to distract the voting public from the fact there might be a connection between Spain's involvement in the Iraq War and the Madrid attacks. On April 3, 2004, the police cornered the terrorists responsible for them in an apartment building. As they stormed the building, the seven suspected terrorists inside detonated explosives and blew themselves up. The apartment building, in the Leganés neighborhood of Madrid, was heavily damaged. A Spanish police officer also died in the explosion.

The "Forest of the Departed"

On March 11, 2005, the first anniversary of the Madrid disaster, a memorial for the 191 victims of the attack and the police officer who died in the Leganés operation was dedicated in the capital. Located in Retiro Park, the monument, called *Il Bosque de los Ausentes* in Spanish ("The Forest of the Departed"), consists of a hill planted with 192 cypress trees interspersed with olive trees as universal symbols of peace and forgiveness. At noon that day, a 5-minute period of silence was observed throughout Spain to commemorate the worst terrorist attack in Spanish history.

The investigative report

Two years later, almost 500 of those who were injured in the attacks were still undergoing

medical or psychological treatment. The investigations into the attacks have progressed only slowly, but in April 2006 the first judicial indictment was finally presented. The investigators concluded that neither ETA nor the international extremist group Al Qaeda were directly responsible for the attack. Instead, the report assigned resposibility to a small local group of radical Muslims who were motivated by Al Qaeda messages on the internet. That the seven Islamicists who blew themselves up in Leganés were the main perpetrators is undisputed. Twenty-nine people who had known of the attacks and assisted in them in one way or another were indicted for murder and attempted murder.

After the bombings, thousands protested against the Basque underground movement ETA, which was initially accused of perpetrating the attacks.

SUICIDE BOMBERS IN THE LONDON SUBWAY

THE JULY 7, 2005 LONDON SUBWAY BOMBINGS

On July 7, 2005, during London's morning rush hour, three separate explosions rocked subway cars arriving in the center of London. Approximately one hour later, a fourth bomb destroyed a double-decker bus. Four terrorists killed more than fifty unsuspecting commuters and injured some 700 additional people in this series of attacks. The London public transort system was shut down entirely for several hours. Radical Islamic terrorism in Western Europe had been taken to a new level. Suicide attacks in Europe were now a reality.

A goodbye hug

The cameras of the London public transport system's video surveillance network recorded the moment when, at 8:30 a.m., four men later identified as the suicide bombers arrived at Kings Cross Station in central London together and then hugged each other goodbye. They appeared to be excited as they disappeared in the corridors of the complex London traffic system. Twenty minutes later, three bombs went off almost simultaneously in three subway carriages. Islamic terrorism had reached the English capital, as many experts had predicted it would. At the time of the attacks, the subway

Investigators looking for evidence near the destroyed bus the day after the London bombings.

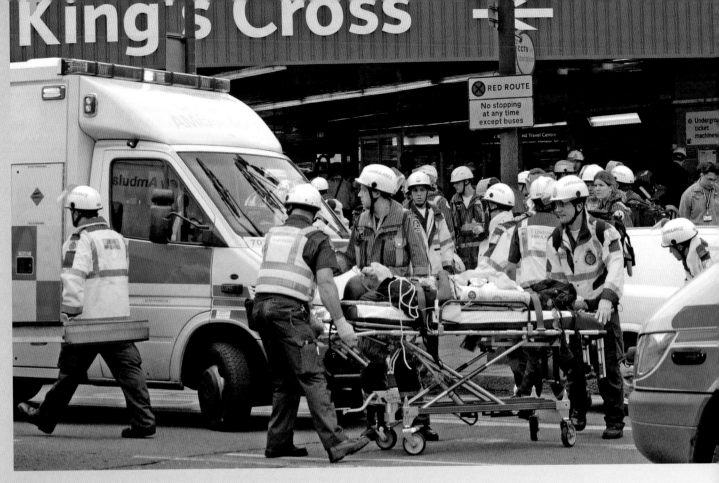

King's Cross

"We are not involved." Pakistani students protesting a major police raid in search of the London bombing terrorists.

trains, crowded with commuters, were approaching the Liverpool Street, King's Cross, and Edgware Road stations.

A difficult evacuation

The bomb that went off on the train traveling Piccadilly line between King's Cross and Russell Square caused the most severe damage. While the other two trains were in stations at the time of the explosions, the Piccadilly line train was passing through a narrow tunnel. This blast alone claimed twenty-eight lives, and the force of the blast threatened the tunnel with collapse. Heat, dust, and foul smoke made it difficult for the rescue teams to get to the scene, so that evacuation of the injured and the other travelers was not complete before early evening. It would be another three days before the dead bodies could all be recovered from the wrecked carriage.

Rescue workers evacuating the injured from King's Cross subway station. The Piccadilly line train where most of the casualties occurred was approaching this station when the bomb went off.

The results of the investigation

In May 2006, the British Home Office and the Parliamentary Intelligence and Security Committee presented their first reports on the events that led to the bombings. Shockingly, these reports made clear that there was never any chance of discovering the terrorists in time to prevent the attacks.

All four of the terrorists, born or raised in Britain, had never attracted any official attention. No coordinating terrorist organization could be identified, and the crimes themselves had seemingly involved no long-term planning. The terrorists had neither traveled widely, nor maintained suspicious relationships with Muslim extremists in Britain. They had never even visited suspicious websites. They had also not required substantial financial support for the attacks. The British Home Office estimated that the suicide bombers had invested a maximum of £8,000, equivalent to around $15,000.

Above: Many people brought flowers to stations in commemoration of the victims of the attack, such as this girl
mourning at the Tavistock Square Station.

Below: Days after the attacks, people were still searching
for their family and friends. Pictures of the missing were
hung on the walls of the King's Cross subway station.

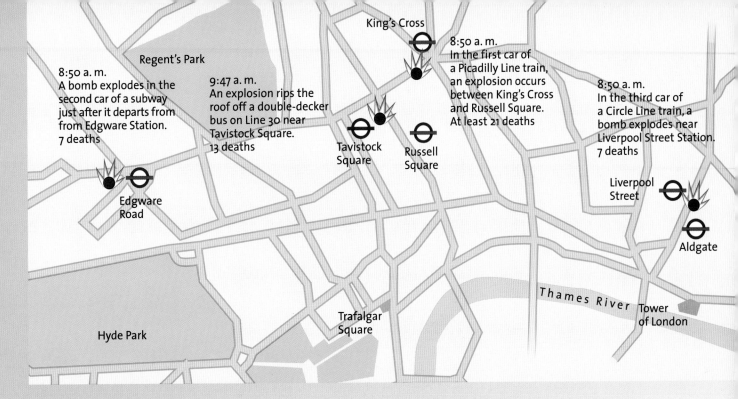

King's Cross

8:50 a.m.
In the first car of a Picadilly Line train, an explosion occurs between King's Cross and Russell Square. At least 21 deaths

Regent's Park

8:50 a.m.
A bomb explodes in the second car of a subway just after it departs from from Edgware Station. 7 deaths

9:47 a.m.
An explosion rips the roof off a double-decker bus on Line 30 near Tavistock Square. 13 deaths

8:50 a.m.
In the third car of a Circle Line train, a bomb explodes near Liverpool Street Station. 7 deaths

Tavistock Square

Russell Square

Edgware Road

Liverpool Street

Aldgate

Trafalgar Square

Hyde Park

Thames River

Tower of London

The fourth bomb

While the ambulances were speeding through the streets of London toward various subway stations with blaring sirens, the fourth terrorist was sitting on the upper deck of a Number 30 double-decker bus. At Tavistock Square, almost one hour after the attacks on the subway, he triggered his backpack bomb. The roof of the red bus was blasted off by the force of the explosion, and thirteen people were killed. The scene of the disaster was horrific.

In less than an hour, the perpetrators brought the public transportation system of one of Europe's major cities to a standstill. A total of fifty-two innocent people lost their lives in these suicide bombings, with several hundred more injured, some of them severely. All of Europe reeled with shock in the aftermath.

Immediate investigation

In the days following the attacks, while the investigations into the who and why behind the attacks were in high gear, many of the seriously injured were struggling for survival in various London hospitals. On July 18th, the fifty-sixth victim died as a result of the attacks.

After some initial doubt as to whether the attacks had involved suicide bombers or remote-triggered devices, it was confirmed that the four terrorists were indeed among the dead. They were all British citizens who had led inconspicuous lives in Leeds up until the day of

the attacks. Three of the young men were of Pakistani origin and the fourth was Jamaican. Two had spent some time in Pakistan not long before the attacks, and it could be established that at least one of them had attended a madrasa (Islamic school) run by Islamic extremists during his stay there. Otherwise, not even their closest relatives were aware of the perpetrators' radicalism and readiness to use violence. On July 16th, it was announced that the person suspected of building the bombs detonated in London had been arrested in Cairo. The British media refered to this man as "the chemist," and as the mastermind behind the attacks.

The London attacks had been meticulously planned.

July 21, 2005: further terror

Exactly two weeks after the terrible explosions in the London subway system, the city was again on red alert. Three subway stations had to be evacuated. A series of small explosions had occurred on three subways and one bus. Fortunately, only one person was injured. Subsequent investigation showed that the perpetrators were copycat terrorists trying to emulate the attacks of July 7, 2005. The execution of their plans was apparently faulty: only the fuses exploded, but not the bombs themselves. After the failed attack all of the suspects were able to escape, even though in at least one instance courageous passengers had chased after one of the perpetrators and almost succeeded in catching him. Eight days after the attempted attack, the police were able to arrest all the suspects in London and Rome.

DISASTERS IN THE AIR

In a world full of bad news, none spreads faster and further than reports of aviation and spaceflight disasters. Invariably, each event raises questions about cause and responsibility. Was it poor maintenance, construction flaws or unpredictable weather? Human error is implicated all too often, raising the possibility that perhaps we, like Icarus, fly too close to the sun.

THE LAST ZEPPELIN

THE HINDENBURG EXPLODES AT LAKEHURST

On May 6, 1937, the *Hindenburg*, an enormous airship of the type known as a dirigible, or zeppelin, approached its landing spot in Lakehurst, New Jersey. The airship had departed three days earlier from Frankfurt, Germany on its first transatlantic flight of the season. On its final descent, the *Hindenburg* caught fire. Within seconds, the zeppelin was a huge ball of flame. Miraculously, sixty-two of the ninety-seven passengers on board survived the catastrophe. The public on both sides of the Atlantic was horrified by the accident, leading to the end of dirigibles in civil aviation.

A comfortable journey

The Hindenburg *operated regular passenger flights between Germany and America for only one year, from 1936 until 1937.*

Beginning in 1930, advances in the design and development of airships had made regular commercial transatlantic air travel possible. Traveling by airship was still very expensive and only a few wealthy travelers could afford it. While the passenger cabins in airships were small and sparsely furnished compared with the luxurious accommodations offered by ocean liners, a dirigible's comfortable common rooms and the panoramic views out the gallery windows more than made up for those inconveniences. Other niceties were also included. The food served on board the giant airships was famous for its exquisite quality and, for a while, the *Hindenburg* even had an ultra-light aluminum grand piano, designed specifically for zeppelins. In 1936, the *Hindenburg* began flying a regular route between Germany and America, and its first season had been exceptionally successful. The 1937 season was projected to be equally or even more profitable.

The last flight of the Hindenburg

The last flight of LZ 129 *Hindenburg* began on the evening of May 3, 1937 in Frankfurt, Germany. There were sixty-one crew members and thirty-five passengers on board. Due to unusually strong head winds, simply crossing the Atlantic Ocean took twelve hours longer than usual. When the airship finally made it to mainland America, the weather forecast warned that

a violent storm was on the way. The captain of the *Hindenburg* tried to fly around the storm at first, but an hour later, he decided to make for land instead.

Hydrogen instead of helium

At the time of her maiden flight in 1936, the *Hindenburg* was the largest flying machine ever made. Until then, the airship *Graf Zeppelin* had been Germany's most famous dirigible, transporting an ever-growing number of passengers across the Atlantic Ocean since 1930. The *Hindenburg* had been brought into service to ease the burden on the *Graf Zeppelin*, and at the same time set a new standard for speed and distance. Although it was only a few feet longer than the *Graf Zeppelin*, the *Hindenburg* was significantly larger in diameter with double the gas capacity. While her predecessors had been filled with highly flammable hydrogen gas, the *Hindenburg* was designed to use inflammable helium. At the time, however, helium could only be produced in large quantities in the United States, where a military embargo had banned all exports to Germany after the election of the Nazi government. Failing access to helium, the *Hindenburg* had to fall back on using dangerous hydrogen instead.

Panic on board

After a three-day flight across the Atlantic Ocean, the *Hindenburg* began its final descent to Lakehurst, New Jersey on May 6, 1937 at 7:15 p.m. local time. The ground crew was standing by, ready to grab the long towropes lowered from the airship to the ground. As the Hindenburg hovered less than 200 feet above the airfield, a small plume of smoke was observed near its tail fin. Seconds later, an explosion rocked the *Hindenburg*'s stern. Within moments, the middle section exploded and the entire zeppelin erupted in flames. The *Hindenburg* continued to descend. In despair, the passengers and crew who had survived the first explosion jumped to save their lives. Steward Wilhelm Balla later wrote in his diary how he watched a mother throwing her two young sons out of the burning airship, with the boys' older sister jumping after them. The boys and their

The Hindenburg's *cockpit as seen from the outside.*

Aviation pioneer

Ferdinand Graf von Zeppelin (1838–1917) was a general and an aviation engineer. After a career in the armed forces he began building buoyant aircraft. These became known as dirigibles after the French word dirigeable, *which means "steerable." His work, based on designs and patents by Hungarian inventor David Schwarz, resulted in a rigid airship that was easily steered and propelled. His first prototype dirigible flew over Lake Constance in 1900. Zeppelin raised funds for his airship development from donations and by lottery. By 1909, his new airships, named "zeppelins" after their inventor, were ready for commercial passenger transport. Most zeppelins, though, were built for military purposes. During World War I, they were used as bombers and reconnaissance aircraft.*

mother would survive the catastrophe, but their sister and father were among the thirty-six people who did not. The last to jump were the *Hindenburg*'s two captains, one of whom died of severe burns the following morning. In all, thirteen passengers, twenty-two of the crew, and one worker on the ground were killed.

The investigation

The exact cause of the catastrophe remains a matter of controversy to this day. The commission appointed to investigate the accident explored a number of different theories, including the possibility of sabotage, but could reach no firm, incontrovertible conclusions. The most plausible theory suggested that the airship's skin could have been statically charged when the zeppelin flew through the thunderstorm. As the airship attempted to land, a static spark could have ignited the hydrogen. However, it was the diesel fuel that powered the *Hindenburg*'s engines that caused most of the deaths by fire. The hydrogen gas that provided lift was completely consumed after just one minute. Ignited by the initial explosions, the diesel fuel continued to burn for hours.

The Lakehurst disaster brought about the end of the zeppelin era. Only one day after the accident, Hermann Göring, head of the German Luftwaffe, ordered the temporary discontinuation of all commercial services. The American embargo, still in place after the disaster, meant that the less dangerous helium gas could not be exported to Germany. With the dangers of hydrogen gas now vividly exposed by the *Hindenburg* catastrophe, the great zeppelins never resumed service.

An eyewitness report
"I saw the two little boys standing there, right next to me, and I heard them cry. I also saw the 13-year-old girl, lying on the ground, her hair burning. Together with a friend, we dashed over there and extinguished the fire as best we could. But it was too late. Three hours later, she was dead, freed from her suffering."
Excerpt from the diary of steward Wilhelm Balla

Live coverage

Miraculously, the *Hindenburg* disaster claimed only thirty-six lives. Nevertheless, the public on both sides of the Atlantic was badly shaken by the fiery crash. This was due in part to the live coverage the *Hindenburg* accident received on the radio, making it one of the first disasters ever to receive such instantaneous attention. Herbert Morrison, a journalist working for a Chicago radio station, happened to be present at the Lakehurst airfield to report on the zeppelin's arrival. Unexpectedly, he became a witness to catastrophe instead. His professional and matter-of-fact account of the landing maneuver became emotional as he reacted to the disaster he watched unfold before him. Clearly shaken, he had to break off his commentary several times. His report, recorded on tape, was broadcast the very same day in Chicago and was re-run on national radio the next day. Today, it is acknowledged as a classic piece of radio history.

The diesel fuel the Hindenburg *had been carrying caused the wreck to continue burning for several hours.*

As the fire burned itself out, emergency workers carried off the victims of the disaster.

The Empire State Building, designed by the architects Shreve, Lamb & Harmon, was constructed between 1929 and 1931. It was the world's tallest skyscraper for over forty years.

NIGHTMARE ON THE 79TH FLOOR

A B-25 BOMBER CRASHES INTO THE EMPIRE STATE BUILDING IN NEW YORK

On a foggy day in June 1945, a B-25 bomber was headed from Massachusetts to New York. Due to thick fog, the plane was unable to land at La Guardia Airport as scheduled. Instead, the pilot requested permission to divert to Newark, across the Hudson River in New Jersey. Thinking he was flying over Manhattan's West Side, just across the river from the airport, the pilot flew dangerously close to the Chrysler Building on East 42nd Street, then continued along 5th Avenue toward 34th Street. The last words from air traffic control to the plane were: "From where I'm sitting, I can't see the top of the Empire State Building."

Built in a time of crisis

The year 1929 had been a great one for the economy. To meet the increasing demand for office space, John Jacob Raskob, founder of General Motors, together with Alfred E. Smith, former governor of New York State and the recently defeated presidential candidate of the Democratic Party, decided to build the world's tallest skyscraper. For the design, they contracted the architectural group Shreve, Lamb & Harmon. Their simple and elegant tower rose in a series of setbacks from a five-story lobby. Its limestone facade was distinguished by subtle art deco ornamentation executed in aluminum and nickel. Only two weeks after construction began, the USA plunged into the Great Depression, effectively ending the ongoing competition for the world's tallest skyscraper. The Empire State Building would retain that title for more than forty years. The building opened its doors for business during the peak of the worldwide financial crisis, which meant that most of its offices could not be rented. Before long, New Yorkers nicknamed it the "Empty State Building." What saved the project from bankruptcy was its observation deck. Millions of visitors paid admission to see the stunning view of the world offered from the impossible height of the Empire State Building.

Fog in New York

Through the thick morning fog on July 28, 1945, the B-25 bomber under the command of Lieutenant Colonel William Smith made its way to Newark. Visibility was very poor. When Smith released his landing gear, he thought he was on course for the final descent. Suddenly, the fog lifted, and Smith realized that his plane was hurtling toward midtown Manhattan's Radio City Music Hall at Rockefeller Center. Smith yanked the control stick back, but the plane could not climb quickly enough. He looked up to see the facade of the Empire State Building racing toward him. Helpless, he crashed the bomber into the 79th floor of the world's tallest building.

The three-man crew was killed on impact. One engine was torn off the plane, cut through the entire building, and exited on the opposite side. It plummeted through the roof of a 20-story building located on 34th Street, starting a fire. The B-25 bomber's fuel tank exploded and burned fiercely. Ignited gasoline poured into the building and ran down its facade. Eleven people on the 79th floor of the Empire State Building died in the flames, another three were killed by falling debris, and twenty-six people were injured.

If the number of casualties seems relatively low, it is because the accident took place on a Saturday morning, and there were only around 1,500 people in the building at the time. Today, there are generally about 15,000 people working in the Empire State Building every day, not counting the 10,000 to 20,000 daily visitors. The streets were also less crowded on a Saturday compared to a typical work day during the week. Finally, this particular B-25 was a training plane, and thus did not carry muni-

The Empire State Building was shrouded in smoke and flames after a B-25 bomber crashed into the 79th floor.

A crowd gathered in front of the Empire State Building looks on in shock.

The gaping hole left by the B-25 that crashed into the Empire State Building shows the force of the impact.

tions. If it had, the scale of the catastrophe would have been much greater.

The July 28th accident would not be the only one of its kind. Less than one year later, on May 20, 1946, another military plane flying in thick fog crashed into the 58th floor of a building on Wall Street. The five men on board were killed.

Drama in the elevator

A separate drama was playing out inside the skyscraper on that fateful day. The plane's detached second engine, together with parts of the landing gear, had crashed into the building and hurtled down an elevator shaft. Before exploding into a ball of fire within the shaft, the falling engine had severely damaged all six steel cables suspending the elevator.

On the 80th floor, elevator operator Betty Lou Oliver had been slightly injured by the fire. Emergency workers and firefighters administered first aid and told her to take elevator No. 6 down to the lobby, where an ambulance was waiting to bring her to the hospital. No one was aware that the cables of this very elevator had already been nearly severed. When the door closed, they heard the horrifying sound of the cables snapping. Forcing the door open, they watched helplessly as the elevator plunged downward, so fast that Betty Lou's feet were lifted off the floor by the initial acceleration. Its ceiling battered by the damaged cables, the cab hit bottom. Oliver was badly injured, but had survived a 985-foot fall: safety equipment and the cushion of air that formed beneath the cab had slowed its descent. Oliver was rescued from a pile of rubble at the bottom of the shaft. Miraculously, she had lived through the Empire State Building 79th floor crash, a catastrophe that had almost killed her twice.

Are elevators dangerous?

The vertical ambitions of New York architecture were only made possible because of the invention of the Otis Safety Elevator, the only way to quickly and conveniently reach the breathtakingly high upper floors of a skyscraper. Today, there are about 54,000 elevators in New York City alone, transporting some 27 million people up and down every day. According to one study, a safety incident occurs approximately once for every 135 million

Two days after the accident, workers on 33rd Street erected scaffolds to repair the Empire State Building's facade.

elevator rides. On average, this means that an elevator is damaged or malfunctions every fifth day. It is exceedingly rare for elevator cars to come loose and plummet down the shaft. For that we have Elisha Graves Otis (1811–1864) to thank, an engineer who in 1854 invented a safety device that uses clamps as emergency brakes for elevator cabs. This keeps them from falling even if their cables fail completely. This device is still in use today in the majority of elevators all over the world.

Why the Empire State Building did not collapse

The story of the B-25 bomber obviously brings to mind the events of September 11, 2001. Why did the building not collapse?

Compared to a modern jet airliner, a B-25 bomber is a very small plane, especially in relation to the massive steel and concrete structure of a skyscraper. In addition, unlike the World Trade Center, the Empire State Building's stability does not depend on any one, single structural element. With few of its vertical girders damaged by the crash, there was never any danger of the Empire State Building collapsing.

A week or so after the crash, the survivors, after much discussion, made the decision to eat their dead friends so that they themselves might live.

CANNIBALS OUT OF DESPERATION

SIXTEEN PASSENGERS SURVIVE A PLANE CRASH IN THE ANDES

On October 13, 1972, a small prop plane belonging to the Uruguayan Air Force crashed in the Andes. The plane had been chartered by a rugby team on their way to a match in Chile. Thirty-three of the forty-five passengers survived the crash, but the search and rescue operation was abandoned early on because no one expected anyone to survive more than a few days in the harsh climate. This was the beginning of a struggle for survival in the snows of the Andes that would not end for another seventy-two days, when sixteen passengers would be rescued. Faced with starvation, they had eaten their deceased fellow passengers to avoid death.

Heading for a match

To give former students the opportunity to continue playing rugby after graduation, a few alumni of Stella Maris College in Montevideo, Uruguay formed a rugby team, the Old Christians. In 1971, the club was invited to play an amateur match in Santiago, Chile. They had such a good experience that they were delighted when they were invited to participate again the following year. Friends and relatives were invited to come join them on their trip to the neighboring country.

On the morning of October 12, 1972, a group of forty people gathered at Carrasco Airport near Montevideo, Uruguay, where they had chartered a small Fairchild FH-227 prop plane for their trip across the Andes. On board, the mood was cheerful. Players tossed a rugby ball around the cabin and everyone was in high spirits. In the afternoon, however, the weather turned bad, and the small plane had difficulty gaining enough altitude to fly over the high peaks of the Andes Mountains. The pilots decided to make an overnight stop. The next day, the weather had improved enough to make the small plane's flight through the peaks of the Andes seem a reasonable proposition.

A fatal navigational error

Nonetheless, the conditions were still far from ideal. The mountain peaks were shrouded in a thick layer of clouds, forcing the pilots to fly by their instruments. They left the Andes behind them, or so they thought, and began their descent through the cloud cover. When they were low enough to have a clear view, they realized that they were still in the middle of the Andes. The instruments had underestimated the speed of the strong headwind, giving them false information. Before the plane could ascend to a higher altitude, its right wing crashed into a mountainside and broke off. Shortly thereafter, the plane lost its left wing as well. Parts of the severed wing ripped a hole in the rear fuselage, and five passengers fell to their deaths. By now, all that remained of the plane was the damaged cabin, which hit the ground and slid over the snow before coming to a stop with a loud crash.

The first nights in the snow

Inside the plane, chaos reigned. Most of the seats had been wrenched from their anchorage and hurled to the front of the plane. Among the pile of seats and fuselage parts, the injured people moaned. Those who had not been badly injured began helping the others. Night was falling, and a night at 13,000 feet above sea level can be as cold as −22 °F. There was almost nothing on board the plane that could provide protection against that kind of cold. During the first night, another five passengers died from their injuries. On the morning of October 14, 1972, twenty-seven of the original forty-five people on board were still alive, many in bad shape. The survivors helped each other as best they could. Still hoping to be rescued, they put together a bucket system for collecting drinking water produced by snowmelt. However, the lack of food quickly turned into a real problem. There was nothing on board except for some chocolate bars and cookies. After about a week in the ice and the cold, the survivors, listening to a small pocket radio, learned that the search for them had been abandoned. As far as the rest of the world was concerned, they were dead.

Desperate struggle for survival

After one week, those with less severe injuries were healing, but the meager food supply was gone. Hunger made the survivors increasingly weak. After much discussion, they decided to

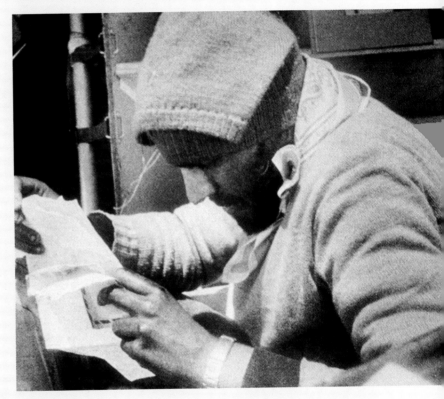

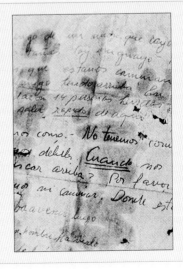

The letter
This is the text of the cry for help the survivors threw over the river: "I come from a plane that crashed in the mountains. I am Uruguayan. We've been walking for ten days. I have an injured friend up in the valley. There are 14 injured people in the plane. We have to get out of here soon and we do not know how. We have no more food. We are weak. When are you going to come up and get us? Please, we cannot even walk. Where are we?"

try to eat the flesh of those who had died. The graveyard they had created became their food supply, a deep freeze locker for survival. After initial hesitation, everyone took part in the cannibalism. At that altitude, in a cold, snowy, hostile environment like the west slope of the Andes, no animal or plant life exists. The survivors had no other alternative if they wanted to live.

Expedition to civilization

After two months of living in such inhumane conditions, sixteen passengers were still alive. Eight had died at the end of October when an avalanche buried part of the plane's fuselage. Another three passengers died in November and December from crash-related injuries. In the meantime, the survivors had set out on a number of expeditions in small groups, but all had returned without results. After sixty-two days on the mountain, Nando Parrado, Roberto Canessa, and Antonio Vizintin set out on yet another attempt to contact the outside world. This time, they would succeed. After three days, Vizintin was sent back to save on food. Eight days later, Parrado and Canessa finally reached the end of the snowfield. They found a river and saw a farmer riding a horse on the other side, grazing his herds. Their shouts for help were not understood and they were unable to cross the rushing waters, so they threw a letter wrapped around a stone across the river. Finally, the man on horseback rode off to alert authorities. Helicopters arrived to rescue those who remained. The survivors had been stranded in the snowy wastes for seventy-two days.

Below: No animals or plants can survive in the snow-covered desert located 13,000 feet above sea level.

Right: Finally, after 72 days in the ice and the cold, helicopters arrived to rescue the survivors.

Reunion thirty years later

On the 30th anniversary of their rescue, after praying together, four of the survivors descended the mountain along the route that led to the river and eventual rescue. Among them is Roberto Canessa (far right), one of the men from the expedition who brought helicopters to the crash site.

INFERNO ON THE RUNWAY

TWO PASSENGER AIRLINERS COLLIDE ON TENERIFE

On March 27, 1977, two airliners collided on the runway of Tenerife. Of the 643 people on board the two planes, only sixty-one survived the fiery inferno that ensued. Ironically, one of the worst disasters in the history of twentieth-century aviation did not occur in midair, but on the ground, on the runway of an airport. It seems that a series of communication problems between the air control tower and the two crews caused the catastrophe.

Terrorist threat on Gran Canaria

On Sunday, March 27th, 1977, two wide-body airliners were on their way to the island of Gran Canaria, a popular Spanish holiday resort. Coming in from Amsterdam, the *Rhine River* was a Boeing 747 jumbo jet belonging to the Dutch airline KLM. Arriving from New York was the *Clipper Victor*, a Pan Am jumbo jet. Together, the two planes had a total of 643 passengers and crew on board. Shortly before they

The burnt-out skeleton of the KLM plane on the runway of Tenerife Airport.

were scheduled to land at their destination, Las Palmas, a terrorist bomb threat temporarily shut down that airport. Air traffic control diverted the two planes to the neighboring island of Tenerife, where they landed in short succession at approximately 2:00 p.m. By that time, Los Rodeos Airport in Santa Cruz, Tenerife was hopelessly overcrowded. It had to deal not only with its regular weekend air traffic, but with all the flights diverted from Gran Canaria as well. Due to lack of space, several large planes were parked close to one other in the area normally used for taxiing to the runway. This meant that the runway would have to be used for taxiing as well as take-off.

The Rhine River blocks the path of the Clipper Victor

The pilots of the two jumbo jets made different decisions regarding their passengers. Jacob van Zanten, the Dutch captain, let his passengers deplane so they could spend the time in the airport building. The American pilot, however, decided to keep his passengers on board so that he could depart as quickly as possible. Both crews were readied for take-off as soon as Las Palmas air traffic control gave them the all

The scene on
the runway one
day after the
catastrophe.

clear signal. Unfortunately, the KLM plane was parked behind the Pan Am plane, which meant that the American plane had to wait until the Dutch passengers were all on board again. When the KLM airliner finally received clearance to taxi into position, it had to use the runway because other waiting planes were blocking the area in front of the departure hall and the taxiway. Shortly thereafter, the Pan Am airplane was cleared to taxi into take-off position as well.

A fatal series of miscommunications

As soon as KLM captain Zanten reached the end of the runway, he made a 180-degree turn and reported to the tower that he was "ready for take-off." Air traffic control responded that the KLM plane should "stay at take-off," because the American plane next in line was still taxiing on the runway. The Pan Am plane was supposed to taxi from the runway to the main taxiway using a specific exit, which, however, the Pan Am captain missed. Instead, the Pan Am plane continued taxiing. Making a bad situation worse, a thick fog rolled in as this was transpiring. Captain van Zanten reported that he no longer had clear sight of the runway. To compound the series of tragic events, he also could

not hear the standby message from the controller in its entirety. It may be that he only heard the last part—" . . . take-off"—instead of the complete message telling him to wait. In any case, the captain thought that he had received permission for take-off and initiated the departure sequence. Meanwhile, his flight engineer overheard fragments of the radio communication between the Pan Am plane and the tower. The controller had told the American crew to report back when it had left the runway. The cockpit voice recorder of the KLM plane recorded the engineer's question to the captain: "Is he not clear, the Pan American?" The captain answered emphatically: "Of course!"

Los Rodeos Airport
Aeropuerto International de Los Rodeos is the smaller of the two airports on Tenerife, located in the north of the island, near the city of Santa Cruz. Los Rodeos Airport already had a reputation as a problematic airport for take-off and landing maneuvers because of the sudden formation of fog banks and local strong winds. In 1977, when the catastrophe occurred, the airport did not have ground radar to facilitate control on the runway when visibility was poor.

The catastrophe unfolds

As the American plane continued taxiing down the runway, the departing KLM plane suddenly appeared out of the fog. The aircraft was accelerating along the runway at a speed of more than 125 miles per hour. Both pilots tried to accomplish the impossible: the American pilot turned his airliner sharply to the left at full thrust in an attempt to get off the runway, and the Dutch captain forced his plane off the ground in an effort to fly over the American aircraft—but it was too late. The KLM aircraft succeeded in lifting off, but its landing gear hit the American plane's fuselage, tearing it open. At 492 feet past the point of collision, the *Rhine River* crashed down onto the runway and slid for another 984 feet before its fuel caught fire. A sea of flames engulfed the aircraft, killing all 248 people on board. The *Clipper Victor*, the upper side of its fuselage ripped open and its tail unit gone, kept rolling for a short distance before it, too, exploded in flames. Of the 396 people aboard the Pan Am jet, only sixty-one survived, almost all of them with severe injuries. The force of the explosion had catapulted some of the passengers out of the Pan Am jet. Miraculously, these were among the very few people who escaped the accident largely uninjured. The runway was covered in debris, all of it on fire. Radio Tenerife instantly broadcast calls to all doctors and nurses on the island to come to the airport to help the injured. Chaos broke out on the streets leading to the airport, and the weather—heavy rain and strong winds—made a bad traffic situation worse. A hangar was turned into a provisional mortuary as firefighters struggled with the fires on the runway. Nine hours would pass before the inferno was finally brought under control.

Causes and responsibility

In its report on the incident, the Spanish civil aviation authority later concluded that the air traffic controllers were not at fault, and that weather conditions were not decisive either. There was no doubt, however, that radio communication problems played an important role in the disaster. The investigation revealed that

Aircraft accidents at Los Rodeos

December 7, 1965: A Douglas DC-3 operated by SPANTAX (Spain) crashed shortly after take-off, killing 32 passengers and crew.

December 3, 1972: A Convair 990 operated by SPANTAX (Spain) flew into a fog bank shortly after take-off. The pilot lost his orientation and crashed the plane, killing 155.

March 27, 1977: In the worst accident in the history of civil aviation, two jumbo jets collided in the fog while taxiing on the runway, killing 583.

April 25, 1980: During landing, a Boeing 727–100 disintegrated when it ran into a rocky cliff shrouded in low-slung clouds, killing 146.

Debris from the Pan Am jet was scattered all over the runway of the Tenerife airport.

the rules regarding standard phrases and regulations for radio communication had not been consistently followed. The tower did not always wait for instructions to be acknowledged, nor did it explicitly ask for confirmation. There were also major allegations made against van Zanten, the veteran captain of the KLM plane, because he did not wait for clearance. As a consequence of the catastrophe, Dutch and American investigation authorities recommended the use of ground radar at Spanish airports. Had ground radar been available on that foggy Sunday afternoon, the fatal series of misunderstandings that led to the death of 583 passengers and crew might well have been recognized and averted in time.

A KLM 747 jumbo jet flying high above the clouds.

The runway was covered by a mass of twisted metal debris, including the landing gear of one of the aircraft shown here.

Challenger lifting off at the Kennedy Space Center in Cape Canaveral, Florida.

A BALL OF FIRE

THE EXPLOSION OF THE CHALLENGER SPACE SHUTTLE

Challenger, NASA's second space shuttle for outer space operations, completed its maiden flight in 1983. In its three-year history, *Challenger* made ten space flights, spending a total of sixty-nine days in outer space and orbiting the earth 987 times. Among its successes were the deployment of the first tracking and communications satellite and the testing of a new NASA space shuttle suit. Then came January 28, 1986, the day of the *Challenger* catastrophe: 73 seconds after a perfect launch for mission STS-51-L, *Challenger* disintegrated, killing six astronauts and one civilian.

Challenger's historic contributions to space travel

The space shuttle was named after the US Navy research ship *Challenger*, which was seen as its forerunner. Prior to this, the *Apollo 17* lunar module had also been named *Challenger*. Prior

A whole country in mourning
"We will never forget them, nor the last time we saw them, this morning, as they prepared for their journey and waved goodbye and slipped the surly bonds of earth to touch the face of God."

Ronald Reagan, US President 1981–1989, quoting John G. Magee, Jr.'s poem *High Flight*.

to this tragic accident, the orbiter had completed ten flights without incident. In fact, this very spacecraft had been involved in several historic milestones in the development of American space travel: Sally Ride was the first American female astronaut in outer space in 1983, and in a separate mission that year, Guy S. Bluford was the first African-American astronaut in space; and in February, 1984 Bruce McCandless II performed the first maneuver outside the shuttle (EVA, or extra-vehicular activity) without a safety line, moving about 100 feet away from the spacecraft. The *Challenger* was the world's first space shuttle to land safely at the Kennedy Space Center in Florida, and also made the first successful launch and landing by night. In the course of three flights in 1985, *Challenger* sent the Spacelab station into orbit, which provided an environment for many tests to be carried out, including experiments with live animals. On yet another mission, *Challenger* transported the European Space Agency's Spacelab-3. During its last flight, this utterly successful space shuttle had a civilian on board for the first time in the history of space travel: a woman named Christa McAuliffe, a teacher from New Hampshire. The plan was for her to teach school children from outer space.

A class from outer space

Over the years, the public increasingly had come to question the benefit of NASA space

The teacher's vision

"One of the things I hope to bring back into the classroom is to make that connection with the students that they too are part of history, the space program belongs to them, and to try to bring them up with the space age."

Christa McAuliffe, first civilian in outer space

missions. The quest for manned space travel devoured billions of dollars, and its original purpose had been nothing more than to get a head start in the Cold War. During the mid-1980s, the popularity of the space program hit an all-time low. People were hardly following the launches and landings of the spacecrafts anymore. In an attempt to revive the popularity of the NASA research program (and to guarantee further government funding), the expensive space program was elevated to the level of a pop media event. One effective promotional idea was to send the "girl next door" into outer space. For the Teacher in Space program thus devised, 37-year-old Christa McAuliffe, teacher and mother of two, was chosen from among 11,500 applicants to become an astronaut. At the same time, American school children were told they would experience the future and be taught directly from outer space. The plan worked. Millions of American classrooms took part—but as fate would have it, they did not sit in on a class taught from outer space. Instead, they experienced the tragedy live on TV and

The *Challenger* crew. From left to right, back: Ellison S. Onizuka, Christa McAuliffe, Gregory Jarvis, Judith A. Resnik; front: Michael J. Smith, Francis R. Scobee and Ronald E. McNair.

On January 28, 1986, within 73 seconds of lift-off, millions of television viewers all over the world witness the dramatic explosion of Challenger.

many required psychological counseling in the aftermath of the catastrophe: 73 seconds after what appeared to be a picture-perfect launch, viewers around the world watched in horror as the *Challenger* disintegrated.

Investigation of the catastrophe

After the accident, then President Ronald Reagan (1911–2004) established the Rogers Commission to investigate its causes. As is customary in the aftermath of fatal catastrophes, a quest was begun to find the one factor that could explain the unfathomable. As early as six months after the tragedy, the first reports were available. It emerged that brittle O-rings on the shuttle's right solid rocket booster caused the catastrophe. It also became clear that NASA ignored several safety measures, as well as the warnings of experts about those very O-rings. The countdown had started and it was not going to be halted.

It is now clear that *Challenger* should never have launched on that January morning in 1986 because there was a frost that day at Cape Canaveral. It has been shown that the unusual cold, in connection with the sudden increase in

heat caused by ignition of the engines, made the booster's rubber O-rings brittle, and this led to leakage. Photographs show trails of smoke being emitted from the space shuttle even before lift-off. With the decision to execute the launch, the fate of Richard Scobee, Michael Smith, Judith Resnik, Ellison Onizuka, Ronald McNair, Gregory Jarvis, and Christa McAuliffe was sealed at the time of lift-off. The leak increased rapidly, and within seconds, sparks impinged on the main tank. After a few more seconds, the tank caught fire, and the 370,000 gallons of hydrogen and oxygen in the shuttle's tank exploded.

The debris was scattered over large parts of Florida's east coast. For months, NASA divers actively recovered parts of the shuttle from the ocean. It was another two months before, in March 1986, they succeed in recovering the cockpit with the remains of the crew. Analysis of the cockpit demonstrated that the seven passengers survived the initial explosion: at least three of them had made use of the emergency oxygen system to breathe. It seems that they fell from a height of 10.5 miles for 3 minutes—quite possibly while fully conscious—

before hitting the surface of the Atlantic Ocean with unimagineable force.

The consequences

As a consequence of the *Challenger* accident and the Rogers Commission's follow-up report, government authorities suspend further shuttle flights. It would be more than two and a half years before *Discovery*, the next shuttle, was launched on September 29, 1988. No fewer than 2,000 improvements had to be made before NASA was allowed to resume space travel. The solid rocket booster that caused the *Challenger* disaster was completely revised, and the cockpit now features an emergency exit, making it necessary for astronauts to go back to wearing pressure suits in order to guarantee they have a sufficient amount of air to breathe during launch and landing. NASA abandoned the practice of sending satellites into orbit with manned spacecrafts, and uses unmanned satellite launchers instead. In 1991, *Endeavour*, the best space shuttle to date, was completed, and NASA experienced no further losses for several years—until the next tragedy occurred in January, 2003, when the space shuttle *Columbia* exploded during a landing maneuver, killing all seven crew members.

The space shuttle Challenger with open cargo doors, orbiting the earth.

Crew members of the USS Preserver recover a large section of the ruptured Challenger from the depths of the ocean on the coast of Florida.

A Crash Landing in Amsterdam

THE MYSTERIOUS 1992 BIJLMERMEER DISASTER

On the evening of October 4, 1992, a cargo plane operated by the Israeli airline El Al crashed into Amsterdam's Bijlmermeer neighborhood, demolishing two multistory buildings. Both of the jumbo jets' right side engines had failed shortly after take-off. When its fuel exploded, it turned the crash site into a sea of flames. For a long time, the public was kept in the dark about the exact nature of the airplane's cargo. Initially, there was talk of flowers, perfume, and consumer electronics. Six years later, however, the airline admitted that materials used in the manufacture of chemical weapons as well as uranium were on board the plane at the time of the accident.

An aircraft circling over Amsterdam

Just minutes after taking off from Amsterdam's Schiphol Airport, one of the two engines on the Boeing 747–200's right wing failed. Captain Yitzak Fuchs transmitted a distress call to the tower and prepared for an immediate return to the airport. The aircraft made a wide turn over Amsterdam, traveling 320 miles per hour. Sud-denly, the second engine on the right side failed as well. This left the plane capable only of flying in circles. Then the aircraft's hydraulic systems began to fail, rendering its wing flaps and rudder units ineffective. No longer able to stay aloft, the plane quickly lost altitude.

The unavoidable crash

"Going down, going down," Fuchs shouted over the radio in his last transmission. The aircraft plummeted straight toward the Amsterdam suburb of Bijlmermeer. Seconds later, it crashed into the Groneveen and Kruitberg apartment houses. The neighborhood was transformed into an inferno as fires at the crash site spread to several other buildings.

The crash of the 13-year-old cargo jet was unavoidable. Investigation showed that it was caused by metal fatigue in the fuse pins that held the engines in place. The question was raised, however, as to why, knowing he was going down, captain Fuchs didn't try to land the heavily loaded jumbo jet in nearby Lake Ijssel. A water landing would certainly have been possible based on the plane's position. Why did he continue flying loops over Amsterdam in an attempt to land on that one particular runway? These are just a few of the many puzzles associated with the event that make the crash of

The Boeing 747, operated by Israel's El Al airline, taking off for her last flight.

Flight LY 1863 from Amsterdam to Tel Aviv something of a mystery still to this day.

Strange activity at the crash site

The three-man crew and single passenger were killed, and at least thirty-nine people died on the ground. Over 230 apartments were destroyed. The enormous heat of the exploding fuel from the plane's full tanks virtually vaporized human bodies—only a few of the victims could be identified without extensive forensic analysis. It is possible, even likely, that there were many more casualties in the neighborhood than were acknowledged at the time, as large numbers of illegal aliens were known to live there. Rescue work continued until midnight, when security officials arrived to close down the accident site. Firefighters, journalists, and onlookers were

After the jumbo jet's crash, several buildings caught fire. All that remained was a smoking pile of rubble.

Press release, April 7, 1998

Amsterdam (dpa)—"On Tuesday, Dutch authorities opened an investigation into the matter of the mysterious 'men in white suits' reported by some witnesses after the crash of an El Al aircraft in Amsterdam in October 1992. Immediately after the plane crashed into some apartment complexes in Amsterdam, eyewitnesses reported seeing the 'moon men' searching through the wreckage. The recent statement of a firefighter who claims to have seen the men in white suits triggered the reopening of the investigation. Before now, only residents of the area had described similar observations. The cargo that the El Al plane, headed for Tel Aviv, had on board, is still unclear. On Monday, an American logistics company confirmed that it had flown some cargo to Tel Aviv immediately after the crash. Prior to this statement, a Dutch TV channel had presented a Swedish study claiming that low-level radioactive uranium had been released during the crash of the Boeing 747 in Amsterdam's Bijlmermeer neighborhood. Dutch toxicologists have expressed doubt as to the accuracy of these results. The crash of the cargo jet, operated by the Israeli airliner El Al, into an apartment complex, killed three crew members, one passenger and thirty-nine residents. In the years following the accident, many residents reported needing medical treatment for hair loss and skin diseases."

driven back, and all buildings with a view of the crash site were evacuated. According to reports, men wearing white protective clothing arrived to search the wreckage. At 5 a.m. the next day, trucks arrived to remove some of the jet's cargo.

What was really on board the plane?

During a press conference in the aftermath of the catastrophe, Dutch Minister of Transport Hanja Maji-Weggen claimed that the plane had only carried flowers and perfume. In fact, many witnesses had reported a cloud of perfume at the site of the accident, but this does not explain the diseases that befell many of the rescue workers and residents of the neighborhood years after the disaster. They reported a significant increase in kidney problems, hair loss, eczemas and miscarriages.

Almost six years after the disaster, further details were made public, confirming that the jet's cargo documents had been manipulated and that the "missing" cockpit voice recorder had been covertly shipped to Israel. The plane definitely carried more than just flowers and perfume. Bit by bit, the airline has admitted to an ever-growing list of military goods that were among the Boeing's cargo. The El Al cargo plane had carried tank parts, components for

The El Al jet crashed into Amsterdam's Bijlmermeer neighborhood, destroying some 230 apartments. At least 43 people were killed.

anti-aircraft missiles, chemical substances for manufacture of the poison gas sarin, and several hundred pounds of uranium.

The "tree that saw it all"

It is unlikely that the whole truth will ever be known. Six years after the catastrophe, the victims suffering the consequences were still waiting for a public investigation of the affair and compensation for their mysterious ailments. By 1998, all that had been accomplished was the dedication of a monument to commemorate the accident. In the midst of the crash site, the area of greatest destruction, a lone poplar tree had survived the disaster. It soon became a location where poems, photographs, and flowers were placed in memory of the victims, some hung from its branches. The "tree that saw it all," a silent, green eyewitness, became the center of the memorial erected in Bijlmermeer, commissioned by the Amsterdam city government.

For the victims, however, it was cold comfort. To them it seemed that international state secrets were given priority over basic civil rights. Their skin diseases, hair loss, and other miseries were treated as if they themselves were responsible. Henk van der Belt, an eyewitness to the catastrophe, put it this way: "What is the point of the memorial? Better that they should investigate this matter, they should give us back our belief that we are still a democracy where people are taken seriously."

THE DEMISE OF A SYMBOL OF PEACE

CONCORDE BURSTS INTO FLAMES

On July 25, 2000, Air France Flight 4590 from Charles de Gaulle International Airport in Paris en route to John F. Kennedy Airport in New York crashed just minutes after take-off. Concorde was the only supersonic passenger aircraft in the history of Western aviation and a shining "symbol of peace and international understanding" (Tony Benn, then British Minister of Technology). When it burst into flames, all 113 people aboard lost their lives.

The engines on Concorde's left wing caught fire just after take-off. The catastrophe was caused by a burst tire.

The safest passenger aircraft in history

Concorde was a joint development by Great Britain and France beginning in the late 1950s. Its top speed was twice the speed of sound, a phenomenal 1,360 miles per hour. The first prototype took its maiden flights in the spring of 1969, and commercial operations began in 1976. To this day, Concorde remains the only Western supersonic airplane to have been used for regular air traffic. Prior to the accident in July, 2000, Concorde was considered the safest plane in the world, a reputation based on its ratio of air miles to passenger deaths (zero). While the Boeing 737 fleet taken as a whole travels more passenger miles each week and logs more flight hours than Concorde flew in its entire brief history, this is due to the large number of Boeing aircraft and their extensive flight network.

A titanium strip on the runway

On that summer day in July 2000, Concorde was scheduled to fly from Charles de Gaulle airport in Paris to New York City. The trouble began even before take-off when Concorde, which had already accelerated to a speed of 185 miles per hour, ran over a 15-inch strip of titanium that was lying on the runway. This strip originated from an American Continental Airlines DC10 that had taken off from the same runway 4 minutes earlier. The affected Concorde tire burst, and a large chunk of it hit the underside of the plane's left wing with such strong force that it damaged one of the fuel tanks. The leaking fuel ignited instantaneously,

either due to a spark from electrical wiring or due to contact with some of the extremely hot parts of the engine. Moments later, as the plane was taking off, engines 1 and 2 simultaneously lost all power, but recovered during the following seconds. When a fire erupted in engine 2, flames trailed behind the plane in long streams, and the crew switched off the engine in response to a fire warning generated by an on-board computer. At this point, the pilot had no choice but to continue the start maneuver. He planned to fly to the nearby Le Bourget airport and attempt an emergency landing there.

Crashing into a hotel

With only three of the four engines functioning properly, however, and the damaged landing gear impossible to retract, Concorde was not able to gain speed or altitude: the plane was moving only 230 miles per hour rather than the 250 miles per hour necessary for take-off and ascent, and that at an elevation of merely 200 feet. Engine 1 caught fire, causing it to fail as well, leaving the plane powered only by engines 3 and 4. This resulted in asymmetric thrust, which lifted the right wing and rolled

Concorde crashes into a nearby hotel, killing four of the hotel's guests.

the plane into a 100-degree bank. In an attempt to bring the aircraft back to a level position, the pilot was forced to reduce power in the remaining engines, but this reduced the airspeed further still and he lost control of the plane. Tragically, Concorde crashed into *Les Relais Bleus*, a hotel in Gonesse, near the airport. All nine crew members, all one hundred passengers on board and four people on the ground lost their lives.

All Concorde Flights Stopped

A few days after the accident, all Concorde flights were grounded until the International Aviation Safety Agency could thoroughly investigate the accident and make recommendations. One Air France aircraft located in New York at the time was allowed to fly back to Paris, although without passengers. In addition to investigating the causes of the accident, the

The firefighters could do no more than extinguish Concorde's burning wreckage. None of the crew or passengers could be rescued.

Records by Concorde

In its time, Concorde set several records: in 1995, it took off from Paris, flew around the globe, and returned to its airport of departure in 32 hours, 27 minutes, and 49 seconds, including all intermediate stops. On February 7, 1996, a British Airways Concorde set a world record of 2 hours, 52 minutes, and 59 seconds between New York and London. In August 1999, during a total eclipse of the sun, three Concorde aircraft crossed the Atlantic Ocean, flying along with the shadow of the moon at Mach 2. The 300 passengers on board experienced the eclipse three to four times longer than observers on the ground.

A British Airways Concorde during take-off from John F. Kennedy International Airport. The flight to London Heathrow Airport on July 26, 2000, one day after the crash, took place without any passengers.

The wrecked aircraft left a scene of devastation and cost Air France millions in damages. In addition to being ordered to pay large sums in compensation, the company suffered tremendous losses while all Concordes were grounded, pending investigation results.

agency also invited proposals on how to improve the Concorde fleet. Analyses showed the need for a few changes; above all, they were to be equipped with tires developed specially for Concorde planes that could not burst.

Long-standing problems with the tires

It was not until 2005 that French authorities initiated proceedings against Continental Airlines on the basis of their use of the titanium strip that was lying on the runway, which was not actually approved (it had been used by the airline because titanium is more robust than traditional metals). In the same year, Jacques Herubel, a former flight engineer, came under investigation. It had come to light that there had been more than seventy incidents involving Concorde tires between 1979 and 2000, but Herubel, the flight engineer in charge, had neglected the issue and failed to take steps to correct known defects.

When the identified defects had been corrected, test flights were conducted in July 2001 and the Concorde was actually in flight again on September 11, 2001 when the terrorist attacks on the World Trade Center in New York City took place. As an indirect consequence, transatlantic air traffic dwindled. With passenger numbers dropping, Concorde service became less profitable and was ultimately discontinued in 2003.

Concorde, the only Western supersonic aircraft ever operated in regular air traffic, was considered the safest airplane until the Paris tragedy.

BURNED UPON RE-ENTRY

THE COLUMBIA SPACE SHUTTLE

On April 12, 1981, the *Columbia* space shuttle inaugurated a new chapter in the history of space travel. Unlike traditional rockets that disintegrate in the upper atmosphere after launching satellites or astronauts into space, the re-usable space shuttle was an orbiting vehicle capable of landing on a runway, much like a plane. Named after a sailing ship that made the first American circumnavigation of the globe in 1792, the space shuttle *Columbia* had flown twenty-seven missions before the catastrophe of February 1, 2003, when it broke into pieces while re-entering the atmosphere. The entire seven-person crew perished.

The damage at lift-off

For three months, a specially appointed commission investigated 50,000 fragments of the *Columbia*'s wreckage, along with computer data and photographs. It concluded that the tragedy that occurred during the final minutes of *Columbia*'s last flight was caused by damage sustained during lift-off, just 81 seconds after the launch. While the damaged parts of the spacecraft had withstood the strain of the sixteen-day mission, they failed during the final minutes when the space shuttle attempted to re-enter the earth's atmosphere. The damage was sustained when insulation material broke off one of the external tanks and penetrated the outer shell of the shuttle's left wing. When hot gas entered the spacecraft through the damaged wing, *Columbia* sustained major structural damage prior to breaking apart. Harold Gehman, head of the commission in Houston, made clear that NASA was aware that the shuttle had a damaged left wing at the time of its attempted return from orbit. The potential repercussions of the damage, however, had not been completely understood. The tear in the wing had been a small one, small enough to allow the shuttle to make it into the skies over Texas, but large enough to allow the hot gas to enter, causing internal temperatures high enough to melt metal. Gehman conceded that it would probably be impossible to prove conclusively that this was the actual course of events that had led to the accident.

Space Shuttle Columbia *during launch, starting out on its 16-day mission to outer space.*

Critical seconds

"Re-entry through the atmosphere is one of the most critical moments in the mission of the shuttle. An error of a few degrees could provoke a catastrophe similar to what happened today."

Umberto Guidoni,
Italian astronaut

A photograph in memory of the Columbia *crew at the Johnson Space Center in Houston, Texas.*

The investigation committee criticized NASA for having ignored the advice of experts and for not having done everything possible to save the crew. In his report of August 26, 2003, Gehman noted that the full-scale investigations revealed several errors in judgment and management. In addition, it was clear that poor quality control was endemic throughout the agency. NASA had grown complacent, accepting risk levels that would have been unheard of in the early days of the space program.

The error messages began 15 minutes before landing

The *Columbia* space shuttle set out on its sixteen-day mission on January 16th with seven astronauts on board. Rick Husband was the commander and William McCool the pilot. Also on board were mission specialists Kalpana Chawla, Michael Anderson, David Brown, and Laurel Clark, who were in charge of conducting more than eighty scheduled scientific experiments during the flight. The seventh crew member was the Israeli officer Ilan Ramon, *Columbia*'s payload specialist. He was the first Israeli astronaut in outer space. Special safety measures had been taken during launch because of concerns about terrorist attacks.

When a spacecraft makes its final descent, it must reduce its speed from 18,000 miles per hour to just 620 miles per hour very rapidly. This deceleration generates enormously high temperatures. The thermal protection system, a heat shield consisting of 20,000 specially manufactured ceramic tiles, is designed to withstand temperatures up to 3,000 °F. On February 1st, *Columbia* began to show signs of overheating as the shuttle approached the coast of California at an altitude of 38 miles. At 19:52 CST, about 15 minutes before the scheduled landing, the temperature sensor for the wing leading edge first detected unusually high temperatures. Only a minute later, hydraulic sensors in the left wing indicated sudden loss of pressure. *Columbia* continued on its journey across California. Four minutes later, the sensors on both

Falling wreckage from the Columbia *caused several small fires on the ground near Athens, Texas.*

Below: Engineers working at the Columbia wreckage reconstruction site. About 55,000 lbs of parts were found after the crash, representing about 24 percent of the shuttle.

left main landing-gear tires failed as the shuttle was flying across Arizona, cutting off most data transmission to mission control. A few seconds before all radio contact was lost, the sensors transmitted data reporting unusually high strain on the left wing. *Columbia* was speeding along at 12,500 miles per hour when witnesses heard a series of deafening explosions. The shuttle broke apart into at least three burning sections continued to fall like shooting stars against the sapphire-blue sky. Seventeen years after the *Challenger* disaster, the USA had lost a second spacecraft.

The search for wreckage

The search for *Columbia* wreckage recovered only about 24 percent of the shuttle; the rest of the spacecraft was declared lost. Immediately after the accident, NASA emphatically warned the public not to go anywhere near the debris, which was scattered over several states. NASA asked any members of the general public that found fragments of the shuttle to photograph or film them, but warned not to touch or remove anything. In an attempt to fend off trophy hunters, officials went so far as to announce that the shuttle's components were toxic. Shortly after the accident, large pieces of the wreck

Wreckage from the Columbia was scattered across five states.

were found in Nacogdoches, Texas. The first body parts were identified only a few hours later when a charred human torso, thigh bones, and helmet were found on a highway near a field full of debris from *Columbia*.

Firefighters from Oregon and California walk shoulder-to-shoulder, combed through fields in Texas in search of pieces of Columbia.

Chronicle of space disasters

January 27, 1967: A fire on board Apollo 1 *killed three US astronauts*

April 24, 1967: The braking parachute of a Russian Soyuz capsule did not open properly during landing. One cosmonaut died.

April 13, 1970: While Apollo 13 was on its way to the moon, an oxygen tank on board exploded. The three astronauts aboard managed to return to earth unharmed.

June 30, 1971: A pressure valve on a Soyuz capsule opened. Three cosmonauts were killed.

September 26, 1983: Shortly before launch, fire broke out on board a Russian Soyuz rocket. The three cosmonauts were

saved because the launch escape system moved the capsule out of danger in time.

January 28, 1986: Shortly after launch, the Challenger space shuttle exploded, killing all seven crew members.

February 23, 1997: A fire broke out on board the Mir orbital station. The cosmonauts reacted quickly, extinguishing the fire within just 14 minutes. No one was injured.

June 25, 1997: An unmanned supply vehicle crashed into the space station Mir. The crew was unharmed.

February 1, 2003: Columbia space shuttle exploded at an altitude of 38 miles during re-entry into the earth's atmosphere, falling to the earth in pieces. All seven astronauts were killed.

DISASTERS AT SEA

The *Titanic* was a ship of superlatives, and its sinking had far-reaching consequences. This chapter includes not only sunken dreams, however, but other marine calamities as well, including oil spills that impact the environment for years. Analysis of these accidents is always geared toward prevention—next time they can be prevented. We grasp at this illusion in order to continue striving for superlatives.

HUMAN BEINGS WERE THE CARGO

THE LAST JOURNEY OF THE SLAVE SHIP HENRIETTA MARIE

Slavery has existed since time immemorial. Throughout human history, people have been the property of others and forced to work against their will. The seventeenth and eighteenth centuries were the heyday of the slave ships, merchant vessels that traveled a triangular route from Europe to West Africa, on to South America, and then to the southeast coast of the USA. Hundreds of thousands of people were shipped in cargo holds to be sold like any other commodity, packed in tightly in the most inhumane conditions imaginable, often with very little food. In addition to the staggering individual tragedies, the very existence of slavery is one of humanity's greatest tragedies.

Four generations of an African-American family living in Beaufort, South Carolina. Once caught, slaves became part of a vicious cycle of exploitation, usually for life.

An open letter

"My paramount object in this struggle is to save the Union; and is not either to save or to destroy slavery. If I could save the Union without freeing any slave I would do it, and if I could save it by freeing all the slaves, I would do it; and if I could save it by freeing some and leaving others alone I would also do that. What I do about slavery, and the colored race, I do because I believe it helps to save the Union."

Open letter by Abraham Lincoln,
published in the *New York Tribune*
of August 23, 1862

The Indian government is well aware that thousands of children aged four to eleven are systematically exploited as forced labor.

Slavery today

In April 2006, the human rights organization Terre des Hommes published a report stating that even in this day and age, more than 12 million people worldwide are slaves. More than half of them are children and teenagers working forced labor in countries such as India, Bangladesh, and Pakistan. In industrial countries, the report continues, prostitutes are often little more than indentured servants, if not technically enslaved. Unfortunately, these well known facts have done little to prompt legal or social change, either in the developing world or countries like the United States and Russia. As long as there is demand for forced labor, and as long as keeping costs low is paramount, this horrific state of affairs is unlikely to change. In addition, many children, especially in Africa, are little more than slaves after rebel groups transform them into child soldiers. While human rights organizations have long called attention to particularly insidious types of abuse, there has been little improvement. Slavery may proved to be the most difficult of human evils to eradicate.

Shipped like cattle

In the summer of 1700, the English slave ship *Henrietta Marie* sank about 30 miles off Key West, Florida. A few days earlier, on May 18th, the ship had made harbor at Port Royal, Jamaica. The two cargo decks aboard the sailing ship had been loaded with more than 300 men, women, and children, all of them slaves purchased on the African west coast. According to estimates, the ship was not even close to its full capacity; it could easily have carried 400 slaves. Slaves were usually captured by other Africans, often by enemy tribes, and forcibly marched to the coastal ports. There, European slave traders paid for the slaves with glass beads, tools, copper or iron bars.

Before the *Henrietta Marie* had made port, Captain Thomas Chamberlain would have had the slaves prepared for sale. They would have been brought up on deck, where they would be scrubbed, shaved, oiled, and have their wounds treated. They would then be taken ashore naked and in chains. Potential buyers would inspect them like cattle, feeling their bellies, examining their teeth, and smelling and tasting their sweat because it was believed that disease could be detected by taste and odor.

Hundreds of Africans were packed in cargo holds with a mere 5 square feet of space allotted per individual on the lower decks of slave ships.

Slavery was an exceptionally high-profit business. Estimates place the revenues from one cargo load at more than 3,000 pounds sterling, which would be around $595,000 in today's currency. The majority of the slaves would then be sent to work either on sugarcane plantations in Jamaica or on cotton plantations in the American Southeast. Their average life expectancy after sale was just five to ten years. The slaves sold, the *Henrietta Marie* departed from Jamaica with a cargo of sugar, cotton, precious tropical woods, and indigo, all purchased with the profits from the sale of the cargo of slaves. On the way back to England, however, the *Henrietta Marie* ran aground and sank. Everyone on board perished.

Sailing into certain death

In 1972, the American diver and treasure seeker Mel Fisher came across the shipwreck of *Henrietta Marie*, but because the ship had not carried any gold, he was not particularly interested in it. It was not investigated more closely until 1983, when the American archeol-

Storing slaves on a slave deck. When the Danish slave ship Kron-Printzen *sank in a storm in 1706, all 820 of the slaves chained in the hold went down with the ship.*

A group of African-American slaves in front of the cabin where they lived. Living conditions were often almost insufferable.

ogist David Moore identified it as a slave ship by the great number of iron shackles scattered across the seabed. The English sailing ship *Henrietta Marie* is the oldest slave shipwreck ever recovered. It was not the only slave ship to sink, of course, and England was not the only nation profiting from the trade in human lives. In 1706, for example, the Danish slave ship *Kron-Printzen* sank in a storm. The seriously overloaded vessel went down with its cargo of 820 slaves still chained in the hold. Needless to say, they all drowned.

Worth less than the food they consumed

The European discovery and colonization of America had greatly increased the demand for a cheap labor force in the New World. At first, it was the original inhabitants of the newly colonized lands who were enslaved. The Native Americans, however, were weak, decimated by diseases like smallpox and measles that came to the New World with the Europeans. The centuries-old solution was to provision cheap labor for the colonies in the form of imported slaves from Africa. Approximately 750,000 African slaves were transported to the Spanish colonies during the sixteenth and seventeenth centuries.

The conditions on the slave ships were so incompatible with human life that some estimates suggest that twice this number of potential slaves perished during the journey across the Atlantic. Slave traders looked at this loss of human life as a kind of selection process that ensured that only the strongest slaves would make it to the new countries. It was also more profitable for the slave traders to save money during the several weeks of an Atlantic crossing by taking along as little food as they possibly could. In a sense, the slaves' lives were worth less than the food required to keep them alive during that passage. After all, slaves only gained value at the moment of their sale in the Americas.

When steam engines were introduced on the plantations during the early years of the Industrial Revolution, working conditions for the slaves actually worsened. They had to adapt the pace of their work to the much faster machines. Living in rudimentary shacks and undernourished, being forced to work more and more hours to keep up with machines such as the cotton gin led to a decrease in the life expectancy of slaves by several years.

Black slaves being unloaded from the American ship Wyandotte *in Key West, Florida. The* Wyandotte *was one of many illegal slave ships that continued to smuggle slaves after their import was banned in the late 18th century.*

Uncle Tom's Cabin

In 1852, Harriet Beecher-Stowe (1811–1896) published her novel Uncle Tom's Cabin, *one of the first to deal directly with the issue of slavery. Beecher-Stowe's book was met with some hostility, especially in the South, where she was accused of fabrication and lies. Her research, however, was sound. Abraham Lincoln (1809–1865), the sixteenth American President, reportedly said to the author: "So you are the little lady who wrote the book that started this great war." Shortly after the end of the Civil War Lincoln was shot and killed by John Wilkes Booth, a supporter of the Southern cause dissatisfied with the war's outcome.*

A Sea of Flames on the East River

THE SINKING OF THE GENERAL SLOCUM

New Yorkers, when asked about the city's greatest disaster prior to the destruction of the World Trade Center's twin towers on September 11, 2001, will reply without hesitation that it was the sinking of the paddle steamer *General Slocum*. On June 15, 1904, a fire broke out aboard the steam cruiser while it was traveling upstream on the East River with more than 1,300 passengers on board. The fire quickly burned out of control. The great majority of the passengers lost their lives, either by drowning in the river or burning to death.

A German church takes an excursion

Around the turn of the century, the area that we now know as the East Village on the Lower East Side of New York was called "Klein-deutschland" (Little Germany). More than 80,000 German immigrants had settled there. The neighborhood had its own German the-aters, bookstores, grocery stores, beer gardens, butchers' shops, sports clubs, churches, and synagogues. Every year in June, St. Mark's Lutheran Church on East 6th Street organized an excursion to mark the end of Sunday school for the summer.

Usually, the congregation rented a boat to take members of the church on an excursion to

Fire fighters tried to extinguish the fire on the General Slocum, *but for the 1,021 victims, help came too late. The fire hoses aboard the ship were later found to have been defective.*

a recreation area where they would swim, picnic, play games, and generally enjoy themselves. On June 15, 1904, the paddle steamer *General Slocum* was hired for this purpose. The ship, named after Union General Henry Warner Slocum (1827–1894), was 250 feet long and licensed to carry 3,000 passengers. On that day in June, it was bound for the picnic gardens of Locust Grove on Long Island.

The steamboat embarked around 9:00 a.m., chugging along upstream. The deck was crowded with children playing, while the adults listened to a band playing German songs. The river was filled with a variety of ships of all shapes and sizes.

Completely unprepared for emergencies

Around 9:30 a.m., just as the ship was passing East 90th Street, a member of the crew spotted a fire in a cargo compartment below deck. The blaze spread rapidly. When the sailors, who had never been trained for such an emergency, reached for the fire hoses, they were so old and brittle that they burst in their hands the minute the water was turned on. Captain William Van Schaick was first informed of the problem 10 minutes after the fire had broken out, well after the first attempts at extinguishing the blaze had failed. By that time, the ship found itself in a narrow section of the East River

The fire on the General Slocum *started in the cargo room and spread rapidly. Panic broke out on board.*

The General Slocum *was a popular excursion boat with a capacity of up to 3,000 passengers.*

A group of experts investigating the burnt-out remains of the General Slocum. 1,021 people died on the ship on June 15, 1904.

When the paint ignited, the paddle steamer erupted in flames. Passengers began to jump overboard after clinging to the railing as long as they could. When their strength was exhausted, they simply let go, falling into the river and drowning. The crewmen, unprepared for the emergency, abandoned ship, having provided no assistance whatsoever to the passengers. The 3,000 cork life jackets on board fell to pieces when the desperate passengers tried to use them. Anyone who managed to put one on sank at once due to the extra weight. Stuck to the ship because of the fresh paint, the lifeboats could not be lowered. Ropes became tangled because the winches were broken. When the ship finally reached North Brother Island, the fire had engulfed the entire vessel. The few remaining people on board were crammed into the corners of the ship that the fire had not yet reached.

known as Hell Gate because of its treacherous currents. Large oil tanks lined the riverbank piers. Afraid of landing and causing an explosion at the piers, the captain decided, in spite of shouts that he should make land as quickly as possible, to instead set course at full speed for North Brother Island, which was approximately 1 mile away.

Panic on board

Panic broke out on board. Very few of the passengers could swim. Parents called for their children, and men and women for their spouses. Later investigations would show that the ship had been painted with a highly flammable paint a few days before the accident.

At the time, North Brother Island was home to the city's quarantine hospital. Nurses and doctors saw the burning ship approaching and rushed to the rescue with ladders to hold out to people trying to make it to shore. The captain and some of the passengers could be rescued. Within minutes, the fire had burned itself out, and what remained of the *General Slocum* keeled over and sank.

Rescue workers wept helplessly as they looked upon the horrific scene of the disaster. A

total of 1,021 people, many of them children, had drowned or burned to death. It is assumed that the actual number of victims was even higher, since children younger than a year old did not require a ticket and were not included in the passenger lists.

In search of those responsible for the catastrophe

In the week after the accident, thousands of people walked by rows of laid-out corpses to identify them. Some had lost their entire families. Many of the bodies were burnt beyond recognition. Sixty-one victims never were identified, and were interred in a mass grave in Queens. News of the catastrophe spread rapidly and money was raised for the survivors.

In the investigations that followed the accident, authorities had to respond to the bitter question of how it was possible that a tragedy of such proportions could occur a mere 650 feet from shore. Just one month prior to the fire, the *General Slocum* had been inspected and declared to be safe and in perfect condition by Captain Van Schaick and the city's inspector in charge of river vessels. Investigators had many questions for the captain. Why had he not docked the ship at one of the riverside piers? Why did he keep going upstream while the fire spread? How was it possible that the crew was not trained at all for an emergency? Why did he survive when so many others died?

These and other questions are the kind that consistently come up in the wake of a disaster. People will always try to understand the incomprehensible, yet the answers are too often the

Dockworkers walk among the victims of the catastrophe, the greatest disaster ever to hit New York prior to the destruction of the World Trade Center a century later.

Making passenger ships safer
In the aftermath of the disaster, US president Theodore Roosevelt (1858–1919) mandated the following safety measures for passenger steamers: each ship was required to have fireproof doors for controlling blazes, automatic fire extinguishing systems on board, better life jackets (at least one per passenger and crew member), fire hoses capable of withstanding a specified water pressure, and lifeboats that were easily accessible and functioning.

same. As with so many other catastrophes, at the heart of the *General Slocum* disaster lay human error. The jury sentenced Captain Van Schaick, the most obvious scapegoat, to ten years of forced labor at the notorious Sing Sing prison for criminal negligence and other violations. Van Schaick had spent three years in this prison when President William H. Taft (1857–1930) commuted his sentence. The captain never recovered, and suffered severe depression the rest of his life.

Divers salvaged bodies from the wreck of the General Slocum. Overall, 175 bodies were recovered from inside the hull.

The End of a Luxury Liner

THE SINKING OF THE TITANIC

At 11:40 p.m. on April 14, 1912, during her maiden voyage from Southampton, England to New York, New York, the super liner *Titanic* collided with an iceberg southeast of Newfoundland. Just two hours and forty minutes later, the most luxurious ocean liner ever built sank into the North Atlantic Ocean. The sinking of the *Titanic* was the largest-scale nautical disaster prior to World War II. Of the 2,208 passengers and crew, 1,504 perished.

The Titanic *leaving Southampton on her maiden voyage into disaster. Just eleven months earlier, she had been launched from Belfast docks, Ireland.*

Who has the speediest ship?

The RMS *Titanic* was part of American banker J. P. Morgan's White Star Line. She and her sister ships, the *Olympic*, which had passed her maiden voyage eight months earlier, and the *Gigantic* (later the *Britannic*), which was still being planned at the time of the tragic incident, would take turns plying the route between Southampton, England, Cherbourg, France, and New York City. All three of these top-of-the-line steamships were classified as RMS (Royal Mail Ships) and could thus transport mail. The contracts with Royal Mail offered additional profit for the shipping company.

Until World War I, the great international shipping companies, mirroring the arms race on the national level, were engaged in fierce competition as to who owned the fastest and most magnificent ship. The three ship designers who created the *Titanic* had designed her not to be the fastest ship, but rather to be the biggest, safest, and, above all, the most luxurious ship afloat. The press applauded the ship as a technological marvel and her safety equipment as the world's most advanced: the *Titanic* was considered, quite simply, to be unsinkable.

The most splendid first class in the world

The steam liner's launch took place on May 31, 1911 in Belfast, Ireland. In the year before her maiden voyage, the construction of the interior and the decoration were progressing at high speed. The ship was registered with British authorities for a total capacity of 3,300 passengers, not including the crew. However, because of the luxurious and spacious interiors of the first class, the *Titanic* actually only had room for 2,400 passengers, 750 of whom could travel first class. These figures show the privileged status of first-class accommodation aboard the *Titanic*. The super liner not only offered spacious suites, but also amenities including a squash court, an onboard swimming pool, splendid smoking and dining halls, libraries, coffee houses, a promenade deck, and private decks that belonged to the suites. Second-class accommodation on the *Titanic* offered the level of comfort found in the first-class sections of older ships. Even in its third-class accommodations, the *Titanic* set new standards: where other ships had had large dormitory style rooms, the *Titanic* boasted passenger rooms for four, with one double bed and one set of bunk beds. The voyage was intended to be comfortable even for second and third class passengers, not least because emigrants to America were the most secure source of income. Rates for a third-class room started at $36, and second-class cabins were available from $60.

Only half booked for her maiden voyage

At the beginning of the nineteenth century, a ship's maiden voyage was a great social event, and thus many passengers aboard the *Titanic*

Chief Purser Hugh Walter McElroy (left) and Captain Edward J. Smith on the Titanic.

Technical specs for the Titanic

Ship type: passenger steamer
Class: Olympic
Purpose: transatlantic liner
Capacity: 46,329 GRT
Displacement: 53,147 t
Length: 882 ft 9 in
Beam: 92 ft 6 in
Draft (at 52,310 long tons): 34 ft 7 in
Height (keel to rim of funnel): 183 ft 8 in
Propulsion and engines: three propellers, two four-cylinder piston steam engines, one low-pressure Parsons turbine
Power: 51,000 hp/38 MW (registered)
Speed: 21 knots (ca. 24 mph)
Consumption: 6,700 tons coal storage capacity; daily consumption: ca. 630 tons
Passengers: First Class: 750, Second Class: 550, Third Class: 1,100
Crew: 897
Construction cost: £1.5 million (ca. $400 million current purchasing power)

Even so, the majestic liner was only a little more than half booked for her maiden sailing. Many people had decided against a trip on the *Titanic* because of a strike in the coal industry, with the result that a mere 1,311 passengers were on board the "largest ship in the world," as she was billed in advertisements, plus 897 crew members, 500 of whom tended to the passengers, while the rest took care of running the ship.

Accompanied by great fanfare and the sound of an orchestra playing—no expense was spared on the occasion of her send-off—the *Titanic* departed from Southampton on the 10th of April 1912, a legend even before her first voyage.

Apparent post-collision stability

Only four days after her departure, at approximately 11:40 p.m., the *Titanic*'s maiden voyage came to an abrupt end when an iceberg was spotted directly ahead by the lookouts, who consequently rang the alarm bell three times. Meanwhile, an officer on duty had already spotted the iceberg himself and had initiated an evasive maneuver. This failed, however, because the *Titanic* was already too close to change its course. At undiminished cruise speed, the ocean liner's starboard side hit the sharp-edged block of ice. One of the firefighters on board would later liken the sound of the collision to the sound of cotton being torn apart. The consequences of the impact were severe; ice-cold water began to pour into the hull. Initially, the foundering could be slowed down by pumps working at full speed, but even so, during the first hour alone about 25,000 tons of water burst into the ship.

In addition to the decks and storage rooms, this cutaway sketch shows the probable spot where the iceberg breached the Titanic.

were not really travelers. People whose main purpose was to cross the Atlantic generally traveled in second and third class, while the majority of the deluxe suites, priced at $4,350, were booked for the pleasure of participating in history by a number of the rich and famous of European and American high society. Among these, the list of distinguished passengers included Isidor Strauss, owner of Macy's department store in New York City; multimillionaire John Jacob Astor IV; writer Jacques Futrelle; Texan oil millionaire Margaret Brown; American actress Dorothy Gibson; and John B. Thayer, the railway magnate.

Although the first five anti-flood compartments were almost completely filled with water, the *Titanic* appeared to maintain its stability, and most of the passengers did not yet perceive the situation as threatening. During the next 60 minutes, an additional 3,000 tons of water flooded into the ship—and still the illusion of stability persisted. But then, all of a sudden, the secondary flooding set in: water began to enter in huge quantities through openings that were never intended to be waterproof, such as scuttles, hatches, and ports, which by now were below the water line. The unstoppable process of sinking then sped up enormously, and 40 minutes later, the *Titanic* was gone.

An unsinkable ship needs fewer lifeboats

The *Titanic* was considered the safest ship ever built, and as a result, she only carried twenty lifeboats, with capacity for about half of the people on board. Constructors, the ship's owners, and public authorities had consciously planned, or at least tolerated, this discrepancy: since the ship was deemed

Titanic was considered the safest ship ever—a fatal delusion that contributed to the insufficient number of lifeboats on board.

A painting of the Titanic sinking off the coast of Newfoundland.

Eyewitness account

"Suddenly a queer quivering ran under me, apparently the whole length of the ship. Startled by the very strangeness of the shivering motion, I sprang to the floor. With too perfect a trust in that mighty vessel I again lay down. Someone knocked at my door, and the voice of a friend said: 'Come quickly to my cabin, an iceberg has just passed our window; I know we have just struck one.' No confusion, no noise of any kind, one could believe no danger imminent. ...Our lifeboat, with thirty-six in it, began lowering to the sea. This was done amid the greatest confusion. Rough seamen all giving different orders. No officer aboard. As only one side of the ropes worked, the lifeboat at one time was in such a position that it seemed we must capsize in mid-air. At last the ropes worked together, and we drew nearer and nearer the black, oily water. The first touch of our lifeboat on that black sea came to me as a last goodbye to life, and so we put off—a tiny boat on a great sea—rowed away from what had been a safe home for five days."

Elizabeth Shutes,
first class passenger

unsinkable, it did not need more lifeboats—or so the fatal line of reasoning. The lifeboats the *Titanic* did carry were mainly intended for saving survivors of other ships in distress. Moreover, lifeboats required space, and that space was instead used for the promenade deck, private decks, and suites. The *Titanic* was originally intended to carry sixty-four lifeboats, but Bruce Ismay, chairman and director of the White Star Line, had campaigned for these to be reduced by half in order to guarantee a better view from the promenade deck. Moreover, he argued, it was unwise to upset passengers who had paid for the luxury of traveling on an unsinkable ship by the sight of too many lifeboats. In the end, the number of lifeboats was reduced to twenty.

The Carpathia receives Titanic's distress call and comes to the rescue

Shortly after midnight, Captain Edward J. Smith consulted with Thomas Andrews, one of the shipbuilders on board. After inspecting the damage, Andrews, exasperated with his failure, had no choice but to predict the quick and inevitable sinking of the ship. Smith then gave the orders to send out distress calls around 12:15 a.m. Later that night, Captain Smith voluntarily stayed with his ship and drowned.

The *Carpathia* was the first to reply to *Titanic*'s distress signals and changed her course to come to the rescue, even though it took her four hours to reach the scene of the disaster. Meanwhile, most first class passengers refused to don life vests: since they could not perceive any tilt of the ship, they did not believe they were in an emergency situation. Sixty-five minutes after the collision, the first lifeboat was lowered. The idea of women and children first did not apply on the *Titanic* that fateful night. Rather, being rescued became a matter of what side of the ship passengers happened to be on and what class they had booked. Some port side officers determinedly imposed the "no men" principle, accepting that this resulted in half-full lifeboats being lowered when there were no more women willing to get on—people found it hard to believe that something so terrible was

A lifeboat is picked up by the Carpathia, *which arrived at the scene of disaster two hours after* Titanic's *last distress call. By this time, the* Titanic *had already sunk.*

The Titanic's *grand dining hall. The ship was considered not only the world's safest, but also the most splendid.*

actually happening. One survivor reported that it took great persuasion to get her 13-year-old son into a boat, as the officer on duty considered him a man. It was easier for men to get into a lifeboat on the starboard side, where many more lives were saved than on the port side. Tragically, though there was lifeboat capacity for 1,178 people, only 705 used them. While the tragedy unfolded, Wallace Hartley, conductor of the ship's orchestra, ordered the musicians to play entertaining music in order to keep people calm. However, when both the passengers and crew realized that the unthinkable was actually happening, they were seized with panic. The ship had been flooded with some 40,000 tons of water, the decks were awash, the funnels were collapsing, and at about 2:18 a.m., the uneven weight of the water burst the hull in two. The bow sank instantly. The stern reared straight up in the air, and at 2:20 a.m., it sank, vertically, to a depth of 12,500 feet.

At 4:10 a.m., the *Carpathia* rescued a total of 705 survivors, but 1,522 people lost their lives in the catastrophe, dying in the ice-cold waters. Arthur Rostron, captain of the *Carpathia*, was left with the tragic duty of recovering the dead still floating in the sea.

Who was to blame?

Few of the victims actually died as the boat sank. Most died in the water, of hypothermia. Apart from lack of experience in the use of lifeboats in an emergency situation, subsequent analyses and investigations blamed the high death toll on an insufficient number of lifeboats. Ever since the sinking of the *Titanic*, all ships have been required to carry enough lifeboats to provide space for every passenger on board.

The commission set up to clarify the issue of liability ultimately held the following to blame for the tragedy: William M. Murdoch, First Officer of the *Titanic*; Joseph Bruce Ismay, Manager of the White Star Line; and Stanley Lord, Captain of the SS *Californian*, a ship that allegedly passed by the *Titanic* in immediate proximity without coming to its aid. Captain Lord, however, denied these accusations throughout his life.

Relieved and cheerful friends and relatives of survivors of the Titanic *catastrophe during their arrival in Southampton.*

Auction sale of artifacts found in the Titanic wreck

On June 10, 2004, an auction was held at the South Street Seaport Museum in New York, in the vicinity of the Titanic *memorial. Finds from the legendary wreck of the ocean liner were for sale.*

Some interesting items among the hundreds for sale included:
- *Original menus: five items from the various restaurants and classes were up for sale*
- *White Star Line china*
- *Property from the luxury liner, including a lifeboat name plaque, a deck chair and a* Titanic *life jacket*
- *Rare photographs and autographs*
- *A collection of items relating to the life and death of John William Gill, one of the passengers*
- *Models of the ship*
- *Props from James Cameron's movie,* Titanic

OIL ON THE COASTS OF EUROPE

THE TANKERS TORREY CANYON AND AMOCO CADIZ POLLUTE THE ATLANTIC COAST

In March 1967, the first massive oil disaster in the history of tanker shipping struck a European coast. The *Torrey Canyon* hit a reef off the coast of England, causing an environmental catastrophe of unprecedented proportions. While maritime safety measures were increased on a global scale in the aftermath of that disaster, supertankers still remain a threat to the environment. Eleven years later, human failure led to the next enormous oil spill: the *Amoco Cadiz* sank off the coast of Brittany, badly polluting that coastline.

The Torrey Canyon accident

In 1967, a new kind of catastrophe reached the coasts of Europe. For some time, the industrial nations' rapidly growing demand for crude oil had made it necessary to build oil tankers of ever increasing size. The supertanker *Torrey Canyon* herself, built in 1959 with a capacity of 60,000 tons, had since been adapted to enable her to carry double her original cargo of crude oil, making the ship correspondingly cumbersome to navigate. Moreover, this enlargement made her a member of a class of ships which, according to international agreement, was only authorized to travel along certain routes that were considered particularly safe. Unfortunately, on March 18, 1967, the *Torrey Canyon* left the safe route owing to a navigational error, and then struck the notorious Seven Stones Reef off the coast of Land's End, the westernmost point of the English coastline. The ship sprang a leak and spilled 120,000 tons of oil into the Atlantic Ocean. For the first time in history, an oil spill polluted European shores.

The woefully inept response to the catastrophe

Even as the accident was taking place, a disastrous lack of experience in responding to this kind of environmental disaster became appallingly evident, as a series of attempts to control the damage actually resulted in compounding the problems. In the first instance, efforts were directed toward making the ship functional again. After several days of this unsuccessful endeavor, the ship broke apart while it was still impaled on the reef. Meanwhile, the oil layer on the sea continued to grow and grow, and also threatened coasts on both sides of the Channel: the Cornish coast in England and the coast of Normandy in France. An effort was therefore made to burn off the oil spill—but this did not have the intended effect, either. Finally, the British Army bombed the wreckage. In an attempt to break up the oil slick, extensive use of detergents was made—but this turned out to be even more detrimental to marine life than the oil itself.

About a week after the accident, the Torrey Canyon *broke into two halves while still stranded on the Seven Stones reef off the coast of Cornwall.*

The bow of the stricken supertanker Amoco Cadiz *projects from the water like the mouth of a gigantic whale.*

The Suez Canal and supertankers

The Suez Canal is a link between the Indian Ocean and the Mediterranean Sea. After World War II, it became the ideal route for transporting crude oil from oil producing regions on the Arab peninsula to industrial consumers in Europe in a quick and inexpensive manner. However, the dimensions of the canal made it necessary to introduce a size limit for ships.

From June 5–10, 1967, during the Six Day War between Israel and its Arab neighbors Egypt, Syria, and Jordan, the Suez Canal became the front line between Israel and Egypt. Ships that sank in the canal in during the clashes made it impassable, and eight years passed before the wrecks were salvaged, thus clearing the passage so that it could be reopened for international shipping.

Around this time ocean carriers started building supertankers, because oil from the Arab countries now had to be shipped to Europe by the circuitous southern route around the African continent. Using this route, which was much longer, profitability could only be achieved by employing very large tankers, and this was attractive since the size limitations for the Suez Canal no longer applied. The world's largest tanker in 1955, the Al Malik Saud Al Awal, *could carry 47,000 tons of crude oil. The world's largest ship fifty years later, the tanker* Jahre Viking, *had a capacity over ten times higher: 564,673 tons.*

The Alaskan oil spill

Until 1989, the USA was spared big tanker accidents. That year, however, oil spills reached American shores. The supertanker Exxon Valdez *had picked up oil from the Alaska Pipeline and embarked on her southbound journey on March 24, 1989. Shortly after midnight, an inexperienced third mate found himself alone behind the wheel, while the captain lay drunk in his berth. He made a mistake, and the tanker left its planned route and struck a reef at full speed. Some 40,000 tons of crude oil spilled into the sea, polluting about 1,250 miles of Alaska's coast. Hundreds of thousan[ds] of marine animals and bird[s] died in this catastrophe, including twenty-two killer whales and about two hundred bald eagles, America's heraldic bird.*

The environmental repercussions of the accide[nt] are still being experienced today. An expedition by American chemists into the disaster area found that the[re] are still approximately 26,5[00] gallons of oil in the sea. The ship's captain, who had bee[n] intoxicated when the accide[nt] happened, got away with paying a $5,000 fine.

Consequences of the first oil spill

The situation after these misguided efforts was shocking: 120 miles of the English coast and 50 miles of the French coast were badly contaminated. More than 15,000 sea birds died an agonizing death, and countless marine organisms were destroyed. Europe, however, had been stirred. From that point forward, the general public took greater interest in environmental health issues. Legal provisions for the operation and traffic of tankers was tightened significantly, and eventually, in 1973, an international agreement was passed. MARPOL73, the International Convention for the Prevention of Marine Pollution from Ships, is internationally recognized and still in force today.

The next apocalypse

In spite of tightened international regulations, supertankers remain environmental time bombs. Their impact depends not only on technology, but also on human action in emergencies. In the early hours of March 16, 1978, some 15 miles off the Breton coast, the rudder unit of the tanker *Amoco Cadiz* failed. The tanker, which carried 223,000 tons of crude oil, drifted helplessly. In the teeth of strong west winds pushing

Despite the bombing of the ship by the Royal Navy, part of the Torrey Canyon *still had not sunk on March 30, 1967.*

the tanker toward the coast, the crew initially tried to repair the rudder unit themselves. Almost two hours after the failure, the captain finally requested a tugboat to help move the ship's bow into the wind so it could steer away from the coast independently. Unfortunately, the requested tug was not powerful enough to bring the supertanker into the right position, and a stronger boat arrived on the scene too late. At 9:00 p.m., the *Amoco Cadiz* ran into a rock off

Two weeks after the Amoco Cadiz *broke apart, the Breton coast was completely polluted by oil. Volunteer helpers fought a desperate battle.*

the French coast. While the crew could be successfully rescued by helicopter, the tanker broke apart the same night. A 225-mile stretch of the Breton coast was contaminated by crude oil, and about 28 million sea animals—fish, mussels, conches, and more—died in a single day.

Major oil spills

YEAR	SHIP	COAST	OIL SPILLED
1967	Torrey Canyon	Cornwall (England)	120,000 t
1976	Urquillo	North Spain	100,000 t
1978	Amoco Cadiz	Brittany (France)	230,000 t
1978	Andros Patria	North Spain	50,000 t
1992	Aegean Sea	North Spain	70,000 t
1996	Sea Empress	Wales (England)	147,000 t
1999	Erika	Brittany (France)	20,000 t
2002	Prestige	Spain	77,000 t

Spilled oil coats and congeals the feathers of sea birds, which is why these creatures die in enormous numbers in the aftermath of an oil spill.

Towboats held the
capsized ferry in
position while
rescue teams
searched for
victims.

FATAL NEGLIGENCE

THE HERALD OF FREE ENTERPRISE

On the evening of March 6, 1987, the channel
ferry *Herald of Free Enterprise* left the Belgian
port of Zeebrugge. Only 15 minutes into her
journey, she capsized after hitting a sand bank
just outside the mouth of the harbor. In spite
of immediate rescue operations, 193 people
died in the ice-cold waters of the English
Channel. Water had entered the ferry's cargo
doors, which had not been closed, causing the
ship to sink within minutes.

The departure of the RORO ferry from Zeebrugge

Ferry traffic between the Belgian port of Zeebrugge and the English port of Dover is a routine operation. Several times a day, the so-called RORO ferries (short for "roll-on/roll-off") make the trip back and forth across the English Channel. These ferries are designed to allow vehicles to drive into the ship's hold on one side and exit through the other side at the destination port, thus avoiding time-consuming maneuvers during the loading and unloading process. Although the enormous doors at the ship's bow and stern are secured during the voyage, the hold of a RORO ferry such as the *Herald of Free Enterprise* cannot be divided into compartments by bulkheads. This means that any water that enters the ship can immediately flood the vehicle deck.

One seaman was asleep

At the time of the accident, the *Herald of Free Enterprise* had been in service as a cross-channel ferry for seven years. At 7:10 p.m. on March 6, 1987, the ferry slowly backed out of the narrow dock of the Zeebrugge port. Its bow doors were still open, which was standard oper-

ating procedure at cast off so that the vehicles' exhaust would have a chance to dissipate. At the mouth of the harbor, the ferry turned around and continued to travel toward the entrance of the port at full speed.

That day, only 459 passengers and eighty crewmen were on board a ship that was designed to carry as many as 1,300 passengers. The vehicle deck carried eighty-one cars, three buses, and forty-seven trucks. The ferry's first officer was in charge of closing the bow doors. According to regulations, he was required to be present on the bridge when the ship was casting off. The bow doors, however, were not visible from the bridge, and since the ferry lacked control lights on the bridge to confirm that the door had been shut, the first officer had delegated the task of checking the doors to a lower ranking seaman. On the evening of March 6,

The catastrophe happened so suddenly and quickly that not a single lifeboat could be deployed.

An eyewitness account

One survivor reported that her husband volunteered to act as a living bridge to allow her and her daughter to climb off the ship. Once they were safe, she begged him to join them, but he replied that there were others in need of his help. She never saw him again.

Seven weeks after the catastrophe, the Herald of Free Enterprise *was righted and towed back to the port of Zeebrugge.*

1987, however, that seaman was on break and asleep in his cabin at the time of departure. There was no one present to notice that the ferry was accelerating at full speed with her bow doors still open.

The ferry begins to list

Water immediately began rushing into the vehicle deck. Some of the truck drivers who had remained in their vehicles would later report two seamen frantically beating the half-closed bow doors with sledgehammers. Apparently, something had jammed, preventing the hydraulic system from closing the doors completely. The truck drivers, wading through knee-high water, tried to escape to the upper deck. At 7:35 p.m., the ferry capsized within 2 minutes, as if struck by a blow from a giant fist. The fact that the ferry had not yet left the sand banks just outside the port's entrance turned out to be a blessing in disguise. The *Herald of Free Enterprise* capsized portside in the shallow water (30 feet), on its side like a stranded whale.

RORO ferries allow for quick crossings of the English Channel. However, the price for the comfort and speed is a higher safety risk.

No time for a distress call

The catastrophe hit the ship so fast that Captain David Lewry had no time to even send a mayday call. When the vehicles began crashing into each other and the lights went out, the passengers on the decks above panicked. The disaster took place within a mere 2 sea miles of the coast, but many of those who died were killed immediately by the impact of the ferry colliding with the sandbar.

The Belgian freighter *Seahorse* was near the scene of the accident, having departed from the docks at Zeebrugge right behind the *Herald of Free Enterprise*. The *Seahorse* began sending distress signals, bringing the first rescue helicopters to the scene just 16 minutes after the disaster. Survivors were flown ashore without delay. Thanks to the cool-headed reactions of the crew and the efforts of a few courageous passengers, more than 400 people could be saved. However, 193 people did not survive the catastrophe. Those not killed by the collision itself died from hypothermia. It is thought that many perished within seconds of entering the icy water. American scientists looking into the reasons for their quick deaths concluded that the cold experienced when a person is plunged into 37.5 °F water triggered hyperventilation, which led to the inhaling of sea water and death by drowning.

The Sheen Report

Following the capsizing of the *Herald of Free Enterprise*, there was a public investigation into the causes of the accident. The findings were published in the Sheen Report in July of 1987. The shipping company Townsend Thorensen was reproached for negligence on many levels. Townsend Thorensen was not only confronted for negligence in handling the high-risk RORO technology, but also for the lack of reliable and complete passenger lists. At the time of the accident, it was not even possible to determine how many people had been on board the ferry.

The Sheen Report's recommendations for improved safety measures were put into practice very slowly. Soon after the sinking, the *Herald of Free Enterprise* was salvaged and towed back to Zeebrugge. There, she was renamed *Flushing Range* and made ready for her final journey to India, where she was dismantled. Her sister ship, *Spirit of Free Enter-*

prise, was also re-named, so as not to scare off future passengers. Under her new name, *Pride of Brugge*, the ferry is still in service on the English Channel.

Many of the victims never had a chance to leave the sinking ship.

Musicians respond
Shortly after the catastrophe, a number of well-known pop musicians joined former Beatle Paul McCartney to form a group named "Ferry Aid." They recorded a new version of the Beatles song "Let it Be" that was a Number 1 hit in the British charts for three weeks. The revenue was donated to the friends and relatives of the victims. Later, British singer-songwriter Robb Johnson wrote the song "Herald of Free Enterprise" about the disaster.

A Cold Death in the Baltic Sea

THE UNSOLVED SINKING OF THE ESTONIA

In the early hours of September 28, 1994, the automobile and passenger ferry *Estonia* sank in a stormy Baltic Sea. Eigh hundred fifty-two people perished in what came to be known as the worst ship disaster in post-war European history. The ferry was traveling on her regular route from Tallinn, Estonia to Stockholm, Sweden. Officially, the *Estonia*'s bow door broke off, and the subsequent inrush of water sank her. Even today, however, speculations abound that the actual causes of the catastrophe have been obscured.

The last voyage

On the evening of September 27, 1994, the cruise ferry *Estonia* was loaded in the harbor of the Estonian capital, Tallinn. Her destination was Stockholm, the Swedish capital, and the scheduled traveling time was approximately fifteen hours. The ferry was only half booked on that day: documentation records 803 passengers, 186 crew members, and 100 vehicles.

Two months after the Estonia sank, her bow door was salvaged from the bottom of the sea.

One of the survivors later reported that the harbor had been locked down immediately prior to the ferry's departure, and that two sizeable trailer trucks, escorted by a military convoy, were directed toward the ship. According to this survivor's report, the loading ramp and the ship's bow door were only closed after those two trucks had been unloaded. The *Estonia* departed on her last voyage at 7:15 p.m., about 15 minutes behind schedule.

The sinking

The Baltic Sea was rough and ice-cold on that autumn night. The waves were 13–20 feet high, and the water temperature was no more than a chilly 50°F. After midnight, the *Estonia* began to pitch violently, with waves crashing over her bow. At about 12:45 a.m., passengers heard thuds and noises that differed markedly from the relatively constant sound of breakers crashing against the ship. Within half an hour, so much water had entered the ship that she tilted at a 25° angle. It appears that the ferry's bow visor had broken off, and the loading ramp behind the visor—designed to function as a safety barrier—could not prevent the inrush of water. At 1:22 a.m., the ship sent out the first Mayday call, and the onboard alarm called the crew to man the lifeboat stations. When the second Mayday call went out two minutes later, however, the *Estonia* was already listing at an angle of 45°, making it nearly impossible to move about the ship and reach the lifeboats. From that point onward, the catastrophe rapidly ran its course. By 1:48 a.m., *Estonia* had already disappeared from radar screens: she had sunk in the 260-foot-deep, icy cold Baltic Sea.

A hopeless rescue operation

The Baltic Sea has a relatively high frequency of shipping traffic, and eleven ships heard the second distress call sounded by the *Estonia*. Rescue operations began at once. About an hour after the sinking, the first ships arrived at the scene of the accident—but even that brief period was too long to survive in the cold sea. Many passengers who were able to abandon ship in time succumbed to hypothermia either in the water itself or in the cold winds aboard

The Estonia

The Estonia *was built in 1980 at the Meyer-Werft shipyard in Papenburg, Germany. For her first twelve years, under the names of* Viking Sally, Silja Star, *and* Wasa King, *she served various ocean carriers on the Baltic Sea. From 1992 onward she was in operation for a joint Swedish-Estonian venture, cruising between Tallinn and Stockholm under the name* Estonia. *At the time, the ferry was the largest and most modern ship operating under the Estonian flag. She was a RORO ferry (roll-on/roll-off), allowing vehicles to drive onto the cargo decks through massive bow and stern doors and leave the ship without having to reverse. Since there are no bulkheads between the cargo decks, any inrush of water would immediately lead to dangerous listing.*

Because of this safety hazard, the Estonia *was supposed to serve only in safe waters and on short distances of no more than 23 miles. Regulating authorities, however, had been tolerating* Estonia's *use on significantly longer routes for fourteen years.*

the life rafts. Most of the passengers, however, were not able to leave the rapidly sinking ship in the first place; they were dragged to the bottom of the sea along with the ferry. No fewer

Survivors were rescued and flown to nearby hospitals by Navy rescue helicopters.

Many of the passengers who managed to get onto lifeboats froze to death in the ice-cold wind before rescue teams arrived.

than 852 people lost their lives, making the *Estonia* accident the deadliest shipping disaster in post-war European history. Only 137 people managed to survive the catastrophe.

Curious inconsistencies

Soon after the accident, an official commission investigated the causes and details of the catastrophe. The commission's conclusions boiled down to an unfortunate combination of constructional flaws and stormy weather. In an attempt to mount a defense against the charges of constructional flaws, Meyer-Werft tried to perform their own analyses, only to discover that important evidence was withheld from independent investigators. It is also worthy of note that the Swedish government commissioned a Dutch company specializing in the neutralization of underwater nuclear waste to seal the wreck in a concrete sarcophagus. This procedure would have made any future investigations impossible; however, it was never carried out.

The rampant rumors about the *Estonia* transporting secret military equipment could neither be proven nor convincingly rebutted. In September 2004, a Swedish TV broadcaster ran a report in which a retired Swedish customs officer claimed that the *Estonia* was, in fact, used for secret transports of Soviet military technology to the West, and that customs officers had been given orders to let certain vehicles pass without checking, even though all other vehicles boarding the *Estonia* were inspected quite thoroughly. Another thread that fuels the conspiracy theories concerns a mysterious black suitcase that rescue divers allegedly sought in the wreck. The existence of such a suitcase was later denied.

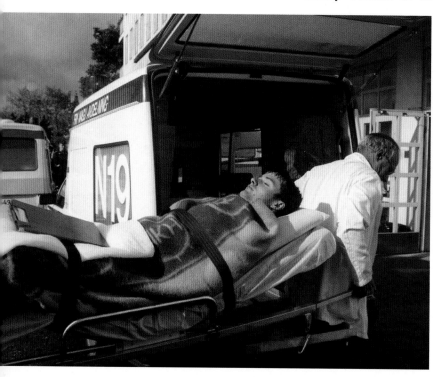

Only 137 of almost 1,000 people aboard the ferry survived this accident, making the sinking of the Estonia *the most severe ship catastrophe in European post-war history.*

The survivors who vanished

Finally, some relatives of those who died in the *Estonia* accident claimed that they received messages after the catastrophe stating that their spouses or children had survived the accident. Some survivors also confirm that the twins Hannely and Hannika Veide, for example, were able to board a lifeboat; the Swedish rescue headquarters also lists the twins among the survivors. They are among a group of people who, disturbingly, were initially recorded as survivors, but seem to have disappeared without a trace at some later stage.

In March 2006, a report by a new commission of inquiry was published that cast further doubt on the first commission's final and official report. The true causes of the catastrophe seem to be unclear to this day.

The map to the right illustrates the Estonia's route across the Baltic Sea. The circle indicates where the ferry sank.

The recovered victims of the tragedy were returned to their home countries. On October 20, 1994, a memorial service was held in Stockholm to commemorate the 28 Swedish passengers who died.

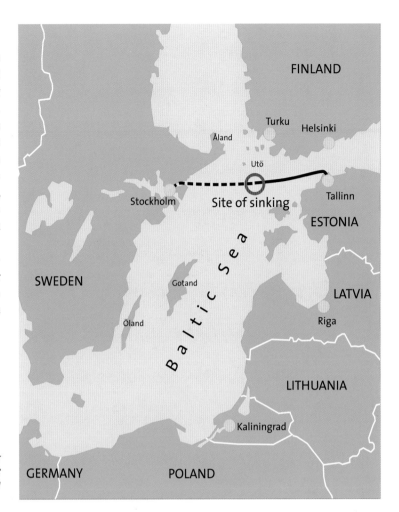

THE PRIDE OF THE RUSSIAN NAVY SINKS

THE NUCLEAR SUBMARINE KURSK EXPLODES

On August 12, 2000, the front section of the Russian nuclear submarine *Kursk* was completely destroyed by an explosion. A torpedo that had been readied for firing caught fire and exploded while still inside the boat. Of 118 crew members, only twenty-three survived the first minutes of the incident. While the world continued to hope for a miraculous rescue of these survivors for several days, it later turned out that only four hours after the accident, even those sailors had no chance of surviving. The pride of the Russian Navy sank to the bottom of the Barents Sea, claiming 118 lives.

Fleet maneuver

The Kursk was part of a naval unit within the Russian Northern Fleet. In August 2000, that unit participated in a maneuver in the Barents Sea.

On August 9, 2000, the Russian Northern Fleet set out for a maneuver in the Barents Sea, part of the Arctic Ocean. The exercise, during which new weapons were to be tested, involved some thirty battleships, including the heavy missile cruiser *Peter the Great*, the aircraft carrier *Admiral Kuznetsov*, and the pride of the Russian Navy, the nuclear submarine *Kursk*. With a length of 492 feet, the *Kursk* was twice as long as a jumbo jet. The gigantic submarine had the reputation of being unsinkable; it was said that not even a direct hit could destroy her. August 12th was expected to be a great day for the *Kursk*: the plan was to test a new, top-secret torpedo. For this reason, a number of distinguished guests were on board, including five high-ranking officers of the fleet's command. Since one of the *Kursk*'s functions was to destroy enemy aircraft carriers, she also carried guided cruise missiles bearing 1,500-pound warheads.

Underwater explosion

Four minutes prior to the explosion, the *Kursk* radio operator requested permission to fire from the Northern Fleet commander on board the missile cruiser *Peter the Great*. Permission was granted, and the commander of the *Kursk* issued the command.

At 9:30 a.m. CEST, Norwegian seismologists registered two explosions in the vicinity of the maneuver, about 112 miles northeast of the Russian seaport of Murmansk. Something had evidently gone wrong when the torpedo was fired. The missile may have had a constructional flaw, or the torpedo hatch may not

have opened properly. In either case, the missile's fuel exploded, killing seven seamen in the torpedo station compartment instantly. The commander immediately gave his final orders: to empty the ballast tanks and prepare for an emergency evacuation. Within a minute of the explosion, the submarine started surfacing at full speed, but no further orders were issued from the command center. Meanwhile, the enormously hot fire that raged in the torpedo compartment triggered the explosion of the torpedo's warhead. An explosion equivalent to 1 ton of TNT blasted away the entire forecastle. The shock wave of the explosion tore through the submarine with enormous force, killing the seventy-nine members of the crew in the first four compartments, including all the seamen on the bridge and in the radio room. Only the compartment containing the propulsion reactor was protected by a massive steel wall.

The Kursk was not reported as missing

At that point, the *Kursk* ceased to surface and instead began to sink rapidly toward the bottom of the sea. Three minutes after the explosion, she crashed onto the seabed, and further members of the crew died on impact. When the reactors shut down automatically, leaving the submarine lying immobilized under the sea, only twenty-three seamen were still alive. The survivors crawled to the back of the boat, where the remaining air had accumulated. The

air was so toxic that they could only survive wearing protection suits, which supplied air for up to four hours. When the emergency batteries failed, the ship went dark.

The Kursk *in her home port of Vidyayevo on the Kola Peninsula, a few months before she sank.*

Divers prepare to investigate the sunken wreck of the Kursk.

Above the water's surface, it seems that no one noticed the catastrophe. Since the *Kursk* had been scheduled to remain submerged for another three hours, she was not missed, and no search and rescue operation was initiated. About four hours after the first explosion, the remaining twenty-three survivors were dead, as well. Not one of the 118 people aboard had survived.

Political obstinacy

The Russian Navy only confirmed the sinking of the *Kursk* two days after the incident, and then initiated rescue operations, which were unsuccessful. After days of indecision, offers of support from Western countries, in particular England and the USA, were finally accepted. At the same time, fleet commanders hinted that the sinking was caused by a collision with a foreign submarine. Five days after the accident, Norwegian and British experts arrived on the scene of the disaster. On August 21st, deep-sea divers reached the wreck lying on the seabed about 328 feet under the sea, and the deaths of the entire crew were officially confirmed.

The salvage operation

In October 2000, the Norwegian diving platform *Regalia* finally arrived at the site of the accident. Russian and Norwegian divers began salvage efforts. They were able to confirm that the two nuclear reactors that had been propelling the *Kursk* posed no further danger, as had been feared; diving robots found no evidence of heightened radioactivity near the wreck. Working on the seabed, the salvage

---

The farewell letter

Divers found a farewell note in the pocket of the uniform jacket worn by Captain Lieutenant Dmitri Kolesnikov. The note begins by stating that all twenty-three survivors have gathered in the ninth compartment of the boat.

Then Kolesnikov wrote: "Mustn't despair. It's too dark to write, but I'll try by touch. It seems there is no chance, no more than 10–20%. We hope that at least someone will read this."

Officers carrying the coffin of a dead officer of the Kursk. The funeral took place on January 17, 2001 in St. Petersburg, over a year after the catastrophe took place.

workers cut access holes into the submarine's hull to facilitate the search for bodies inside the boat. Norwegian divers, however, could only work on the outside of the wreck. For reasons of military secrecy, only Russian divers were permitted to go inside. After salvaging twelve bodies, work was halted. It was not until May 2001 that Moscow officially confirmed what Western experts had suspected all along: it was not a collision with a NATO submarine that had caused the sinking of the *Kursk*, but the explosion of a torpedo inside the vessel. A Dutch salvaging company was contracted to recover the wreck and towed it to a dock in Murmansk, where the bodies of more than a hundred seamen were finally salvaged and laid to rest.

Grieving relatives visited the site of the disaster after it was officially confirmed that none of the crew survived the sinking of the *Kursk*.

THE CURSE OF TECHNOLOGY

Technological progress is supposed to enhance the well-being of all humanity, but it has a dark side. Blind faith in technology can lead to all manner of horrific scenarios. The Chernobyl disaster of 1986 was a wake up call for those who believe progress is always for the good. Ignorance and human error also play a role in technology-related disasters. Chemicals can run off and poison rivers, or explode, spreading poisons that bring disease and death.

The Bridge over the Firth of Tay

A TECHNOLOGICAL MARVEL THAT COULD NOT STAND UP TO THE POWER OF NATURE

On the stormy night of December 28, 1879, a mail train with seventy-five passengers on board made its way across the Firth of Tay Bridge. The bridge ran across the mouth of Scotland's longest river where it meets the North Sea. Completed in just two years, the Firth of Tay Bridge had been hailed as a masterpiece of engineering. Sadly, it soon became tragically clear that the engineers had gravely underestimated the strength of the prevailing crosswinds, as well as their effects on a bridge and train. On December 28, 1879, these winds reached hurricane strength. As the mail train crossed the central span, the bridge broke in half. The middle section of the bridge, and the train that was traveling across it, crashed down into the swirling currents of the Tay. There were no survivors.

A technological marvel

The Firth of Tay (Scottish *firth* = strait, inlet) is a broad estuary extending far inland just to the south of the Scottish city of Dundee. In the middle of the nineteenth century, as British railroads became busier and the track system more crowded, the Firth of Tay was increasingly viewed as a major obstacle to a fast connection between Dundee and Edinburgh. The Edinburgh and Northern Railway, which was one of the companies involved in expanding the Scottish railroads, stepped in with a solution. Its head engineer, Thomas Bouch (1822–1880), boldly proposed the construction of two enormous rail bridges, one across the Firth of Tay and

The collapse of the Tay Bridge has been depicted in several movies, including the 1942 film Hatter's Castle.

Queen Victoria of England (1819–1901) crossed the Tay Bridge in 1879, the year of the disaster. She later knighted its engineer, Thomas Bouch.

another across the nearby Firth of Forth. Once in place, they would considerably shorten the time required to travel between Dundee and Edinburgh. Bouch's plans were approved and construction of the Tay Bridge began in 1871. Given the state of technology at the time, the sheer size of the structure made every phase of its construction an adventure. When it was finished in 1877, it was, at 10,709 feet, the longest railway bridge in the world.

Queen Victoria knights an engineer
The construction was plagued by financial and technical difficulties from the outset. Financial concerns led to skimping on the quality of the building materials. The number of supporting pillars was reduced for technical reasons having to do with unstable geological strata on the estuary floor. This made the span-width of the

The construction of the bridges over the Tay and Forth considerably shortened the travel time between Dundee and Edinburgh .

Out of fear of further catastrophes, the structural components of the bridge over the Firth of Forth were heavily reinforced in 1883.

middle section much greater than Bouch had planned. Nonetheless, on September 26, 1877, the first train rolled across the new bridge. The British public welcomed this triumph of technology with great enthusiasm. Queen Victoria (1819–1901) was among those most impressed by the structure. In 1879, she crossed the bridge on her way back from the Scottish Highlands, and knighted its engineer shortly afterward. From then on he would be Sir Thomas Bouch.

The fateful night

Only a few months after the royal train had passed over the bridge, the unbelievable happened. A powerful hurricane raged over the North Sea on December 28, 1879, traveling toward the Firth of Tay. The already gale force winds became stronger and stronger, reaching their apex around 7 p.m., just as the Edinburgh mail train with its six passenger cars approached the bridge. Before it could cross, the train had to stop at a control point to ensure that it would be the only train on the bridge's single track. The control system in place was simple. The train driver picked up a staff from the bridge guard and handed it back on the other side. Since there was only one staff, there could only be one train on the bridge at a time.

On that stormy night, the driver took the staff and continued across the bridge with his seventy-five passengers. A short time later, the bridge guard noticed that all the telegraph wires across the Tay had been cut. This was a bad sign, because the telegraph cables had been built into the very structure of the bridge itself. Without delay, the guard sent two employees across the bridge to look into the problem. After walking half a mile, the men found themselves staring into a void. There was nothing in front of them. The central span of the bridge had collapsed into the swirling currents of the Tay, taking the entire train with it. Bridge and train had disappeared completely into the depths; no trace of the people on board could be found.

Causes and consequences

Five months later, the commission that was set up to investigate the catastrophe came to a devastating conclusion: the disaster had been caused by onstruction errors and sloppy work. The cast iron used was the wrong kind and too

The Firth of Forth Bridge

At the time of the Tay Bridge disaster in 1879, Thomas Bouch's next giant bridge, across the Firth of Forth to the south, was already in the works. After the Firth of Tay Bridge collapsed, construction of the second bridge was stopped. Engineers John Fowler (1817–1898) and Benjamin Baker (1840–1907) were given the job of designing a more stable structure. Construction began anew in 1883. Exceptionally strong, the Firth of Forth Bridge consists of three lozenge-shaped cantilever elements made of interwoven steel girders. Visually striking, these have been compared to three dinosaurs striding one after another across the estuary. Due to general insecurity in the wake of the Tay catastrophe, the stability of the new bridge was given the highest possible priority. Modern analysis has shown that, from an engineering perspective, the Firth of Forth Bridge is probably five times stronger than it would need to be to meet present-day safety requirements.

low quality for a structure of this type. Air holes that had formed in the iron during the smelting process were simply covered over with a mixture of metal filings and resin. When the faulty girders and pillars were painted, these flaws were completely concealed. In addition, the commission concluded that the design by engineer Thomas Bouch greatly underestimated the lateral forces that could be generated by a strong storm. His estimate of the wind speed of a hurricane was just 20 percent of the actual figure, which was readily available at that time, having been calculated by the French and Americans. That a train crossing the bridge was particularly vulnerable because of the increase in surface area exposed to cross-winds was a possibility Bouch never even considered. He was removed from office, lost all his honors, and died, embittered, only a few months after that terrible night.

In 1887, a completely new bridge across the Tay was built 60 feet upstream from the site of the original bridge. The new Tay Bridge is still in use today.

"Now I am become Death, destroyer of worlds"

ATOMIC BOMB TESTS IN THE AMERICAN SOUTHWEST

The USA carried out 1,039 atomic bomb tests between 1945 and 1992, most of them in the deserts of Nevada near Las Vegas. Tests were also carried out in the South Pacific, but these proved to be too expensive. The decision was made to limit testing to areas within the continental United States. Over the years, more than 380,000 soldiers were assigned to observe bomb tests so that the effects of radiation could be studied. Many of them developed cancer and died.

Atomic bomb tests in the desert

One of over 900 nuclear explosions that took place in the Southwestern US desert between 1945 and 1992.

At the time of the testing, Nevada was the seventh largest state by area, but it was also one of the emptiest. Most Nevadans live in Reno and Las Vegas, leaving nearly all the rest of the state uninhabited desert. The average population den-

Visitors look down from the rim of an enormous crater to see for themselves the effect of "the bomb."

sity was less than eight persons per square mile. This made Nevada the primary atomic test site next to the South Pacific, but other southwestern states were also involved. On July 16, 1945, the first atomic bomb test in history took place in an expanse of desert near Almagordo, New Mexico. This test, dubbed "Trinity," detonated an implosion-type plutonium bomb, the culmination of the Manhattan Project based at nearby Los Alamos. Trinity tested the prototype for the kind of bomb that would be dropped on Nagasaki, Japan (see p. 178).

Trinitrotoluene (TNT)

The explosive force of an atomic bomb is usually calculated as equivalent to x number of tons of TNT. TNT is an explosive with primarily military applications. It has a detonation speed of 22,000 feet per second. A bomb like the ones exploded in the desert during the atomic tests could be as powerful as 20,000 tons of TNT, with a detonation speed of 8,575 miles per second. TNT also has a number of commercial uses because it is relatively stable and so easily detonated.

Over 900 tests—underground, above ground, and atmospheric—took place near the Nellis Air Force Range in the Yucca Mountains about 100 miles northwest of Las Vegas. Not coincidentally, the Yucca Mountains are the site of America's largest radioactive waste dump.

The uranium bomb known as "Little Boy" dropped on Hiroshima on August 6, 1945 was never tested. In contrast to plutonium bombs, a uranium bomb was considered a "sure thing." There was also simply not enough uranium available at the time for a second bomb. This is why the American military refers to the Hiroshima bombing as history's "second atomic test," one that cost 250,000 people their lives.

The "Trinity" atomic test

General Leslie Groves, military head of the Manhattan Project that developed the atomic bomb,

The USA was not the only country testing atomic bombs

The atomic bomb testing area in Kazakhstan, with an area of 18,000 square miles, is almost as large as all of Belgium. Between 1949 and 1989, the Soviet Union tested 461 atomic bombs there, of which 113 were atmospheric explosions. Following the 1963 atmospheric atomic test ban, a further 348 atomic bombs were detonated underground. To this day the region is heavily contaminated by plutonium. As was the case with the USA, the Soviet Union claimed to be testing the bombs for peaceful purposes, such as melting glaciers or excavating deep tunnels and mines. Like the Americans, the Russians documented every test on film using a number of different measurement devices. Both sides of the Iron Curtain used animals as test subjects. Pigs, horses, sheep, and dogs were exposed to atomic blasts so that the effects could be studied. To this day, the population of the area around the test site has a cancer rate twice as high as the national average.

was deeply impressed by the Trinity test. "The war is over," he said, "as soon as we drop one or two on Japan." For this first test, the explosive material was set on a 100-foot-tall tower, where it could be detonated from a distance. Observers donned sunglasses and applied suntan lotion to protect themselves from the searing flash of light

When asked his thoughts following the Trinity test, Dr. J. Robert Oppenheimer, director of the Manhattan Project, memorably, quoted the Bhagavad Gita: "Now I am become death, the destroyer of worlds."

J. Robert Oppenheimer and General Leslie Groves inspect the location of the 100-ft-tall tower at ground zero of the Trinity atomic test site.

Soldiers were sent to a detonation site shortly after a bomb test so that they might become hardened to the effects of an atomic explosion.

that would accompany the explosion. The test was set for 16:00 hours (4 p.m.), but the bomb was actually detonated 90 minutes later. Dance music was played to entertain invited guests, but the explosion provided the greatest thrill. The observers, standing just 10 miles away, cheered when the 7.5-mile-tall mushroom cloud rose into the sky. It set off a shock wave so great it was felt 190 miles away. The plutonium bomb, which had an explosive force equivalent to 20,000 tons of TNT, melted the sand around it to a glassy crust. The tower had virtually disintegrated, with the force of the explosion leaving a crater 10 feet deep and 1,000 feet wide in its place. The results of the Trinity test were at first kept top secret; the general public never knew it had taken place.

The legacy of atomic testing

In the following years, atomic tests were documented in tremendous detail using a variety of methods. Nevertheless, all bets were off when the wind was blowing to the west. An atomic

test could be postponed or even cancelled to avoid "by every means" the possibility of nuclear fallout drifting toward the urban areas of Las Vegas or Los Angeles.

An eyewitness account of an atomic explosion
"The effects could well be called unprecedented, magnificent, beautiful, stupendous, and terrifying. No manmade phenomenon of such tremendous power had ever occurred before. It lit every peak, crevasse, and ridge of the nearby mountain range with a clarity and beauty that cannot be described but must be seen to be imagined. Seconds after the explosion came, the air blast pressed hard against the people watching, to be followed almost immediately by the strong, sustained, awesome roar which warned of doomsday and made us feel we puny things were blasphemous to dare tamper with the forces previously reserved for the Almighty."

Thomas Farrell, general

Over the years, however, areas with above-normal levels of radioactivity, called "hot spots," were identified across the country, as far away as New York. The Mormon community of St. George in the neighboring state of Utah suffered more than any other municipality. The people of St. George remember seeing mushroom clouds and detonation flashes as children. They also recall an inordinately high rate of leukemia among their schoolmates and siblings. It was already too late for most of them by the time scientists on the other side of the state line confirmed the direct link between cancer and atomic tests. Since 1988, the US government has paid $50,000 for each cancer death in St. George. Many families refuse it as blood money.

The soldiers stationed at the Nevada test site were often less than 2 miles from ground zero. The Atomic Energy Commission prescribed a distance of at least 7 miles, but military leaders wanted them closer. Soldiers were sent to the blast site 45 minutes after detonation so they could "harden" themselves to the effects of an atomic bomb attack. 380,000 soldiers took part in the tests. Many died of cancer.

Jonathan Parfrey, director of the organization Physicians for Social Responsibility, calculates 11,000 cancer deaths that are a direct result of the atomic tests, as well as 100,000 to 150,000 serious illnesses. He has since documented an additional 120,000 cases of a variety of thyroid cancer caused by absorption of the radioactive isotope Iodine 121, a product of nuclear fission.

The "mini-nuke" tests

The land and people of the USA still suffer the effects of the atomic tests. Aggressive forms of certain cancers are rampant among the scientific observers and soldiers. Civilian cameramen, who recorded hundreds of explosions on film, have suffered a similar fate. Earth and water are thoroughly contaminated by radioactive materials. Nonetheless, plans are in place to start testing atomic weapons again. In 2003, the Senate passed a bill permitting development and testing of "mini-nukes," as the government of George W. Bush playfully calls them. As yet, no new American atomic tests have been reported. Russia is also working to develop new atomic weapons, because, as head of state Vladimir Putin says, long-term world peace can only be secured by a strategic balance of power.

The bomb "Grable" was detonated on May 25, 1953 at a test site in the Nevada desert.

Table of the number of atomic tests per country

COUNTRY	NUMBER OF TESTS	YEARS
USA	1,039	1945–1992
Soviet Union	718	1949–1990
France	198	1960–1996
PR of China	45	1964–1996
United Kingdom	45	1952–1991

Paradise and the Bomb

THE ATOMIC TESTS AT BIKINI ATOLL

In 1946, Americans wanted to learn more about the destructive power of atomic weapons. Toward that end, they detonated the first in a long series of atomic bombs over the paradise islands of Bikini Atoll, having first moved its inhabitants to a neighboring island. The tests were the work of physicist Edward Teller (1908–2003). Unlike J. Robert Oppenheimer, the "Father of the Atomic Bomb," who resigned from his position following the horrors of Hiroshima and Nagasaki, in 1946 Teller was still an enthusiastic supporter of the atomic bomb, which he referred to as his "child." Although in 1945 he had claimed that the bomb could blow up mountains, he ended up leaving them all in place. Instead, he blew up Elugelab, an island in the Bikini Atoll, sinking it with a hydrogen bomb.

The bomb "Able" and the beginning of the Cold War

"Able" was the first atomic bomb detonated in the South Seas. It was dropped from an airplane on June 30, 1946, exploding on Bikini Atoll, which is part of the Marshall Islands. Able was a 23 kiloton (kt) bomb. The kiloton, equivalent to 100 tons of TNT, had become the standard unit of measurement used to describe the size and power of an atomic weapon. Over the next twelve years, sixty-seven atmospheric tests would take place in what was known to the military as the Pacific Proving Grounds. According to the Pentagon, the combined magnitude of the bombs detonated was equal to 7,000 Hiroshima bombs. In addition to all the irreparable damage done to the islands, the atomic bomb tests in the Pacific paved the way for the Cold War. The tests changed the nature of the relationship between the United States and the Soviet Union, setting off an arms race between the two superpowers that only came to an end with the fall of the Berlin Wall in 1989. As long as the Cold War continued, the world was forever poised on the brink of a nuclear catastrophe.

For the good of mankind

The American government chose the Marshall Islands as a test site because they were far from the continental United States and unlikely to unleash protests back home. The arrival of the American military, scientists, and bomb experts was comparable to an invasion. Some 42,000 Americans came to the Marshall Islands, where they could study their new "plaything," only twice-used, undisturbed by world reaction. Somewhat paradoxically, the government and press back home were provided with a near-perfect documentary record. Over 600 cameras were positioned around the atoll and unmanned aircraft were flown directly into the mushroom clouds to take photographs. For the good of humanity, some 5,000 animals, including goats, pigs, and rats, were securely tied to ships anchored around the target islands. Investigators wanted to see whether they vaporized, carbon-

On June 30, 1946 the first atomic bomb exploded at Bikini Atoll began a long series of tests that would result in the radioactive contamination of the entire island chain.

In 1945, physicist Edward Teller claimed that the atomic bomb could bring down a mountain.

tions to the citizens of the Marshall Islands. Would that we could dry our tears with dollar bills, say the islanders, resigned to their fate. Over the years, the inhabitants of the Bikini Atoll have naturally noticed that the more sympathy the atoll awakens in the international community, the more they can depend on money coming in from outsiders to support them. The islanders now demand money from the USA for conditions such as high blood pressure, diabetes, and arthritis. However, since "only" thyroid cancer has been proven to be directly related to radiation poisoning, funding from the United States has been more difficult to come by as the population directly exposed to radiation ages and the years since the atomic tests increase. Recently, Congress refused to pass a bill that would have provided $365 million to clean up Bikini Atoll by removing tons of contaminated earth.

During the twelve years of testing in the Pacific, around 5,000 animals, including goats, pigs, and rats, were exposed to atomic blasts so that the effect of a nuclear attack on living beings could be studied.

ized, glowed, or were torn into pieces by the blast. Did they die in agony from the effects of Edward Teller's "baby?" The project was very much Teller's own, conducted under a banner of righteousness that absolved its instigators from all responsibility forever. The father of the hydrogen bomb maintained to the end that the Pacific atomic tests were conducted for the good of mankind.

The inhabitants were in the way and had to be removed

Naturally, the islands of the atoll chosen as a test site had to first be cleared of all its inhabitants. The native population was swiftly resettled on other islands. Today, these people still dream of being permitted, some day, to return to their homeland. The real tragedy, the worst part of the catastrophe, was played out among the local populations. Many sickened and died from radiation poisoning, and many continue to suffer the long-term effects of radiation today. In addition, some islands were so thoroughly contaminated with plutonium that they will remain uninhabitable for thousands of years.

The government of the United States has since paid out more than $1 billion in repara-

Cesium

Cesium is an element with the symbol Cs and atomic number 55. It has the largest atomic radius of all the stable elements on the Periodic Table. The softest of all elements, it is highly malleable, and has a very low melting point of 83 °F. Its radio-active isotope Cesium-137 has a half-life of 30 years. Cesium accumulates rapidly in plants and soil exposed to atomic explosions, particularly in mushrooms and other fungi. Highly carcinogenic, Cesium-137 does not occur naturally; it is a by-product of nuclear fission.

The children and grandchildren of the evacuees from Bikini Atoll still dream of returning to the islands of their ancestors.

Yearning to return

The worst criticism comes not from the evacuated or ill inhabitants, but from international aid agencies. Each person affected by the tests receives a monthly payment from the United States. It is enough to live on, and then some. No one has to work. The subsidies from the United States have damned the population to a life of passive inactivity. The notable passivity of the atoll inhabitants is also a function of their constant, hopeless yearning to return to their homeland. In the meantime, sixty years have come and gone since the evacuations. The lives that the children and grandchildren of the evacuees lead today have little in common with those of their ancestors prior to 1946.

430,000 cancer deaths due to atomic testing

Up to now, there are no precise statistics calculating the number of deaths caused by atomic radiation. No exact count is possible. The Pentagon, citing the Military Secrets Act, will not release any information. Independent organizations like the International Physicians for the Prevention of Nuclear War (IPPNW) cannot calculate more precise results on their own because they lack access to the data. Their estimates run to many thousands of cancer victims from Bikini Atoll and the Marshall Islands as a whole. Worldwide, as many as 430,000 people have died of cancers caused by the fallout from atomic weapons testing.

The nuclear club

With the outbreak of the Cold War, the nuclear weapons club made up of the two superpowers, The United States and the Soviet Union, rapidly gained new members. In 1953, Great Britain developed a bomb; France and China followed in 1964. These five countries are referred to officially as nuclear weapons states. Each is a signatory of the Nuclear Non-Proliferation Treaty and all five sit on the United Nations Security Council, where each holds veto power. More recently, other nations have joined the club, but as non-signatories do not share the privileges of the original five. Israel, India, and Pakistan now have nuclear weapons. Iran has been trying to join the nuclear club for many years. So far, with no special status in the United Nations and no seats on the Security Council, the role of the latecomers has been limited to the threat they pose to world peace.

Islands wiped off the face of the earth

The "King of Kwajalein" is the nominal chief of Bikini Atoll, where the USA still maintains a rocket base. The chief lives in exile, of course, renting his islands to the United States for the sum of $12 million a year. Most of the money flows into his private bank account. Some of it supports his royal plantation, and whatever is left is distributed among his people. No one really takes him seriously, least of all the Americans. Were they to do so, it might suggest that the United States had some expectation of eventually returning Bikini Atoll its rightful ruler.

The flag of Bikini Atoll has three black stars in its upper right corner. They are there in memory of the three islands that were wiped off the face of the earth by the 1954 test of the 15-megaton hydrogen bomb named "Bravo." Two years earlier, a similar bomb obliterated two islands in the nearby Eniwetok Atoll.

The bomb acquires sex appeal

In the war-loving, technology-worshipping years after World War II, the atomic bomb acquired a certain cachet, a kind of sex appeal. The Sands Hotel in Las Vegas hosted a Miss Atom Bomb beauty contest whose winner greeted the crowd from an enormous ball of cotton shaped like a mushroom cloud. The Atomic View Hotel in the Nevada desert offered exclusive access to the best views of the many underground bomb tests in the area. Their advertising campaign promised that one could see an atomic explosion without ever leaving the hotel swimming pool. One of the first modern bikini swimsuits was presented to the fashion world just days after the first nuclear test in Bikini Atoll, for which it was named—its designers extolling the explosive effect it would have. Soon "sex bombs" had "atomic breasts." Bill Haley and the Comets, a 1950s rock and roll band, went so far as to sing a song about a nuclear apocalypse survived by thirteen women—and a man named Bill.

Soldiers observe a 1958 hydrogen bomb explosion off the Marshall Islands.

The 11-megaton "Romeo" bomb was exploded over Bikini Atoll on March 26, 1954, sending an enormous mushroom cloud into the air.

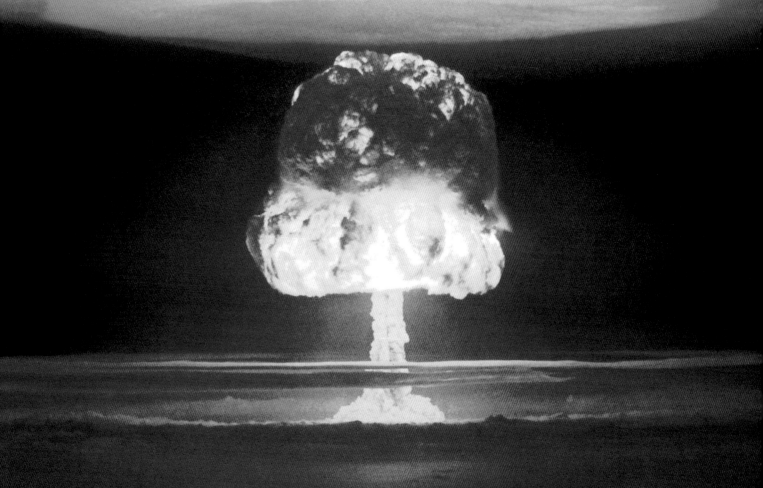

THE MIRACLE OF LENGEDE

DRAMATIC RESCUES AFTER THE 1963 MINING DISASTER

On October 24, 1963, Klarteich 12, one of the wastewater lagoons belonging to the Mathilde iron mine in Lengede, Germany, flooded the mining shafts dug beneath it. Over 121 million gallons of water and muck quickly filled the mine. Of the 129 miners at work that day, seventy-nine were able to escape. Another twenty-one men were dramatically rescued over the course of the next fourteen days. The Miracle of Lengede went down in history as one of the most technically complex mine disaster rescues ever attempted.

Miners trapped underground for days were sent food and dry clothing through a shaft drilled down from the surface.

The water floods in

For almost 100 years, mining had been an important local industry for the small German town of Lengede and its 9,000 inhabitants, most of whom made their living from the mines. Overnight, tragedy made this little-known place in Germany famous around the world. On the evening of October 24, 1963, a breach in the base of a wastewater lagoon caused water to flood into the mineshafts dug deep below. The weight of the water above caused a funnel effect that hindered initial efforts to divert the lagoon water elsewhere. Instead, an enormous amount of water from the lake flowed into the mine. On that day 129 miners were working underground. At the first sign of danger, they sounded the alarm. The crew chief underground received an emergency phone call from the pit foreman, but was unable to relay the message any further because the line leading deeper into the mine was dead. Panicking, seventy-nine miners were able to save themselves by finding safety shafts away from the rushing water. Above ground, workers succeeded in damming the breach, halting the flow into the mine. It was soon clear that fifty miners were still missing.

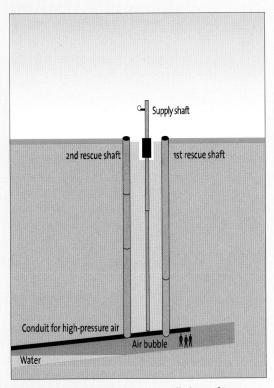

The miners in the air pocket were pulled to safety through a shaft drilled down from the surface. To preserve the air pocket, compressed air had to be pumped down into the chamber.

Rescue by raft

That very night, some of the pit bosses, acting without official permission, entered the mine with flashlights to search for their lost colleagues. They were able to find seven miners floating on a raft they had quickly cobbled together out of debris. One by one, they were floated out of the mine through an 263-foot-

A capsule for digging out buried miners was developed in 1955. Shaped like a torpedo and large enough to lift out one man at a time, the "Dahlbusch bomb" saved many lives at Lengede.

The Miracle of Lengede in film

The first film on the subject of the Lengede rescues was a German television documentary made in 1969. The bulk of the film consisted of archival footage and original photographs made by television and news crews present at the 1963 disaster. Their participation marked the first time that a catastrophe of this kind was reported live, on site, over the course of several days.

Forty years after the accident, a fictionalized two-part television film titled The Miracle of Lengede (2003) was a surprise hit, proof that the miraculous rescue of the miners had remained firmly in many people's memories. That film won the Golden Kamera award as the best German television film of the year, as well as many other prizes. The film was shown internationally in thirty-five countries, including many with a strong mining heritage, including the Czech Republic, Hungary, Spain, and Sweden, .

long gallery flooded almost to the height of its roof. As dawn broke, the number of missing was down to forty-three. Despite a night of nearly nonstop drilling into the mine searching for signs of life, there was no sign of any additional survivors. The rescuers above ground continued working, but the mood was no longer hopeful, but despairing.

Three saved in an air pocket

The next day, drilling continued in the surrounding turnip fields. Rescuers listened at every hole, but heard nothing but dripping water. Meanwhile, the technical corps of the fast-learning rescue squad studied the layout of the mine to determine where air pockets might be found in the maze of galleries and chambers. The theory was that there might be air pockets large enough to sustain miners who had escaped the flood several days. The most likely location was directly underneath the athletic complex of the neighboring village of Barbecke. A drill was brought in, and four survivors were discovered. When it became clear that someone down below was knocking on the drill bit, the rescue team was jubilant. They quickly set to work, carefully boring the rescue shaft through rock. It would have to be broad enough for a so-called Dahlbusch bomb, a hollow, torpedo-shaped capsule big enough to hold one individual. It had been invented eight years earlier at a mine in Gelsenkirchen, Germany. It required a shaft 20 inches in diameter that had to be dug carefully to keep it from caving in, so drilling had to proceed at a painfully slow pace. The drill broke through to the air pocket on the seventh day after the flood.

Three men were still alive; the fourth had drowned. On the eighth day, greatly relieved, the survivors finally returned to the surface.

Death knells

There seemed to be little hope for the rest of the missing miners given the number of days that had now passed since the disaster. The director of the mine gave them up for dead, and sent the drill and rescue teams home. A period of mourning was declared: flags were hung at half-mast and nearby towns were draped in black. A memorial service was planned. Villages for miles around tolled their bells in memory of the lost miners. The miners who had been saved, however, were not at peace. They believed that some of their colleagues could have fled into an abandoned part of the mine known as "Old Man." The Old Man was not stable. Its timbers had been removed to allow its galleries to collapse naturally within the mountain. The mine director, although he remained convinced that there were no further survivors, was eventually forced to reopen the rescue effort due to overwhelming public pressure. More than 400 journalists had traveled to Lengede to report on the catastrophe. Many had produced reports highly critical of the decision to declare the remaining miners dead. With little hope of success, drilling began anew, this time directly above the location of the Old Man.

Inside the Old Man

Deep inside the mine, a small group of survivors hung on, despairing, in the cold and dark of the Old Man. Twenty-one men had fled there during the flood, among them electrician Adolf Herbst and miner Bernhard Wolter. Both had been listed dead for more than a week. Herbst was working a double shift on the day of the disaster because he had his engagement party the following day. Instead, he was trapped for nine days underground. Every day, the group of survivors became smaller. Sections of the abandoned mine collapsed daily, killing and injuring his already weakened colleagues. Then, on November 3, ten days after the flood, a drill hole reached a chamber in the Old Man. Located 164 feet below the surface, the chamber was only 16 x 6.5 feet with a 10-foot-high ceiling. Although locating and safely drilling into the crumbling chamber was a difficult and error-filled process, and the first attempt to dig a shaft was more than 7 feet off-target, the Miracle of Lengede now became reality.

Mr. Wolter, please report!

After food and other necessities had been sent down into the chamber, the careful digging of a shaft for the Dahlbusch bomb began. Bernhard Wolter, chosen to speak for the trapped men, communicated with the surface via microphone. Rescuers were in nearly constant contact, calling down "Mr. Wolter, please report!" in order to adjust the drill angle and transmit other important information. Due to the instability of the abandoned mine, drilling proceeded as if in slow motion. The eleven survivors had to endure four more days in the Old Man before the rescue shaft reached its goal. Two volunteers went down into the mine to help the completely exhausted miners, one by one, into the Dahlbusch bomb. On November 7, two weeks after the disaster, the eleven men stepped out into daylight. For twenty-nine of their colleagues, no rescue was possible.

Top: Jubilant crowds followed the ambulances taking the survivors to nearby hospitals.

Bottom: Red Cross workers support an exhausted, but relieved, miner after his trip to the surface in the rescue capsule.

Mining disasters around the world

Every year, mining accidents claim a high death toll. Miraculous rescues, unfortunately, are quite rare. In January 2006, for example, lightening set off an explosion in the Sago coal mine in Tallmansville, West Virginia. Following the initial round of rescues, twelve miners were still missing. As in Lengede, relatives and friends of the missing men gathered at the accident site in the hope that they might still be rescued. When the rumor broke that all of them were still alive, the crowd reacted with a joy that made the news to come all the more devastating. It became clear soon thereafter that eleven of the twelve men had not survived. For all but one Sago mine family, tragically, there was no Miracle of Lengede to celebrate.

An American military aircraft sprays the herbicide Agent Orange over a forest during the Vietnam War. The goal of the defoliation campaign was to stop the enemy from disappearing into the jungle.

Agent Orange and the Seveso Dioxin Cloud

THE EXTREMELY TOXIC COMPOUND KNOWN AS DIOXIN HAS THREATENED MANKIND FOR THE PAST HALF CENTURY.

Dioxin is one of the most toxic substances ever created. Over the past fifty years, its effect on people and the environment has been catastrophic. During the Vietnam War, it served as a key component in the chemical defoliation compound known as Agent Orange. In 1976, in the Italian city of Seveso, dioxin was released in a toxic aerosol cloud after an accident at a chemical factory. More recently, the deliberate dioxin poisoning of an Ukrainian presidential candidate led to public uproar and widespread unrest.

Operation Ranch Hand

In the 1960s, American troops were embroiled in the longstanding conflict between communist North Vietnam and the more western-oriented South Vietnam. The Vietnam War was fought for the most part in terrain that was as much as three-quarters covered with dense jungle. The heavy vegetation, and the cover it provided for North Vietnamese guerrillas, was the American army's most pressing problem. Operation "Ranch Hand" was devised to drive the enemy out from under the forest canopy through defoliation of those dense forests. From 1962 to 1971, airplanes and helicopters dropped or sprayed herbicides over large areas. The most effective defoliation mixture was the one that went by the now infamous code name "Agent Orange." Agent Orange was a cocktail of chemicals that included a small amount of

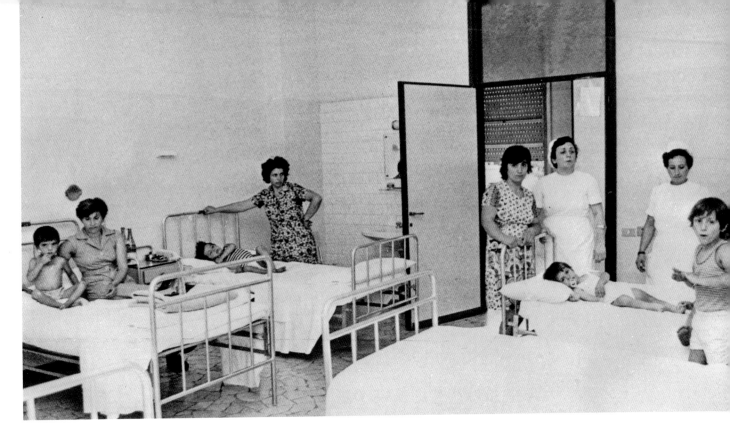

dioxin. Over the years, given the sheer quantity of Agent Orange used, the amount of dioxin released into the environment amounted to several hundred pounds. Due to the exceptional stability of dioxin, which only breaks down very slowly, the long-term effects of Agent Orange were catastrophic. Even today, decades after the end of the war, around 100,000 Vietnamese suffer from dioxin-related medical conditions, or from genetic diseases related to their parents', or even grandparents' exposure. Dioxin attacks human DNA, leading to many generations of serious birth defects. American soldiers exposed to Agent Orange were also affected.

The poison cloud of Seveso

Dioxin was also involved in one of the worst environmental catastrophes of the twentieth century. At 12:37 p.m. on July 10, 1976, human error caused a mixing vat in a small chemical factory near Seveso, Italy to explode. The factory (ICMESA, or Industri Chimiche Meda Società Azionaria), which usually made cosmetics, was enveloped in a cloud of poison gas that drifted slowly over the town of Seveso and several surrounding villages. For a full week, the factory tried to keep the accident secret. Finally, they began to evacuate the region. The cloud carried 4.5 lbs of highly toxic dioxin, enough to make the region around Seveso unin-

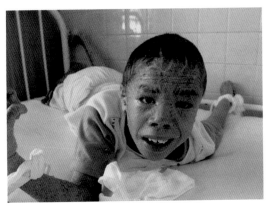

Vietnam is still struggling to overcome the long-term effects of dioxin poisoning. Birth defects caused by genetic damage have continued into the third generation.

Super-poison dioxin

After World War II, the German professor Wilhelm Sandermann (1906–1994) conducted research into the chemistry of wood and related organic compounds. He first described the compound TCDD (tetrachlordibenzo-p-dioxin) in a 1957 paper. Dioxin is a by-product of the chemical reaction that produces resins used to protect wood. Of all the known dioxin compounds, TCDD is by far the most toxic. Ingesting as little as one microgram per kg/2 lb body weight can be deadly. The poison attacks the cells and their DNA, causing severe liver damage, and a disfiguring skin condition called chloracne. A connection between dioxin and cancer has long been suspected, though research is inconclusive. Dioxin breaks down very slowly, leading to long-term effects on the environment. Areas affected by dioxin contamination remain toxic for many years.

A policeman wearing protective clothing and a gas mask sets up signs around the town of Seveso warning people away from the area affected by the poisonous cloud.

habitable for many years. Hundreds of people suffered severe skin damage, and 75,000 poisoned animals had to be slaughtered. Long-term effects comparable to the dioxin-related conditions observed after the Vietnam War have not yet been studied for the Seveso disaster.

The missing barrels of poison

The decontamination of the area affected by the Seveso dioxin cloud began in October 1976. It took until 1982 for all affected materials, including the poisoned earth itself, to be removed. Initially, no attempt was made to clean up the area immediately around the exploded vat. In the summer of 1982, volunteer workers wearing heavy protective clothing took on this highly dangerous task. The debris was packed in barrels and transported north toward France. Shortly thereafter, the press discovered that the barrels had disappeared, and a far-reaching scandal ensued. Officials searched for the barrels for months, eventually finding them in May 1983 in northern France. In 1985, following the introduction of new incineration technology that leaves little or no residue, the barrels of poison were finally burned in Basel, Switzerland.

sostanze tossiche

DIVIETO

TOCCARE O INGERIRE PRODOTTI ORTOFRUTTICOLI, EVITANDO CONTATTI CON VEGETAZIONE TERRA E ERBE IN GENERE.

DIVIETO DI ACCESSO ALLE PERSONE NON AUTORIZZATE

I TRASGRESSORI saranno deferiti all' Autorità Giudiziaria ai sensi dell' Art. 650 C.P.

Attempted assassination with dioxin

In 1991, as the states constituting the Soviet Union began to break away, the Ukraine, like the others, regained its status as an independent nation. Nevertheless, political relations with its former partner states remained in place for many years. In 2004, the Ukranian national presidential election developed into a forum for deciding whether the Ukraine should orient itself to the west or to the east.

One candidate, Viktor Yanukovitch, favored a closer relationship with Russia. His opponent, Viktor Yushchenko, wanted to open up the country to Western democracies. When Yanukovitch won a run-off election, non-violent protests demanding a recount broke out all across the Ukraine. Known to history as the Orange Revolution, the protests led to new elections that were won by Yushchenko.

The election itself, however, was overshadowed by suspicions that Yushchenko was the victim of an assassination attempt involving deliberate poisoning with dioxin. Following a dinner with the head of the Ukrainian secret service, Yushchenko fell ill with symptoms of severe poisoning. He was so debilitated that continuing the campaign proved to be impossible. The effects on his health were especially visible in his face. Within the span of just a few weeks, a vital, handsome politician aged dramatically, owing to the progress of what looks like dioxin-related chloracne. Suspicions regarding deliberate poisoning were confirmed in December 2004 following a series of medical tests in a Vienna hospital. A blood sample taken from Yushchenko showed a dioxin concentration 1,000 times the normal level. Later investigation by the medical board of the Ukraine confirmed the diagnosis.

Victor Yushchenko before and after being poisoned with dioxin.

The worst chemical industrial disaster in history took place at the Union Carbide factory in Bhopal, India, in the early hours of December 3, 1984.

A Deadly Cloud at Midnight

THE BHOPAL DISASTER

Just after midnight on December 3, 1984, the most extreme industrial accident of all time released a poison cloud of chemical gas in the Indian provincial capital of Bhopal. A tank in a pesticide plant operated by the Union Carbide Company released 40 tons of methylisocyanat into the atmosphere after automatically opening its safety ventilators in response to a sudden increase in internal pressure. The chemical compound is so heavy that the poisonous cloud could not dissipate. Instead, it rolled across the city at ground level, bringing suffering and death to thousands. Over 3,800 people died immediately, with hundreds of thousands gravely injured. The scope of the tragedy remains difficult to comprehend, and many of those affected still await compensation.

The American chemical industry invests in India

Bhopal is the capital of the province of Mahya Pradesh, located in central India. It is an industrial city with a university and over 1.5 million inhabitants, though at the time of the disaster the population was about half its current level. The chemical industry is the region's largest

> **Eyewitness account**
> "People were desperate to save their lives so they just ran. Those who fell were not picked up by anybody, they were trampled by other people. Even cows were running to save their lives, crushing people as they ran."
>
> Champa Devi Shukla, leader of the Bhopal victims' rights movement

The Curse of Technology

employer. In 1934, Union Carbide Corporation (UCC) was one of the first American investors in India when it formed the highly profitable Union Carbide India Limited (UCIL). The chemical plant in Bhopal, which was built in the 1970s, employed 9,000 people. In 1984, UCC reported profits of $9.5 billion, making it the largest chemical firm in the world.

Poison gas rolls into residential areas

It all ended tragically shortly after midnight on December 3, 1984 when methylisocyanat (MIC) was released into the atmosphere. Controversial studies have determined that 3,828 people die at once, and hundreds of thousands were overcome by the gas. The next day, Warren Anderson, president of Union Carbide, arrived from Connecticut accompanied by a rescue team. On his arrival in India, however, the government placed him under house arrest with orders to leave the country within 24 hours. Nonetheless, Union Carbide remained long enough to organize medical and technical rescue squads, working together with local aid agencies in Bhopal.

Of the 500,000 people exposed to the gas, around one-fifth still suffer the after-effects in the form of chronic or incurable illnesses. Many have been blinded, and the cancer rate among survivors is well above average. In addition, more than two decades after the catastrophe, every fourth pregnancy in Bhopal ends in stillbirth. Over the years, Union Carbide has reluctantly paid out $690 million in reparations, of which only a small part ever reaches the actual victims owing to government corruption.

How the accident happened

MIC had been manufactured in the Bhopal plant only since 1979. Prior to that, it had been imported from the United States. Workers were the first to smell the MIC on November 3, and they began to search for a possible leak in one of the holding tanks. In the course of mere minutes, the temperature and pressure in tank 610 climbed to such a high level that the safety mechanisms kicked in and began to release the gas into the atmosphere. About 24 tons of MIC and 12 tons of other toxic compounds formed a deadly cloud that settled close to the ground. Within seconds it began to roll slowly toward the residential part of the city.

Subsequent investigations showed that the tank pressure had increased after water was introduced into the mixture of chemicals. There are three possible ways that this could have happened. The tank may have been rinsed out, but not properly dried before use. Sabotage, perhaps by a disgruntled worker, is another possibility (a water hose from elsewhere in the plant was found attached to one of the MIC tank's regulating meters). Finally, it is possible that the workers looking for the leak introduced water into the tank in error.

Old and inadequate technology

In 1984, there were thirty-seven public telephones in the entire city of Bhopal, only two of which were capable of dialing long distance.

The afflicted residential quarter collapsed into chaos as the cloud of poison gas drifted close to the ground through the narrow streets and alleys.

In the years leading up to the incident, Union Carbide had shut down many divisions of the Bhopal plant because they were less profitable than expected. Restructuring led to large parts of the complex being closed or left operating with equipment that had not been properly maintained. This was the situation on the day of the accident. Inadequate technological support gravely affected the safety systems. For a place where dangerous chemicals were handled daily, the emergency procedures were woefully inadequate. In addition, a recent mass lay-off of skilled workers and foremen had led to a dearth of experience at all levels. The new managers, for the most part, had no experience in the chemical industry. In addition, the atmosphere inside the plant had been troubled even before December 3. Many small acts of sabotage had recently been discovered.

The conclusion of many investigating bodies was that, given the conditions inside the plant and in the city of Bhopal, almost any accident would have quickly developed into a catastrophic disaster of comparable proportions. The director of the chemical plant was arrested and a warrant was issued for Union Carbide president Warren Anderson on a charge of negligent homicide.

The twentieth anniversary of the Bhopal disaster was commemorated on February 12, 2004. Activists estimate the death toll at 33,000.

This gives some sense of the paucity of infrastructure in the area at the time of the disaster, a lack that had tragic consequences in the face of a catastrophe of this magnitude. The local population, mostly poor and uneducated, had never been given any information about the plant or the risks involved in the production of chemical pesticides. No one knew what to do in case of an accident, let alone one of this magnitude. If people had known that the best reaction to a toxic cloud is to lie flat on the ground with a wet cloth over their face, many lives could have been saved. Instead, people ran around in blind panic. Physical exertion led them to inhale more of the poisonous gases, and more deeply, than if they had laid on the ground and waited for it to pass.

People continue to suffer and die

The aftermath has been horrific. Union Carbide and the new owner of the plant, Dow Chemical,

Methylisocyanat (MIC)

Methylisocyanat is a highly flammable, colorless liquid with a pungent aroma. Among other applications, it is commonly used in bug sprays. When MIC comes in contact with water and heat, the compound breaks down into the toxic gases cyanide and nitrous oxide, both of which are also highly explosive. MIC is categorized as a contact poison capable of breaking down into its component gases at temperatures as low as 68°F. When inhaled or otherwise in contact with a person or animal, the skin, respiratory system, and eyes become severely inflamed; the eyes are usually most severely affected. MIC can burn away the corneal tissue, leading to vision impairment and blindness. When the chemicals enter the body itself, nausea, vomiting, abdominal cramps, and severe sore throat are the initial symptoms. Dizziness and loss of consciousness can result. In the worst cases, a toxic build up of fluid in the lungs (edema) leads to death. MIC affects all mammals, making its introduction into the environment potentially catastrophic.

have never released precise information regarding the components of the toxic cloud, claiming these are industry secrets. As a result, the victims do not know the exact poisons to which they were exposed, nor in what concentration. This lack of knowledge keeps doctors from providing appropriate medical care. The international environmental watchdog organization Greenpeace published reports on the Bhopal disaster in 1999 and 2002. They claim that the area around the factory is thoroughly contaminated with heavy metal residue and other toxic substances. Dow Chemical nevertheless has no plans for decontamination. The profits from the Bhopal plant are declining and the costs of cleanup too high. In the meantime, the chemicals have found their way into the local drinking water. During the dry season, the contaminated dust blows the toxic substances into the air, far and wide. In Bhopal, children born with birth defects are a regular occurrence. The medical journal *Lancet* catalogued statistical increases for a wide range of birth defects, including cleft palate, three eyes, webbed fingers, extra fingers, one testicle instead of two, irregular skull shape and Down's syndrome.

As you read this, people continue to suffer and die in Bhopal as a result of the 1984 disaster.

Women wearing masks demonstrate in Bhopal in 2002, demanding that Union Carbide president Warren Anderson be brought to trial for homicide.

2,500 fetuses stillborn after the Bhopal disaster are stored at the Gandhi Medical College in India.

Extracts from a 2005 statement by the Union Carbide Corporation (UCC)

The 1984 gas leak in Bhopal was a terrible tragedy that understandably continues to evoke strong emotions even twenty-two years later. In the wake of the gas release, Union Carbide Corporation, and then-chairman Warren Anderson, worked diligently to provide aid to the victims and set up a process to resolve their claims.

Shortly after the gas release, Union Carbide launched an aggressive effort to identify the cause. The engineering consulting firm Arthur D. Little, Inc. conducted a thorough investigation. Its conclusion: the gas leak could only have been caused by deliberate sabotage. Someone purposely put water in the gas storage tank, and this caused a massive chemical reaction. Process safety systems had been put in place that would have kept the water from entering into the tank by accident.

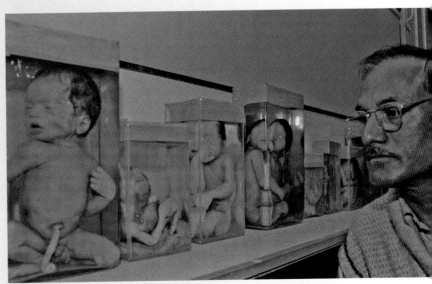

Destroyed reactor 4 was encased in a "sarcophagus" of iron and concrete that, over time, has begun to disintegrate. Not until 2001 could technicians shut down all the reactor blocks in the Chernobyl nuclear power plant.

Nuclear Meltdown

THE CHERNOBYL DISASTER

In the early hours of April 26, 1986, one of four reactors in the Chernobyl nuclear power plant in the Ukraine exploded. The threat that opponents of peaceful uses of nuclear power have always warned against had become reality: nuclear meltdown. The radioactive materials set free by the explosion were spread over a wide area by the heat from the burning complex, and a toxic cloud climbed more than 5,600 feet into the sky. Over the next several days, this atomic cloud drifted over most of Europe. The long-term health effects, which are still being investigated today, will continue to be a factor for many generations to come.

A deadly test

On April 25, 1986, arrangements were made for a series of experiments to be conducted in reactor block 4 of the Chernobyl nuclear power plant. The goal was to determine what would happen in case of a complete loss of electricity. Would the power plant's turbines contain enough residual electricity to keep the cooling system running until power could be restored? In order to conduct the test under the most realistic conditions possible, all emergency control systems were turned off. The test was delayed, however, by unexpected local power requirements during the afternoon and evening. This meant that it had to be carried out much later than originally planned, and by night shift workers who were poorly prepared for the task.

Some families voluntarily remained in their home villages located within the 18.5-mile restricted zone.

2006 near meltdown in Sweden

Twenty years after the Chernobyl disaster, the danger of nuclear catastrophe in Europe is far from over. On July 26, 2006, there was an electrical short-circuit near the Swedish nuclear power plant Forsmark-1. This random event caused the reactor to be cut off from the electrical grid. Theoretically, when this happens, the emergency generators should kick in, but two of the three diesel-powered units failed to turn on. Fortunately, the next level of the safety system functioned perfectly, automatically shutting down the reactor and turning on the emergency cooling system. This kept the reactor from overheating as the Chernobyl reactor had done. In response to the accident, Sweden shut down four of its ten remaining nuclear power plants in to ensure that their safety systems were functioning at all levels. Reports of the "near meltdown" traveled quickly around the world. Careful investigation of the incident by the Swedish nuclear inspection company SKI led to a reassessment of the degree of danger involved. Although the incident was to be taken seriously, there was never a threat of nuclear meltdown at Forsmark-1.

A series of operational errors led to the reaction rate in block 4 increasing until it got out of control. Staff wanted to end the experiment, but the power plant's interim chief engineer ordered them to continue. By the time the emergency control system was finally reactivated manually, at 1:23 a.m., it was too late. Key components had melted in the extreme heat generated during the test and it was no longer possible to stop the reactor. A few minutes later, an enormous explosion of steam blew the 3,000-ton roof off reactor block 4. The 1,500 tons of radioactive graphite inside the reactor ignited in a fiery holocaust. The fire drove radioactive particles so high into the atmosphere that they could be detected thousands of miles above the Earth's surface.

Late reaction

On April 27 and 29, 1986, scientists in Finland and Sweden reported higher than normal levels of atmospheric radiation. Since they had no information as to its cause, they immediately launched an investigation of Swedish nuclear plants to search for damage. Not until late in the evening of April 28 did the Soviet Union announce that there had been an accident involving a nuclear core meltdown in a reactor 62 miles north of Kiev. Inhabitants of the Chernobyl region received this news at the same time as the international community: until that point, they had had no idea what was happening.

This computer simulation shows the extent of the radioactive cloud on the day of the disaster.

Evacuation of the inhabitants of the affected areas began some 36 hours after the explosion. The 50,000 inhabitants of the city of Pripiat, less than 2 miles from the power plant, were transported out of the danger zone by an enormous fleet of buses. In the following weeks, 67,000 people would be evacuated. A restricted zone 18.5 miles in diameter is currently in place around the reactor site, and Pripiat is an abandoned ghost town.

The Liquidators

In order to put a halt to the immediate after effects of the accident, the fire in the destroyed reactor had to be extinguished and the exposed radioactive material encased. A number of workers were brought in, many of whom had little idea of the danger they were being exposed to. This group, later known as the Liquidators, consisted primarily of young men fulfilling

As late as 1990, animals were still being born with serious defects in the region around Chernobyl. Most lived only a few hours.

As early as November 1986, reactor blocks #1 and #2 at Chernobyl were back in operation. Workers were brought to the power plant in special buses.

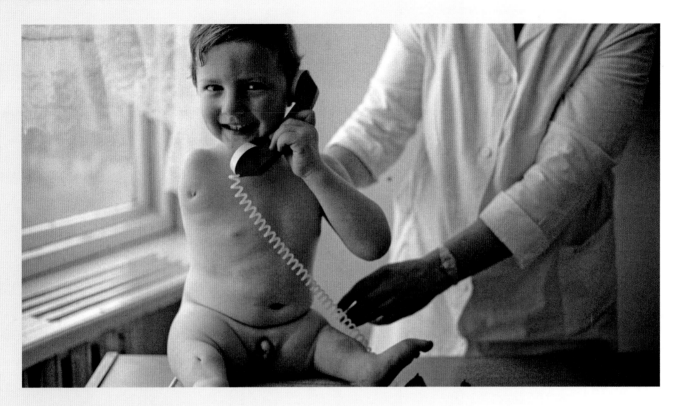

their military service obligation, reservists, students, and miners. Although the exact number of Liquidators remains unknown, it is estimated that as many as one million men were involved in the project through the early 1990s. The government officially recognizes only 60,000, all of whom are entitled to receive free medical care based on their service at Chernobyl. At least 50,000 workers have died of conditions caused by working in reactor block #4. Twenty years after the disaster, experts calculate that 500,000 people have died from the direct or indirect effects of the explosion and meltdown. The official government report, however, recognizes only 4,000 victims.

This photo of a Chernobyl child was published around the world. The boy was later adopted by a British family.

Chernobyl AIDS

From the very first days after the accident it was feared that leukemia and thyroid cancer would be on the rise for decades after the disaster. Twenty years after the rain of radioactive material, studies show that cancer rates are as much as 50 times higher than normal. An even bigger problem has been widespread immune deficiency among children in the affected areas. This phenomenon, called Chernobyl AIDS, has been the subject of increasing attention. Affected children are so debilitated that their bodies are virtually incapable of fighting off illness. They are chronically fatigued, lack the ability to concentrate for more than a few minutes, and suffer from many psychological conditions. Diseases affecting the respiratory, digestive, skeletal and muscle systems are on also the rise.

The Liquidators should have been outfitted with heavy protective clothing. However, in the early days after the accident, this seldom happened.

A Chemical Plant Catches Fire

THE WATER USED TO PUT IT OUT CONTAMINATES THE RHINE RIVER

On November 1, 1986, the nightmare feared by anyone who lives near a chemical factory became bitter reality for the people of Basel, Switzerland. The chemical plant was on fire! The water used by the owners, the Sandoz Company, to put out the fire washed many tons of toxic material into the Rhine River, which flowed directly outside the factory complex. The people of Basel were at first not informed of the danger. In the meantime, the poisoned waters of the Rhine flowed several hundred miles downriver, exterminating everything that lived in the water and contaminating the drinking water supply of more than 5 million people. The trust that had existed between the residents, the chemical industry, and local government was irreparably damaged.

Fire at the Sandoz plant

Shortly after midnight on November 1, 1986, fire broke out in Warehouse 956 on the grounds of the Swiss chemical firm Sandoz. Located near the city of Basel, the complex stored over 1,300 tons of chemicals. For hours, the fire's progress was announced by continual explosions, accompanied by fireballs rising 130 feet into the air. All at once, it was abundantly clear to the people of Basel that they had been, in the truest sense of the phrase, "sitting on a powder keg." More horrifying than the fire was the disorganized way police and other officials handled the situation. Not a single fire alarm functioned the night of the catastrophe, leaving residents ignorant until it was too late. The alarms were in the process of being upgraded, officials explained later, and were not operational. Instead, police wagons cruised the streets of Basel shouting out that everyone should stay inside their houses.

Firefighters at work on the grounds of the burning chemical plant wore heavy protective gear.

Opposite: Large chemical storage complexes and tanks dominate the Rhine side of the harbor of Basel.

Millions without drinking water

On November 13, 2005, the village of Jilin in northeast China suffered an environmental disaster similar to the Sandoz accident, only much, much worse. A series of explosions rocked Factory Number 101 of the Jilin Petroleum and Chemical Company. At least five men were killed, and more than 10,000 people had to be evacuated for safety reasons. As in Basel, the true extent of the catastrophe developed over the next two weeks. The explosion had released 100 tons of the chemical benzol into the Songhua River, where it formed a toxic carpet over 50 miles long. As the poisonous soup moved downstream, it left behind masses of dead fish. On the eleventh day it reached the major city of Harbin, where it contaminated the water supply. After the government shut down the pumps, 3.8 million people had to go four days without any running water.

A catastrophic lack of information

On the morning of November 1, officials gave the all clear: citizens of Basel were allowed to leave their houses. Unfortunately, the only thing that had been brought under control was the fire. The air still stank horribly and the water of the Rhine was stained dark red: the water used to extinguish the fire had run off directly into the river. Sandoz did not take the fears of the general public and concerns of the Basel city government seriously. Instead, corporate representatives chose to play down the dangers. The government had determined that the air was now safe to breathe, meaning that atmospheric levels of chemical compounds were no longer in the danger zone. As for the color of the Rhine, Sandoz claimed the red water was caused by an inert, non-toxic dye. It was only over the following days, as thousands of dead fish began to wash up on the banks of the river, that independent investigators were brought in to comment. There was a loud outcry as people realized that Sandoz had comforted them with empty words. Massive demonstrations took place at tumultuous press conferences. Protesters overturned tables and set glasses of poisoned Rhine water on the speaker podium. The Sandoz representatives had to leave buildings through rear doors with a police escort. The firm suffered as a result, as the name Sandoz was now irrevocably intertwined with the catastrophic lack of information that led to environmental disaster.

Long-distance effects

In the end it was clear that the substance that had turned the Rhine red was indeed a dye, but one commonly added to poisonous chemical compounds as a marker. For days, the red-orange Rhine reeked to the heavens. A bolus of 30 tons of pesticides and 440 pounds of highly toxic mercury compounds moved slowly down the river, causing a massive fish die-off for hundreds of miles. Rhine cities had to shut down their drinking water supplies, many of which were fed by reservoirs on the banks of the river. The effects of the contamination on the environment and people could be measured as far away as Cologne, some 375 miles away.

Years after the poisons have dissipated, large stretches of the Rhine are still biologically dead. In some parts, however, nature recovered much sooner than expected.

It could have been much, much worse

On the riverbed of the Rhine near Basel, all life was exterminated. The red, toxic mud had to be laboriously vacuumed up from the riverbanks. A foundation was set up to restore the water quality of the Rhine, with Sandoz contributing generously to the project. Surprisingly, in some areas, the Rhine recovered from the contamination much faster than expected. This was the one piece of good news that no one who had seen the extent of the damage could have anticipated. Then came the results of a more thorough investigation of the accident itself, which concluded that, for the citizens of Basel, things could have been much, much worse. A tank of World War I era phosgene, an early nerve gas employed in chemical warfare, had been located right next to the burning storage warehouse. Had the heat of the fire caused the tank to explode, thousands would have been killed. Basel had just missed suffering a calamity of unimaginable proportions.

Theories as to the cause of the accident

What actually caused the fire remains unclear today, though many theories have been proposed. As is the case with many accidents without a clear cause, the possibility of sabotage has been mentioned. This suspicion received

powerful support from an interview with former CIA agent Vincent Cannistraro. He claimed that the German Democratic Republic's Ministry for State Security had set the fire under orders from the Soviet Union in order to divert world attention from the Chernobyl accident that had occurred on April 26, 1986, six months earlier. There is other evidence as well. Footprints were discovered leading from the perimeter fence to the site of the fire. However, the team of experts investigating on behalf of the Zurich police came to a completely different conclusion. They saw no evidence of outsiders, having determined that the footprints were those of workers who were in the habit of climbing over the fence for cigarette breaks. Instead, the Zurich police believed that fire broke out when a dye known as "Prussian Blue" burst into flame. As later experiments showed, the dye is a fire hazard, much more so than had previously been assumed. Apparently, a worker had been fooling around with an open flame near a pile of sacks filled with the dye, unintentionally setting off a smoldering fire. A smoldering fire can go undetected for a long time before suddenly bursting into full flame, leading to disaster.

Several Greenpeace activists rappel down a bridge on December 17, 1986 in an attempt to block traffic on the Rhine. They were protesting against the river's contamination following the Sandoz accident.

An immediate effect of the Sandoz catastrophe was a massive fish die-off extending for hundreds of miles down the Rhine.

In service since 1991, the ICE (Inter City Express) train is the flagship of the German railroad. The high-speed train was designed as an alternative to short distance flights.

A TECHNICAL ERROR WITH HORRIFIC REPERCUSSIONS

AN EXPRESS TRAIN CRASHES ON A BRIDGE

On June 3, 1998, the Inter City Express (ICE) train "Wilhelm Conrad Röntgen" was traveling its regularly scheduled route between Munich and Hamburg when the first car suddenly derailed near the small town of Eschede. One of the following cars crashed at full speed into the pillars of a street bridge that the train happened to be passing under at that moment. The bridge collapsed onto the tracks, causing the rest of the cars to smash into the bridge. One hundred and one people died in the crash, and most of the 100 survivors were seriously injured. Investigations showed that a defective wheel on this most technologically advanced of all modern high-speed trains is what caused the worst train accident in German history.

No one pulled the emergency brake.

On the morning of June 3, 1998, ICE 884, named "Wilhelm Conrad Röntgen" after the famous German scientist, was traveling at a speed of 125 miles per hour on its way to the city of Hamburg. It had left Munich early, at 5:47 a.m., but was now slightly behind schedule. At 10:56 a.m. the passengers in the first car were startled by a loud bang. A piece of metal had been driven through the floor of the carriage. The travelers were worried and uncertain as to what to do. They did not think to pull the emergency brake. One passenger went in search of the conductor, finding him in the third car. He did not pull the emergency brake either, because regulations stated that he needed to first confirm the seriousness of the damage.

A wheel tire falls apart

The cars of the ICE were outfitted with a new type of wheel. Passengers had complained that the older type caused the carriages to shake and rattle. The new wheels had a ring of hard rubber between the wheel and the outer tire to reduce vibration. It was the inner wheel separating from the outer tire that caused the first car to derail. Part of the wheel was driven through the carriage floor in the process. Another piece of the wheel slammed into a track switch, sending part of its safety mechanism through the floor as well, where sheer force rammed it through to the roof. This blow forced the rear wheels of the car off the track. The derailed wheel hit the next switch on the track, changing its setting, forcing the next car in line onto a parallel track. The train was now crossing a small street bridge just outside the small town of Eschede.

The crash on the bridge

Two minutes after the first bang had startled the passengers in the front car, the third car in the train crashed into the bridge pillar, causing the entire bridge to collapse. The fifth car was smashed to pieces by falling stone and concrete.

The memorial in Eschede

In 2001 a memorial was erected at the site of the train disaster. A cherry tree was planted for each of the 101 victims alongside a wall inscribed with their names. Steps lead from the cherry grove up to the street, which ends in a symbolic gate. The inscription reads:

"ICE 884 'Wilhelm Conrad Röntgen' crashed on this spot on June 3, 1998 at 10:58 a. m. 101 people lost their lives, entire families were destroyed, and hundreds of passengers were seriously injured. Many will carry the scars of that day for their entire lives. The accident made clear the fragility of human life, its transience, and its insufficiency. Rescue workers and citizens of the town labored selflessly under dangerous conditions for many days, offering help and consolation. Their example and effort made Eschede a monument of solidarity and respect for all humanity."

Traveling at 125 miles per hour, the high speed train crashed into a bridge pillar. The force of the impact caused the train to fold like an accordion.

A great many people worked in independent small groups to free the injured and dead from the mountain of wreckage.

The psychological burden of the rescue workers

The psychological and emotional suffering of rescue crews often goes unrecognized. In the case of a horrific disaster like the Eschede train wreck, not only the wounded are pulled from the crash site, but also dead bodies, many of which were mutilated beyond recognition, and arms and legs amputated by the accident. While in action, the work crews were barely aware of the emotional effect of such grue-some work. Only days later, when they could finally rest, did painful memories begin to plague their waking hours and sleepless nights. Counselors and members of various religious denominations that had been sent to the crash site to help care for distraught relatives were also available to the rescue workers. The individual and group therapy sessions they offered eventually attracted more than 500 of those who had worked at the crash site after the accident.

The remaining cars crashed into the wreckage, folding up like an accordion. Within seconds, a towering pile of wreckage was all that remained of the bridge and train. The train driver in the engine, which had braked automatically, rolled with the first two cars into the Eschede train station. The driver had assumed that some sort of technical flaw had caused the engine to brake automatically, and had no idea of the scale of the tragedy behind him. The stationmaster in Eschede had to tell him that he had rolled into the station with only the front part of the train.

Help arrives quickly

Four minutes after the disaster occurred, the sirens in Eschede howled, bringing the first of many inhabitants of the small town to the wreck. With their bare hands, they began to pull the passengers from the crushed carriages. A few minutes later, a more general alarm went out, bringing the army, fire department, and any rescue equipment that could be found quickly to the crash site.

Within an hour, the critically injured were being flown to nearby hospitals by helicopter. Fortunately for many of the passengers, the nearest university hospital happened to be holding a conference for trauma surgeons that day, all of whom made ready to receive the accident victims. In the meantime, more than a thousand people had arrived to help with the rescue and recovery efforts. Of the 300 or so passengers on the train, ninety-eight would die, as well as three railroad workers who had been stationed near the bridge. A further eighty-eight passengers suffered serious injuries.

Who was responsible?

Two years after the accident, three people were brought to trial for their role in the disaster of June 3, 1998. These included two railroad employees and the director of the firm that had manufactured the wheel tires. The trial was concluded in May 2003, with a declaration that

no guilt could be conclusively proven for any of the three. The German Railroad replaced all the rubber-padded wheels immediately, and no ICE train will ever carry the name "Wilhelm Conrad Röntgen" again.

Professional rescue workers, along with many volunteers, worked to the point of exhaustion freeing wounded passengers from the train wreck.

The extent of the emotional toll that such a catastrophe extracts from rescue workers is often underestimated. At Eschede, the problem was anticipated and counseling was available to anyone who helped at the site.

Inferno in the Tunnel

CATASTROPHIC FIRES IN ALPINE HIGHWAY TUNNELS

Over a period of only ten weeks in 1999, two catastrophic fires broke out inside two different highway tunnels in the Alps. On March 24th, a tractor-trailer caught fire in the Mont Blanc Tunnel between France and Italy. The resulting inferno burned for 53 hours, hot enough to melt concrete, and claimed twenty-nine lives. On May 29th, a tractor-trailer truck rear-ended a line of vehicles in the Austrian Tauern Tunnel, setting off a chain of collisions that eventually involved sixty vehicles, some of which caught fire. Twelve people were killed. The two disasters launched an extensive investigation into tunnel safety standards in Europe and throughout the rest of the world. Nevertheless, in October 2001, a fire in the Gotthard Tunnel in Switzerland once again claimed human lives.

Hellish heat

On March 24, 1999 Belgian driver Gilbert Degrave drove his tractor-trailer loaded with margarine and flour into the 7.2-mile-long Mont Blanc Tunnel. The 35-year-old tunnel had only one lane for traffic in each direction through a single tunnel passage. A few miles into the tunnel, Degrave noticed that drivers coming toward him were signaling to him by blinking their headlights. They were trying to tell him that his truck was giving off smoke, but at that point he had no idea what was wrong. Finally, at kilometer 5.6, about half way through the tunnel, he pulled over to have a look and saw diesel fuel dripping from his exhaust pipe. Suddenly, his entire truck burst into flames. Luckily for

Viewed from the south exit, vehicles burn inside the Gotthard Tunnel like loaves of bread in an oven.

Firemen were forced to wait outside the tunnel until enough of the heavy smoke dissipated to make it possible to approach the site of the accident.

Degrave, a car coming from the other direction picked him up and he made it out of the tunnel safely. Thirty-nine others were not so fortunate. Their cars were stuck in the middle of the tunnel, which was fast becoming an inferno filled with dense smoke and hellish heat. At the center of the fire, temperatures reached as much as 2,190 °F. Two trucks, nine cars, and a motorcycle were engulfed in the flames.

Bad decisions with deadly consequences

The fire department was stopped by smoke and heat one half mile from the site of the accident. A serious of poor decisions made an already bad situation worse. Officials on the Italian side blew air into the tunnel, thinking this would help clear the smoke. Instead, this increased the amount of oxygen in the tunnel, causing the fire to burn still hotter. Many of the victims died because of similarly bad choices. As later investigation would show, most of the victims suffocated in their vehicles. They had felt safer in their cars and trucks than in the tunnel and had chosen to stay in them rather than trying to flee. Safety experts later accused Degrave, the driver of the truck that caught on fire, of lethal stupidity. Instead of stopping his smoking vehicle near the entrance or exit, he pulled over right in the middle of the tunnel. Had he made it a few more miles toward the exit, the inferno might have been avoided.

Fire in the Tauern Tunnel

The Mont Blanc tragedy was hardly out of the headlines when a very similar accident took place in another highway tunnel in the Alps. The 4-mile-long Tauern Tunnel, completed in 1975, is among the most heavily traveled tunnel in all of Austria. At the time of the accident it had a single lane in each direction.

On May 29, 1999, a container truck came to a sudden stop at a construction site some 2,600 feet from the northern tunnel exit. The car directly behind it was able to stop in time, but the vehicle behind it, a heavy tractor-trailer, could not. The impact of their collision rammed the car into the container truck, which was loaded with cans of paint. The flammable cargo exploded. Further vehicles approaching at fairly high speeds set off a chain of collisions that included sixty additional vehicles crashing into the wreckage.

Panic broke out as people fled, screaming, through the burning tunnel. Had the accident not happened so close to an exit, the situation would have been much worse. Instead, eighty people were able to escape the flames on foot, many of them in a deep state of shock.

As was the case at the Mont Blanc Tunnel disaster, rescue crews were at first driven back by the extreme heat and smoke, and could not reach the crash site. Fire engines were forced to turn around by temperatures that reached 1,800 °F. In addition, all rescue efforts had to be called off when part of the concrete ceiling caved in. It was a miracle that only twelve people perished in the inferno. Fifty escaped with injuries. Investigation showed that eight of the victims died as a result of the massive collision, and only four had died in the fire.

Seven-year wait for compensation

The Mont Blanc Tunnel fire raged for a total of 53 hours. The fire was so hot that it melted concrete. The victims were all burned beyond recognition, with the gold crowns in their mouths and rings on their fingers completely melted.

It took years before an explanation for the accident was offered. In the end, it was concluded that a cigarette butt carelessly tossed away by the Belgian truck driver set off the fire. There were still other causes for the catastrophic extent of the resulting inferno: the safety mechanisms in the tunnel were generally poor; the air blown into the tunnel from the Italian side fanned the flames: and the Belgian truck was poorly insulated against fire, despite its easily ignited cargo. In 2006, ten persons and three companies were convicted on charges of negligent homicide. Those left behind by the thirty-nine victims of the blaze were awarded approximately $24 million in damages.

Consequences

Soon after the Mount Blanc catastrophe, all tunnels with one lane of traffic in each direction through a single passage were viewed as ticking time bombs, each one a disaster waiting to happen. The only decided safety improvement after the tragedy was the boring of a second tunnel passage for traffic flowing in the other direction. In case of an accident, the second tunnel could serve as an emergency escape path. The cost of such modifications were, of course, immense. Simply clearing the tunnel after the fire cost $560 million and took three years. During that time, it was closed to traffic.

For three days, firefighters fought through the sea of flames inside the Mont Blanc Tunnel.

Four days after the accident the last rescue vehicle leaves the Mont Blanc Tunnel. Years of repair work lay ahead.

Thick smoke pours from a ventilation shaft in the Gotthard Tunnel

The almost 11-mile-long Gotthard Tunnel in Switzerland is an important link in the main transport route from Germany to Italy. Despite the anticipated heavy traffic, when the tunnel was being built from 1970 to 1980, for financial reasons it was decided to build one tunnel passage instead of two. At 9:45 a. m. on October 24, 2001, two tractor-trailers crashed into one another in a head on collision. One of the trucks was loaded with tires and plastic awnings. These caught fire in the crash, producing heavy clouds of thick, black smoke. The fire quickly spread through a 985-foot-long section of the tunnel. The ventilation system was not able to halt the spread of the smoke. Temperatures inside the inferno reached 1,830 °F. Using high-pressure hoses and fans to bring down the temperature, firefighters were finally able to approach the site of the blaze on the following night.

Investigation of the accident threw a harsh light on the potential for danger posed by overreliance on truck transportation throughout Europe. One of the two truck drivers involved in the Gotthard Tunnel accident did not have a license, and the driver of the other truck did not have a legal work permit.

A dark, black smoke plume climbs high into the sky above the Buncefield Depot.

An Oil Storage Terminal Explodes

THE FUEL DEPOT IN HEMEL HEMPSTEAD BURNS FOR TWO DAYS

On December 11, 2005, a powerful explosion shook the area around the enormous oil storage complex in Hemel Hempstead, England, just north of London. It was the beginning of the worst fire in European postwar history. It took firefighters two days to bring the sea of flames under control. Miraculously, there were only a few injuries. Initial fears that the fire was started by a terrorist attack were not borne out by the investigation that followed.

Explosion on a Sunday morning

It happened early on a Sunday morning shortly after 6 a.m. The inhabitants of the many small towns around the oil storage complex in Hemel Hempstead were literally thrown out of their beds by the shock wave from a tremendous explosion. Windowpanes shattered and the earth quaked. The largest oil storage terminal in Europe had just exploded. The explosion was so loud that it could be heard in London, 25 miles to the south. The initial explosion was followed 20 minutes later by two more.

A towering column of fire

A giant column of fire rose above the fuel storage complex known as the Buncefield Depot. Witnesses report that it climbed 325 to 650 feet into the air. A thick cloud of smoke filled the sky, and the air smelled strongly of gasoline. Police blocked off highways and many other streets in the area near the accident site. The black cloud grew larger and spread over a large part of Southeast England. It was later visible in satellite images transmitted from outer space.

Extinguishing the fire takes days

The work of putting out the fire could only begin a full day after the explosion. Part of the reason for the delay was that firemen could not get very close at first due to the extreme heat. Another reason was the need to coordinate every phase of the operation. A fuel fire can only be extinguished with masses of foam. Fighting a fire on the scale of the Hemel Hempstead disaster meant that foam had to be collected from every part of the country. In the end, some 60,000 gallons of chemical foam concentrate were used to extinguish the blaze. Two days after the first explosion, the fire that consumed twenty fuel storage tanks was finally out.

Few casualties

Miraculously, no one died in the inferno, though more than forty people were injured. These figures would have been quite different had the accident not taken place early on a Sunday morning. On a typical work day, hundreds of employees would have been inside the storage complex close to the area where the tanks exploded. A second bit of luck was the weather at the time of the accident. Wind conditions were such that the smoke plume rose very high in the sky, where it quickly dissipated over a large area in the upper atmosphere. This greatly reduced the environmental damage that might have resulted had the smoke cloud stayed low to the ground.

What caused the explosion?

Even as the inferno still blazed, speculation was rife as to the cause of the explosions. Recent terrorist attacks in New York and Madrid sparked fears that the Hemel Hempstead disaster was also the result of terrorism. Did an airplane crash deliberately into the fuel depot? Eyewitnesses spoke of hearing an airplane fly overhead shortly before the first tank blew up, but, given that Luton Airport is not far away, this was not considered conclusive evidence. It was a month before experts from London could conduct a more thorough investigation. They found no evidence of a terrorist attack. It seems most likely that a leaky tank was the cause. Gasoline mixed with air forms an extremely volatile compound; it would take very little to cause it to burst into flame. No one knows just what ignited the blaze. Static electricity, or even someone using a cell phone, might have been enough to set it off.

Many buildings near the fuel depot were severely damaged by the pressure wave of the explosion.

The intense heat of the fire melted the storage tanks, causing them to cave in like tin cans.

Sources

Anton, Ralph. "Die Versenkung der *Lusitania* am 7. Mai 1915." *Kaiserliche Marine, 2000–2006.* <http://www.deutsche-schutzgebiete.de/lusitania.htm>

apl/AFP. "Briten wählen Concorde zur schönsten Design-Ikone." *Spiegel online.* March 17, 2006. <http://www.spiegel.de/reise/aktell/0,1518,406490,00.html>

Barth, Heinrich and Heinrich Schiffers. *Die große Reise. 1849–1855.* 2nd edition. Stuttgart: 1986.

Boccaccio, Giovanni. *The Decameron.* Transl. Mark Musa and Peter Bondanella. New York: 2002.

Boisjoly, Roger M. "Memo on O-Ring Erosion." *Online Ethics Center for Engineering and Science.* 1995–2005. <http://onlineethics.org/moral/boisjoly/MTImemo1.html>

Brandenburger, Maik. "Bombenlast." *Mare. Die Zeitschrift der Meere.* February/March 2006. 10–26.

Brantley, Steven R. *Volcanoes of the United States.* USGS General Interest Publication, online version 1.1. 1999.

"The Burning of Rome, 64 AD." *EyeWitness to History.* 1999. <www.eyewitnesstohistory.com>

Creutz, Rudolf and Johannes Steudel. *Einführung in die Geschichte der Medizin in Einzeldarstellungen.* Iserlohn: 1948.

Davie, Michael. *Titanic: The Death and Life of a Legend.* New York: 1986.

dpa/AFP: "Raumfähre Columbia beim Landeanflug abgestürzt." *ZDFheute.de magazin.* February 1, 2003. <http://www.heute.de/ZDFheute/ inhalt/12/0,3672,2032396,00.html>

Fontane, Theodor. "Die Brück' am Thay." *Lyrische Werke. Gedichte von Theodor Fontane.* <http://www.fontanetheodor.de/lyrik_8.html>

Gardener's Chronicle and Agricultural Gazette. 1845.

Harms, Robert. *Das Sklavenschiff. Eine Reise in die Welt des Sklavenhandels.* Munich: 2004.

Heine, Heinrich. *Sämtliche Werke.* Munich: 1964.

Kingston, Jeremy and David Lambert. *Katastrophen und Krisen.* Klagenfurt: 1980.

Kortländer, Bernd. "Interpretationen: Gedichte von Heinrich Heine." (studying material). Ditzingen: 1995.

Labunska, I., A. Stephenson, K. Brigden, R. Stringer, D. Santillo, and P.A. Johnston. "The Bhopal Legacy – Toxic contaminants at the former Union Carbide factory site Bhopal, India: 15 years after the Bhopal accident." *Greenpeace.* November 1, 1999. <http://www.greenpeace.org/usa/press/reports/ the-bhopal-legacy-toxic-cont>

London, Jack. "The Story of an Eyewitness: Collier's Special Correspondent." *Collier's, the National Weekly,* May 5, 1906.

Merlin, Tina. *Sulla pelle viva. Come si costruisce una catastrofe.* 4th edition. Verona: 1997.

Moody, Nekesa Mumbi. "An Awakening: India Arie's Eyewitness of AIDS in Africa Teaches and Transforms Her." *Essence.* December 2005.

Morrisroe, Patricia. *Mapplethorpe: A Biography.* New York: 1997.

Müller, Karlheinz and H.G. Korth. "Viermastbark 'Pamir'/DKEF." *Seefunk und Seeschifffahrt.* July 1, 2005. < http://www.seefunknetz.de/dkef.htm>

N.N.: "Bhopal's Health Disaster Continues to Unfold." *The Lancet,* September 14, 2002: Volume 360, Nr. 9336.

N.N.: "Russia to Develop New Nuclear Weapons, Putin Says." *Global Security Newswire by the National Journal Group.* May 11, 2006. <http://www.nti.org/d_newswire/issues/2006/5/11/45258cb9-d17a-4cb3-be71-a6c5915bdf80.html>

N.N.: "Trinity. Der erste Atombombentest." *IPPNW. Internationale Ärzte für die Verhütung des Atomkrieges, Ärzte in sozialer Verantwortung e.V.* 2006. <http://www.ippnw.de/Atomwaffen/Atomtests/article/Trinity.html>

Ohler, Norbert. *Sterben und Tod im Mittelalter.* Munich: 1994.

Scarantino, Alexis J. "Historia del Accidente – dia a dia." *¡Viven! El Accidente de los Andes.* <http://www.viven.com.uy/571/historia.asp>

"Union Carbide Corporation: Statement regarding the Bhopal tragedy." *Bhopal Information Center.* 2001–2005. <http://www.bhopal.com/ucs.htm>

Vandenberg, Philipp. *Nero: Kaiser und Gott, Künstler und Narr.* Munich: 1981.

Winau, Rolf. "Seit Amors Köcher auch vergiftete Pfeile führt. Die Ausbreitung der Syphilis in Europa." *Fundiert.* 2002: Vol 1. 58–65.

Winkle, Stefan. *Geißeln der Menschheit. Kulturgeschichte der Seuchen.* Düsseldorf/Zürich: 1997.

Yong, Chen. *The Great Tangshan Earthquake of 1976.* New York: 1988.

Zaun, Harald. "Ein tragischer Tag für die NASA-Familie." *Telepolis* February 2, 2003. <http://www.heise.de/tp/r4/artikel/14/14097/1.html>

Picture credits

133 Michael T. Sedam, 134 Bettmann, 135 Bettmann (t), Hulton-Deutsch Collection (b), 136 Tim Page, 137 Bettmann (large), Hulton-Deutsch Collection (small), 138 Jon Jones/Sygma, 139 Bettmann (r, l), 140 Bettmann (t), Peter Turnley (b), 141 David Turnley, 142 Corbis, 143 Lan Shu Wing/Next Photo/Corbis Sygma (t), Howard Sochurek (b), 144 Bettmann, 145 Wally McNamee (t), 146 CDC/ PHIL, 147 Michael Freeman (t), Jehad Nga (b), 148 Anna Clopet (t), Tarmizy Harva/Reuters (b), 149 Hulton-Deutsch Collection, 150 Gideon Mendel/ActionAid, 151 Louise Gubb/Corbis Saba (t, b), 152 Gideon Mendel (t), Peter Turnley (b), 153 Michael Freeman, 154 Gideon Mendel (t), Karen Kasmauski (b), 155 Lee Snider/Photo Images, 156 Bettmann, 157 Bettmann (t, b), 158 Bettmann, 159 Bettmann (r), Lester V. Bergman (l), 160/161 Reuters, 162/163 Hulton-Deutsch Collection, 163 Bettmann (small), 164 Bettmann, 165 Bettmann (t, b), 166/167 Hulton-Deutsch Collection, 167 Hulton-Deutsch Collection (b), 168/169 Hulton-Deutsch Collection, 168 Underwood & Underwood (t), 169 Reuters, 172 Hulton-Deutsch Collection (t), 174/175 Bettmann, 174 Corbis (l), 175 Bettmann (t), 175 Corbis (b), 176 Bettmann (t, b), 177 Bettmann, 179 Bryn Colton/Assignments Photographers, 180 Bryn Colton/Assignments Photographers, 181 Reuters (t, b), 182 Reuters (t), Corbis Sygma (b), 183 Bernard Bisson/Corbis Sygma, 184 Issey Kato/Reuters, 185 Tokyo Shimbun/Corbis Sygma (t), 185 (b), 186 Corbis Sygma (large), Nichinichi/ Shimbun/Corbis Sygma (b), 187 Hulton-Deutsch Collection, 188 Sean Adair/Reuters, 189 Reuters (t), Ron Sachs/CNP (b), 190 Reuters, 191 Reuters, 192 Peter Turnley, 193 Peter Turnley, 194/195 Neville Elder, 196 Pablo Torres Guerrero/El Pais/Reuters, 197 Andrea Comas/Reuters (t, b), 198 Dusko Despotovic, 199 Vincent West/Reuters (l), Carlos Dominguez (r), 200 Sion Touhig, 201 David Parry/Newscast/Handout/Reuters (t), Mian Khursheed/Reuters (b), 202 Dylan Martinez/Reuters (t), Toby Melville/Reuters (b), 204/205 Group of Survivors, 206/207 Bettmann, 206 Corbis, 207 Bettmann (t), Underwood & Underwood (b), 208/209 Bettmann, 208 (t), 209 Bettmann (t, b), 210/211 Bettmann, 210 Underwood & Underwood, 211 Bettmann (t, b), 212 Bettmann, 213 Bettmann (t, b), 214 Group of Survivors, 215 Group of Survivors (t), Bettmann (b), 216 Group of Survivors, 217 Group of Survivors (large), Reuters/Max Montecinos (small), 218 Hulton-Deutsch Collection, 221 George Hall (t), 222 Roger Ressmeyer, 223 Corbis (large), Bettmann (b), 224 Corbis, 225 NASA (small), Bettmann (b), 226 Corbis Sygma, 227 Vanderplas Ton/Corbis Sygma, 228 Patrick Robert/Sygma, 229 De Telegraaf/Corbis Sygma, 230 Buzz Pictures/Corbis Sygma, 231 Langevin Jacques/Corbis Sygma (t), Cardinale Stephane/Corbis Sygma (b), 232 Reuters (t), 232/233 Bisson Bernard/ Corbis Sygma (b), 233 Orban Thierry/ Corbis Sygma (t), 234/235 Robert McCullough/Dallas Morning News, 234 Mark M. Lawrence (l), 235 Brooks Kraft (t), 236 Reuters (t, b), 237 Brad Loper/Dallas Morning News (r), Bob Daemmrich (l), 238/239 Vauthey Pierre/ Corbis Sygma, 240 Corbis, 241 Sophie Elbaz/Sygma (t), Historical Picture Archive (b), 242 Louie Psihoyos (t), Bettmann (b), 243 Corbis, 244 Bettmann, 245 Bettmann (t), 246 Underwood & Underwood (t), 247 Bettmann, 248 Ralph White, 249 Bettmann, 252 Bettmann, 253 Underwood & Underwood (t), 254 Bettmann, 255 Vauthey Pierre/Corbis Sygma (t), 255 Corbis (b), 256 Bettmann, 257 Alain DeJean/Sygma (t), Martin Harvey (b), 258 Reuters, 259 Reuters, 260 Reuters (t, b), 261 Jacques Langevin/ Corbis Sygma, 263 Epix/ Corbis Sygma (t), 264 Corbis Sygma (t), Il Talehti / Corbis Sygma (b), 265 Corbis Sygma (b), 266 Trh Pictures Bradle/ Corbis Sygma, 267 Corbis Sygma (t), Reuters (b), 268 Reuters, 269 Reuters (t), Tutov Yuri/ Corbis Sygma (b), 270/271 Bettmann, 272 Hulton-Deutsch Collection, 273 Bettmann (t l), Hulton-Deutsch Collection (t r), Hulton-Deutsch Collection (b), 274/275 Hulton-Deutsch Collection, 275 Angelo Hornak (t), Colin Garratt; Milepost 92 1/2 (b), 276 Corbis (t, b) 277 Corbis, 278 Bettmann, 279 Corbis, 280 Corbis, 281 Corbis (t), Bettmann (b), 282 Jack Fields, 283 (t, b), 290/291 Hulton-Deutsch Collection, 292 Tom Pietrasik, 293 Alain Nogues/Corbis Sygma, 294 Raj Patidar/Reuters, 295 Reuters, 295 Pallava Bagla (b), 296 Igor Kostin/Sygma, 297 Igor Kostin/ Sygma (t), 297 Corbis (b), 298 Igor Kostin/Sygma (t, b), 299 Igor Kostin/ Sygma (t, b), 300

Jacques Pavlovsky/Sygma, 300/301 Charles E. Rotkin, 302/303 Charles E. Rotkin, 302 Jacques Pavlovsky/Sygma, 303 Reuters (t), Frank Lukasseck/zefa (b), 304 Règis Bossu/Sygma, Règis Bossu/Sygma (b), 306 Règis Bossu/Sygma, 307 Règis Bossu/Sygma (t, b), 308 Reuters, 309 Grazia Neri/Corbis Sygma, 310 Ruet Stephane/Corbis Sygma (t, b), 311 Sestini/ Grazia Neri/Corbis Sygma, 312 Hertfordshire Police/Handout/Reuters, 313 Chiltern Air Support Unit/Handout/Reuters (t), Stefan Rousseau/PA/WPA Pool/Reuters (b)

Diederichs, Uwe: 305 (t)

DRK-Archiv: 282, 283 (t), 284, 285

Fillery, Burga: 31 (t), 76 (l), 83 (b), 166 (b), 203, 265 (t)

Getty Images: 4 Ernst Haas/Hulton Archive (l), 10/11 Ernst Haas/Hulton Archive, 42 Keystone/Hulton Archive (t), 43 China Photos, 52 Nicolas Asfouri/AFP, 53 Miguel Riopa/AFP (t, b), 54 Miguel Riopa/AFP, 55 David McNew (t), Miguel Riopa/AFP (b), 63 Howard Sochurek/Time Life Pictures, 64 Keystone, 65 Howard Sochurek/Time Life Pictures (t), 67 Keystone (r), 69 David Lees/Time Life Pictures, 76 Keystone (r), 77 Keystone/Hulton Archive, 78 Hulton Archive (t), 93 (b) Carlos Barria-Pool, 94 Marianne Todd, 105 Illustrated London News (t), 145 Martha Fein (b), 170 Keystone (l), 170/171 Hugo Jaeger/Timepix/ Time Life Pictures, 171 Harrison/Topical Press Agency/Hulton Archive, 172/173 Harrison/Topical Press Agency/Hulton Archive, 173 London Express (b), 178 Keystone, 218/219 CORR/AFP, 219 CORR/AFP, 206 Central Press, 221 CORR/AFP (b), 245 HultonArchive/Illustrated London News (b), 246/247 Hulton Archive/Illustrated London News (b), 250 Time Life Pictures/Mansell, 251 Hulton Archive (t), Time Life Pictures/Mansell (b), 253 Hulton Archive (b), 262 Jaacko Avikainen/AFP, 263 Kimmo Mantyla/AFP (b), 288 Dick Swanson//Time Life Pictures, 289 AFP (t), Hoang Dinh Nam/AFP (b), 291 STF/AFP (b)

INDEX

This is a Parragon Publishing book

Copyright © Parragon Books Ltd 2007
Queen Street House
4 Queen Street
Bath BA1 1 HE, UK

Original edition:
Packaging: ditter.projektagentur GmbH
Picture research: Claudia Bettray
Design and layout: Claudio Martinez

US edition produced by: APE Int'l, Richmond VA
Translation from German: Dr. Maureen Basedow,
    Russell Cennydd, and Markus Flatscher

ISBN: 978-1-4054-9520-2

Printed in China